The Buyer's Workbook

Miriam Guerreiro
Professor
Fashion Buying and Merchandising Department
Fashion Institute of Technology

LaDonna Garrett
Assistant Professor
Fashion Buying and Merchandising Department
Fashion Institute of Technology

Fairchild Publications
New York

ORIGINAL DRAWINGS BY JANET FOUTIN.
BOOK DESIGN BY LESIAK/CRAMPTON DESIGN.

ISBN: 1-56367-000-3 (Book only)
         1-56367-025-9 (Book with 3.5 inch diskette)
         1-56367-026-9 (Book with 5.25 inch diskette)
         1-56367-027-5 (3.5 inch diskette only)
         1-56367-028-3 (5.25 inch diskette only)

GST # R 133004424
Printed in the United States of America

Contents

Foreword

Buying and merchandising has always been a "people" business. The idea of taking money and converting it into merchandise to satisfy people's needs makes for a fulfilling and challenging profession. This is especially true now as we are experiencing profound changes in the global community.

Most experts agree that by the year 2000, the population — age thirty-five and over — will increase by fifty percent. Our aging population will have a new set of spending priorities: health care, college tuition, mortgages and other debts, and savings for retirement. Buyers and merchandisers of fashion products will have to fight creatively for the consumer's attention.

All buyers seek to dominate their trading areas. They achieve this by having the most exciting assortments of merchandise for their consumers. The thrill is in outsmarting and beating the competition to the draw on new fashion trends and key items. The student must keep this in mind as the necessary planning abilities are acquired. When these faculties become second nature, the student will develop those qualitative skills and talents that make this field so exciting.

This text gives the student the tools that are needed to merchandise, that is to plan to satisfy the consumer's needs. It deals with the considerable amounts of quantitative information that skilled merchants use in planning investments and assortments. However, it cannot convey accurately the excitement, the energy, the enthusiasm, and the talent necessary for great merchants to excel — that must be supplied by the participants — the teachers and the students.

Robert Salem
President of Sportswear—Missy Division
Leslie Fay

v

Preface

Any program designed to teach the hows and whys of fashion buying must include the study of present buying practices and techniques, a constant examination of consumer behavior and study of present and future economic trends. Because buyers must cater to the needs and wants of the consumer, they must develop techniques to predict this need in advance of the consumer. Also necessary is a continuing awareness of market conditions, factors that must be considered in stock planning, building and maintenance, and the department's and the store's degree of willingness to assume risk. It must be understood that the major responsibility is to perform within the guidelines and policies set by management.

A department store buyer is an executive who is responsible for the merchandising of a department, which involves providing merchandise that will meet the needs of their specific target consumer. The assumption is made throughout *The Buyer's Workbook* that the student has previously completed coursework which has discussed the fundamentals of how profit is obtained. The goal of this text is to go into greater depth to show how this bottom line or profit actually is achieved by the buyer's decisions and follow through. It is also necessary to stress that successful buying depends a great deal on the ability of the buyer to work as a manager in addition to possessing certain basic qualities to achieve this. A buyer must be able to communicate effectively, to foster team spirit among the staff, to provide proper incentives to achieve successful action and to delegate work responsibility properly. Those functions help to achieve the buyer's desired end, which is, of course, profit.

Despite creatively prepared lectures and discussions, the main behavioral objectives of a teaching program are not achieved unless students can apply what they have learned — the "pay-off" is performance. Teachers and students will agree that there is a wide disparity between comprehension and the ability to apply. In truth, however, a fashion merchandising and/or retailing course can never simulate completely the realities of the marketplace. However, it should do more than cover the "what, where, and how" of the buyer's life. Certainly a more desired objective is the student's participation in the decision-making and application of commonly faced professional experiences — using current retail techniques as well as up-to-date business forms.

The Buyer's Workbook is intended as a yardstick to evaluate student performance — to prove the student's understanding and ability to apply sound retailing techniques. The primary intention of the text is its use as the basis of a workshop — a psychodrama — in which students and teachers are the players: the former are the buyers, the latter are the merchandise managers. Each chapter is an exercise, which exemplifies the application of an important phase within the range of a buyer's responsibilities. This text is intended to be the roadmap to a program of theory and discussion.

In addition to demonstrating an understanding of the tools of merchandising and the ability to use and interpret these principles, the specific objectives for the student in "the game" are to be able to:

- Apply the techniques of planning, selecting, and maintaining a stock.
- Select from various alternatives to solve merchandising problems and accept the "penalties" and/or "rewards" for their performance.
- Exhibit creative aspects of merchandising, and to show awareness of consequences of the decision-making process.
- Apply merchandising principles and practices discussed in the prerequisite courses.

The Buyer's Workbook involves students in a department store fashion buyer's activities and applications, which includes supporting these activities and applications with appropriate data. This data will be provided by previous course work, by the instructor, and by the student's own research.

Although Jarrod & Young is a fictitious store, its background is fairly common to American retailing. The merchandising figures are up-to-date, and all business forms, practices, language, and responsibilities are in current use.

We feel that by using a new department as the foundation for the assignments, the student ("buyer") is in the best position to express creativity and gain understanding of each phase of a buyer's responsibilities. The sequence of the text and the assignments are in logical progression and respond to:

- The buyer's role.
- The store's policies and its retail mix.
- The major steps of planning, buying, selling.

Assignments include those concerned with retail operations that are related to merchandising.

1994   Miriam Guerreiro
                                        Professor
                                        Fashion Institute of Technology

                                        LaDonna Garrett
                                        Assistant Professor
                                        Fashion Institute of Technology
                                        New York

Acknowledgments

We acknowledge with gratitude the participation of the many merchandising executives in the preparation of this text to ensure the accuracy and currency of the techniques and business forms. We are especially thankful to the National Retail Federation for the permission to reprint sections from the MOR, and the Richter Merchandising Services, Inc., for permission to reprint the retailing/merchandising forms used throughout the text.

We would like to thank the following people for their valuable, constructive, and beneficial reviews: Glenda L. Lowry, Marshall University; Eithel M. Simpson, Purdue University; Marsha E. Stein, Teikyo Post University; Gloria Cockerell, Collin County Community College; Andrea Weeks, Business & Systems Analyst, Strouds Linens.

A special thank you to Gertrude Ribet, Assistant Professor; Gloria Hartley, Assistant Professor; Mary McMahon, Adjunct Instructor, and all of the Fashion Institute of Technology, Fashion Buying and Merchandising Department, New York.

Lastly, we wish to express our sincere gratitude to Ms. Janice Johnson for her role in the organization and word processing of this workbook.

List of Figures

The Buyer's Workbook

CHAPTER ONE

Background of the Game

OBJECTIVES

- *Understand the career path of a department store buyer.*
- *Differentiate the job responsibilities of each level for the retail executive — trainee, assistant buyer, department manager, associate buyer, and buyer.*
- *Identify the criteria for promotion to each executive level.*
- *Explain the functions and interrelationships — both external and internal — of the store divisions.*

THE ORGANIZATION JARROD & YOUNG

Jarrod & Young of Des Moines, Iowa was founded in 1878 by William Jarrod, an itinerant peddler who was part of the "Westward Ho" movement of the 19th century. During a stop in Des Moines in 1875, Jarrod met Lucy Belle Smith and they were married the following year.

After several unsuccessful business ventures, Jarrod opened a dry goods store typical of the times. From the beginning it was a success. In 1900, needing money for expansion, he sold a 40% interest to his brother-in-law, Roger Young, for $50,000. The store name was changed from Jarrod Dry Goods to Jarrod & Young.

Over the years the store expanded, and by 1918 it was a full-scale department store, occupying a six-story structure with 200,000 square feet of selling space. During the 1950s, in response to the population movement to suburbia, the store embarked on an expansion program and opened six branches over the next thirty years. The first branch was opened in 1956 in Cedar Rapids, and could be characterized as a miniature of the main store. Later, branches were opened in Davenport, Ames, Council Bluffs, and Iowa City. Finally, in 1980, the Sioux City branch was opened, which was within the trading area of Omaha, Nebraska. All the store structures are two-story buildings, with the exception of Council Bluffs, which has three selling floors.

Last year, the total volume for the Jarrod & Young chain was $300,000,000, which, when broken down by store is:

Des Moines (Flagship store)	$ 105,000,000
Cedar Rapids	51,000,000
Ames	39,000,000
Council Bluffs	35,000,000
Iowa City	30,000,000
Sioux City	18,000,000
Davenport	18,000,000

The organization went public in 1962 and its stock is sold over-the-counter.

The retail mix of Jarrod & Young can be summed up as:

- The store locations are prime — positioned in each area's best shopping locations, including malls.
- The buildings are extremely well maintained. Exterior windows reflect the concern of management — they are professionally planned and represent merchandising know-how.
- The interiors are well planned, with merchandise that is stocked and displayed in a manner consistent with upscale retail practices.
- Merchandise price ranges are from moderate to better, with most price zones at moderate levels. There are no basement operations.
- An organizational structure that features six distinct divisions with clearly defined responsibilities (see Figures 1-1, JARROD & YOUNG STORE ORGANIZATION CHART and 1-2, MAJOR RESPONSIBILITIES OF JARROD & YOUNG'S STORE DIVISIONS, pages 3 and 4).
- All departments are staffed by sales associates who are professionally trained by a department that is supervised by the director of human resources and services. Every employee is required to complete an initial training program before going on the selling floor.
- Strong emphasis is placed on customer services and the store operations system, which includes:

(a) Merchandise being delivered via United Parcel Service.

(b) Advertising expenditures allocated as follows:

(1) All print: newspaper & magazines	65%
(2) Radio	10%
(3) Direct mail	15%
(4) In-store promotions	10%

Advertising format for Jarrod & Young is in good taste and is consistently part of a well-conceived plan that uses multiple mediums to the best advantage.

(c) Gift wrapping is available at minimal cost.

(d) In-store promotions, (i.e., video monitors, trunk and fashion shows, and fashion clinics are exhibited at all stores.)

The majority of Jarrod & Young's customers are from lower-middle to upper-middle income groups, with incomes ranging from $35,000 to $75,000. As a department store organization, the continued customer patronage strategy is to appeal to the widest possible age group. This strategy has worked well over the years. Customers trust the integrity of the organization, and appreciate the store's efforts to be current and even fashion forward in its thinking. Customer attitudes are most favorable, and the store motto: *"Jarrod & Young Serves with Pride and Integrity"* has consumer acceptance. Additionally, the profit and loss records evidence the following averages:

- Profit before taxes   7.5%
- Profit after taxes   4 %

FIGURE 1-1 JARROD AND YOUNG STORE OGANIZATION CHART

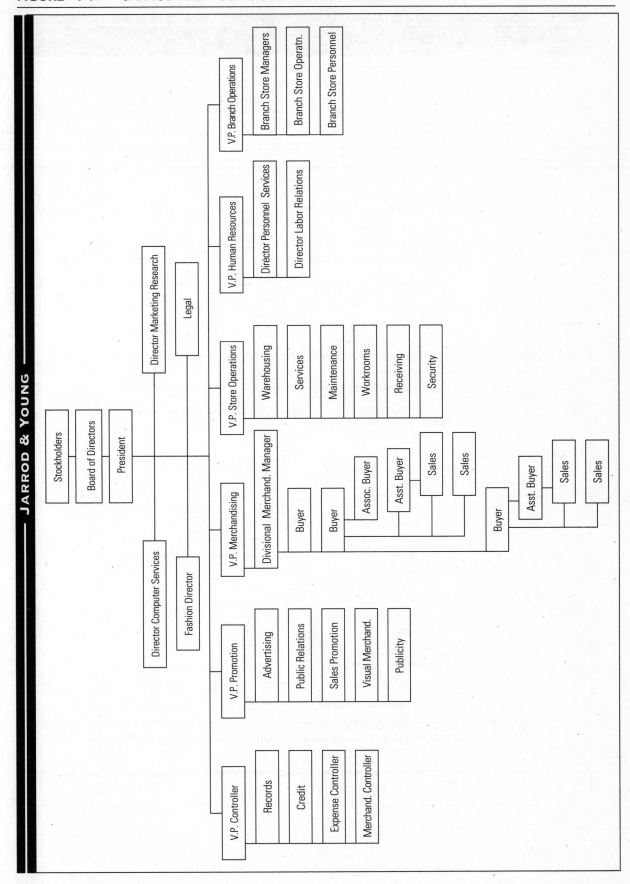

═ JARROD & YOUNG ═

Division	Responsibilities
MERCHANDISING	• Merchandise development, selection, pricing, and selling • Controlling inventory (joint responsibility with Operations). • Sets merchandising policies: quality standards, price ranges, fashion leadership position, exclusivity. The **Merchandising Division** is the only division that generates income for the store.
CONTROL	• Payroll • Expense planning and control • Credit office • Internal auditing • Accounts payable • Inventory monitoring and reconciliation • Statistical: generates purchase journal The **Control Division** initiates and monitors all areas covering finance and general accounting within the store.
PROMOTION	• Advertising, copy, and layout • Catalogue, radio, television • Display: interior and windows • Store design and decor • Public relations/Special events The **Promotion Division** works closely with the **Merchandising Division** to generate customer traffic and a favorable store image.
HUMAN RESOURCES	• Training • Employee selection and development • Rating and reviews • Termination • Job Analysis • Benefits The **Human Resources Division** recruits, develops, evaluates, and manages the store's personnel.
STORE OPERATIONS	• Customer service — sales, service desk • Telephone and mail order • Warehouse • Restaurants • Receiving and marking • General operations activities: security, housekeeping, delivery, alterations The **Store Operations Division** provides general support services, internally and externally, that allow the store to function. The **Branch Store Division** operates as a microcosm of the other divisions — solely for branch store locations. Within each branch are offices for **Advertising, Operations, Personnel,** and **Control.** Branch department managers perform the operational and merchandising functions.

THE BUYER—YOU

Nicole Anderson (you), a resident of Des Moines, is a graduate of the University of Iowa with a major in Retailing. As an undergraduate, she worked part-time at Jarrod & Young in various capacities: as a sales associate in junior sportswear, as a clerical in the accounts payable division, and, during her senior year, as a clerical in the office of the divisional merchandise manager of dresses.

Following her graduation from the University, Nicole applied for the executive training program at Jarrod & Young. As a well-known and highly regarded employee, she was recognized as having the potential to become a fine merchant and was, consequently, accepted. The training program covers a six-month to nine-month period during which the training class has two three-month assignments, in addition to the formal classes. The training program includes a trainee assignment, which covers:

- *Managing the selling floor:* assigning and supervising sales associates; moving merchandise.
- *Managing the flow of merchandise:* overseeing transfers to branches; expediting goods from receiving to floor.
- *Analyzing merchandise controls:* developing familiarity with all manual and computer generated merchandising forms; operating terminals, interfacing with branch managers.
- *Studying and discussing sales promotions as a method of increasing sales and profits:* conducting/participating in seminars; examining current sales promotion efforts with the results for constructive criticism and future improvements.
- *Strengthening markup techniques:* evaluating vendors for development and improvement; developing private labels and merchandise exclusives.
- *Monitoring inventories for profit:* constantly checking the rate of sell-through of classes, sub-classes, and styles to increase turnover.
- *Increasing gross margin:* increasing turnover, decreasing shortage; examining in detail all factors involved to achieve these goals.
- *Demonstrating an understanding of the operating statement:* capability of explaining each element in the operating statement.
- *Studying the conditions that exist when an assistant buyer is performing well:* sales associates operating efficiently; branch managers communicating well, floor being well stocked and well maintained; buyer being satisfied with the assistant's results.
- *Discussing major areas of retailing with various department heads:* participating in management organized meetings to discuss the function and operations of various store divisions and departments.

An executive program trainee is the first step on JARROD & YOUNG'S BUYING OR MANAGEMENT CAREER PATH (see Figure 1-3, page 6).

Upon completion of the program, Nicole received her first assignment — assistant buyer in the 7 to 14 children's department of the main store, which is located on the second floor. Nicole's responsibilities as an assistant buyer were outlined in the job description (see Figure 1-4, JARROD & YOUNG'S MERCHANDISING DIVISION JOB DESCRIPTION — ASSISTANT BUYER, page 8).

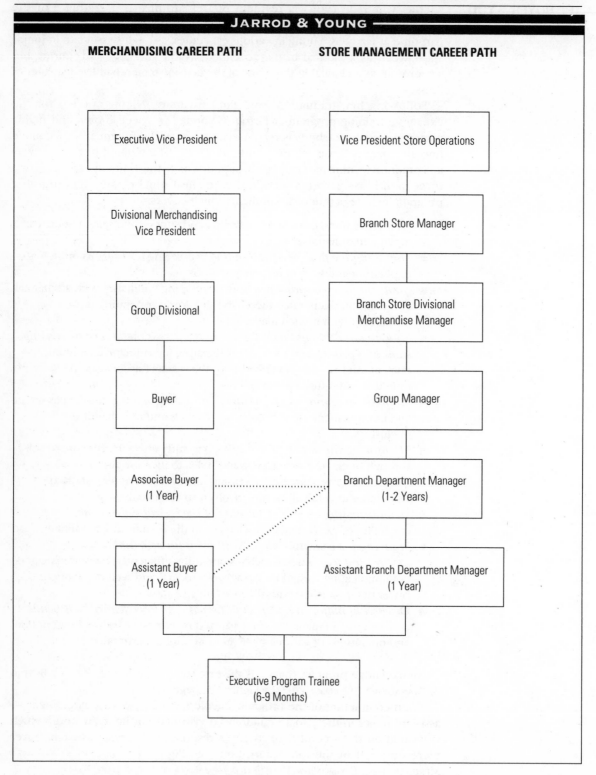

JARROD & YOUNG

MERCHANDISING CAREER PATH   **STORE MANAGEMENT CAREER PATH**

Executive Vice President | Vice President Store Operations

Divisional Merchandising Vice President | Branch Store Manager

Group Divisional | Branch Store Divisional Merchandise Manager

Buyer | Group Manager

Associate Buyer (1 Year) | Branch Department Manager (1-2 Years)

Assistant Buyer (1 Year) | Assistant Branch Department Manager (1 Year)

Executive Program Trainee (6-9 Months)

The time frame in each job is subject to modification because of special circumstances, unusual needs, etc. Quoted times for each level are given only to suggest a frame of reference. The merchandising career path develops trainees for executive positions, (e.g., buyers, divisional merchandise managers, etc.) in the merchandising division. The store management career path prepares trainees for executive positions in the store operations and branch operations divisions.

In this capacity, Nicole enjoyed the challenge of the position, which was helped in no small degree by the buyer, Jeff Smith. As the buyer for the department, Jeff was responsible for evaluating Nicole's performance as an assistant buyer (see Figure 1-5, Jarrod & Young's Assistant Buyer Performance Evaluation, page 9). Through hard work, Nicole consistently scored very good or outstanding ratings on her performance evaluations. In a short time, Jeff allowed Nicole to use her judgment about reordering several classifications of merchandise, to fill in advertising information sheets, and generally treated her as an associate.

After a year and two months as assistant buyer in the main store, Nicole was assigned to the Cedar Rapids' store, the largest branch, as the branch department manager of "Women's World." This department features half-size dresses, career clothes, and sportswear. In this capacity, she was responsible for some reordering of best-selling styles, accounting for the proper flow and display of merchandise, and acting as a source of information for two flagship store buyers. As a branch department manager, Nicole had to supervise and report to more people than she did as an assistant buyer. Merchandising, management, and operations duties were now part of her job responsibilities (see Figure 1-6, Jarrod & Young's Merchandising Division Job Description — Branch Department Manager, page 11).

Because of her merchandising talents, high performance ratings, and the skillful way she handled assignments, Nicole was returned to the main store after a relatively short time period — nine months. Due to personnel shifts, an associate buyer's position was vacant and Nicole was selected over twenty candidates for the most sought-after position of her trainee group — associate buyer for junior dresses.

Once again, she was lucky. Her new buyer, Jane Armstrong, was a young, secure, outgoing executive, who was ready to pass on her accumulated merchandising knowledge. Nicole was assigned two classifications to merchandise: (1) two-piece dresses with jackets, and (2) two-piece dress suits with either pants or skirt bottoms.

The position worked out exactly as it is detailed in Jarrod & Young's Merchandising Division Job Description — Associate Buyer (see Figure 1-7, page 12). When the buyer went on foreign buying trips, Nicole assumed control of the department: she reordered, bought new merchandise, planned several successful ads, analyzed merchandising results, and conferred with the divisional manager during the weekly open-to-buy meetings.

One month ago, after one and a half years as an associate, Nicole was called into George Johnson's office, the divisional merchandise manager. Mr. Johnson, an astute merchant, greeted her cordially, asked her to sit down and said, "Nicole, we have been following your career, and I am happy to say that after approximately three years of training, you are now promoted to the position of buyer."

Nicole took a deep breath and expressed her joy and thanks to Mr. Johnson. Finally, all that studying, training, and hard work was starting to pay off!

JARROD & YOUNG

JOB TITLE: Assistant Buyer

REPORTS TO: Buyer

SUPERVISES: Assists buyer in supervising trainees, clerical staff, and sales/stock personnel

OBJECTIVES	Under the direction of the buyer:
	• To work in all aspects of merchandising within the department.
	• To coordinate all activity necessary to achieve profitability goals.
	• To be responsible for the department in the buyer's absence.
	• To prepare for additional buying responsibilities.
	• To gain knowledge of the selling floor and merchandise control procedures.
	• To interact with all support areas within the store: visual merchandising, advertising, fashion office, operations, and sales associate.
RESPONSIBILITIES	Planning and Buying
	• Works with buyer on needed merchandise, reorders basics when indicated. Sees vendors and new lines. Follows up on outstanding orders.
	• Selects merchandise, with buyer's guidance, for assistant's classification(s).
	• Administers basic order programs where applicable.
PROMOTION AND MERCHANDISING	• Works with buyer on advertising program by writing copy and sign orders; handling departmental displays and following up with three-day selling report for divisional merchandise manager after appearance of ad.
	• Acts as liaison between the buyer and customer to provide information concerning customer requests.
	• Visits branch stores at request of buyer.
CONTROL AND ADMINISTRATION	• Places new merchandise in stock, verifying order information, and ticketing. Handles damaged stock disposal properly by price adjustment, vendor return, etc. Maintains two-way communication with selling personnel, reporting input to the buyer.
	• With a knowledge of warehousing procedures, regularly checks on proper merchandise processing and distribution for stores, lost and special merchandise, order file, and invoice office.
	• Communicates with branch stores on price change merchandise information, advertised merchandise, adequate merchandise coverage, etc.
	• Assumes responsibility for purchase journal work, (e.g., checking markup computation, discounts, transportation and goods returned and vendor charge backs).
	• Records daily, weekly, and monthly performance figures and want-slip analysis. Handles goods returned and inter-store transfer books, as well as merchandise loans.
	• Carries out stock counts as directed by the buyer and handles unit control review and interpretation where applicable.
	• Assists buyer with preparation for inventory.
INTERNAL RELATIONSHIPS	Under the direction of the buyer:
	• Cooperates with sales manager (where applicable) in the merchandising operation of the selling floor.
	• Works with service manager on scheduling, adjustments, and selling services.
	• Works with operations personnel in the flow and stocking of merchandise and in departmental housekeeping.
	• Works with branch stores in the distribution and sale of merchandise in stores.
	• Follows through all promotional activities with visual merchandising, the fashion office, and advertising.
EXTERNAL RELATIONSHIPS	• Tracks group buys and private label programs from the RBO.
	• Follows-up order delivery, vendor returns, and cancellations with vendors.

FIGURE 1-5 JARROD & YOUNG'S ASSISTANT BUYER'S PERFORMANCE EVALUATION

JARROD & YOUNG

EXECUTIVE PERFORMANCE EVALUATION MX 10535 (1/77)
ASSISTANT BUYER

NAME

Spring ....
Fall ....

1 = Unacceptable	2 = Marginal	3 = Good	4 = Very Good	5 = Outstanding
[x] ☐ ☐ ☐ ☐	☐ [x] ☐ ☐ ☐	☐ ☐ [x] ☐ ☐	☐ ☐ ☐ [x] ☐	☐ ☐ ☐ ☐ [x]
1 2 3 4 5	1 2 3 4 5	1 2 3 4 5	1 2 3 4 5	1 2 3 4 5

1 2 3 4 5   MERCHANDISE RESPONSIBILITY

☐ ☐ ☐ ☐ ☐ 1. Initiates plans/actions to optimize sales.

☐ ☐ ☐ ☐ ☐ 2. Understands the importance of floor presentation by proper classification, color, or trend.

☐ ☐ ☐ ☐ ☐ 3. Understands the components of coordinated merchandise presentation by proper arrangement/assortment.

☐ ☐ ☐ ☐ ☐ 4. Understands the importance of proper stock levels relative to the business.

☐ ☐ ☐ ☐ ☐ 5. Sees that stock is filled in, labelled accurately as to price and size, counted per schedule, and is neat and accessible.

☐ ☐ ☐ ☐ ☐ 6. Department records are kept up to date correctly (RTVs, markdowns, recaps, turnover, etc.)

☐ ☐ ☐ ☐ ☐ 7. Plans actions and recommendations for assigned classification, which reflect an understanding of the department's current potential, trends, seasonal needs, and past experience.

1 2 3 4 5   MERCHANDISE KNOWLEDGE

☐ ☐ ☐ ☐ ☐ 1. Understands the Open-to-Buy concept.

☐ ☐ ☐ ☐ ☐ 2. Understands merchandising reports/information and effectively utilizes them.

☐ ☐ ☐ ☐ ☐ 3. Understands the flow of paperwork and related systems.

☐ ☐ ☐ ☐ ☐ 4. Able to project and forecast in a concise and precise manner (rates of sale, reorders, etc.)

1 2 3 4 5   LEADERSHIP RESPONSIBILITY

☐ ☐ ☐ ☐ ☐ 1. Sales staff is constantly apprised and informed of merchandise selection and trends.

☐ ☐ ☐ ☐ ☐ 2. Is flexible and can adapt to the changing needs of the business within the context of the department's goal and objectives.

☐ ☐ ☐ ☐ ☐ 3. Buyer is well informed of the merchandise situations (on hand, on order, best seller by store, stock conditions); the action of the competition; department problems and recommended solutions.

☐ ☐ ☐ ☐ ☐ 4. Suburban department managers are kept informed (through communication, store visits, etc.)

☐ ☐ ☐ ☐ ☐ 5. Interacts well and deals effectively with other divisions in the store.

☐ ☐ ☐ ☐ ☐ 6. Takes constructive criticism well and tries to correct shortcomings.

☐ ☐ ☐ ☐ ☐ 7. Is well motivated and a self-starter.

☐ ☐ ☐ ☐ ☐ 8. Maintains high standards for self and department.

1 2 3 4 5   PLANNING AND ORGANIZATION

☐ ☐ ☐ ☐ ☐ 1. Is well organized and apportions time constructively and wisely.

☐ ☐ ☐ ☐ ☐ 2. Meets deadlines and schedules.

☐ ☐ ☐ ☐ ☐ 3. Reacts to the changing needs of the business by taking actions which reflect a basic understanding of priorities.

☐ ☐ ☐ ☐ ☐ 4. Learns quickly and effectively.

ACCOMPLISHMENTS

What specific measurable results has this individual accomplished in the appraisal period (sales growth, profit):

....
....
....
....

OBJECTIVES

What specific business objectives are to be achieved by the next evaluation period:

....
....
....
....
....
....
....
....
....
....

FUTURE GROWTH AND DEVELOPMENT

What ideas and thoughts do you have for this individual's professional development:

....
....
....
....
....
....
....
....
....
....
....
....

1	2	3	4	5	**OVERALL EVALUATION**
☐	☐	☐	☐	☐	Performance as a merchant
☐	☐	☐	☐	☐	Performance as a leader
☐	☐	☐	☐	☐	Potential for advancement

Discussed With Assistant Buyer:

Signature .... Date

Rater's Signature .... Salary Action

FIGURE 1-6   JARROD & YOUNG'S MERCHANDISING DIVISION JOB DESCRIPTION —
BRANCH DEPARTMENT MANAGER

JARROD & YOUNG

JOB TITLE: Branch Department Manager

REPORTS TO: Group manager, Branch store divisional merchandise manager

SUPERVISES: Branch assistant department manager, Sales associates

OBJECTIVES	• To achieve maximum departmental performance through direct selling and motivation of sales associates. • To achieve departmental profitability goals through shortage and expense control. • To maintain a high level of customer service. • To increase customer traffic through effective merchandising floor and display. • To develop operations personnel.
RESPONSIBILITIES	Departmental Merchandising • Consults with the buyer regularly on such merchandise points as: strengths and weaknesses, fast and slow sellers, markups and/or markdowns, displays, advertising plans, disposition of damaged merchandise, and departmental layout and fixtures. • Acquires merchandise and sales promotion information from buyers. • Communicates merchandise and storewide promotion information to salespeople. • Controls availability of the signs and material ordered from the display department by the buyer as well as acquiring any supplemental display material; arranges display material within the department. • Ensures availability of all advertised merchandise in the department and reports results. • Requests merchandise from flagship store to fill branch needs. Suggests to buyer the merchandise appropriate for transferring to different branch locations. • Determines in-stock condition of basic merchandise and notifies the group manager and buyer of stock needed to address department requirements. • Holds daily morning meetings with salespeople to discuss merchandise and recap yesterday's selling performance. • Reviews merchandise want slips and reports to the branch store merchandise coordinator.
MANAGEMENT AND DEVELOPMENT	• Works with group manager to schedule sales and stock personnel. • Supervises assistant branch department manager and sales associates. • Maintains high morale within the department though weekly discussions of methods for strengthening customer service, sales, and teamwork. • Encourages development of operations personnel through exposure to management functions.
DEPARTMENT CONTROLS	• Reviews departmental paperwork. • Interacts with security to reduce potential shrinkage. • Maintains departmental stock-keeping in forward and floor stock areas. • Requisitions stock-keepers from assistant manager of operations. • Oversees stock counts, receipts, transfers, RTV's, and markdowns.
INTERNAL RELATIONSHIPS	• Interprets store policies to the sales and stock personnel. • Consults with the branch store group manager concerning selling needs and scheduling sales personnel. • Supervises assistant department manager and sales force daily.
EXTERNAL RELATIONSHIPS	Interprets store policies to the customer. • Handles customer adjustments in accordance with store system and policies. • Handles accidents, writes reports, and follows through with the medical department if necessary. • Services customers in the department. • Monitors level of customer service within the department.

JARROD & YOUNG

JOB TITLE: Associate Buyer

REPORTS TO: Buyer, Divisional merchandise manager

SUPERVISES: Assists buyer in supervising assistant buyers, trainees, clerical staff

OBJECTIVES	Under the direction of the buyer:
	• To coordinate and implement all activities necessary to achieve profitability goals for selected classifications within the department.
	• To supervise all merchandising activities initiated by the buyer for the entire department.
	• To prepare for full buying responsibilities.
	• To identify and support new resources for selected classifications, which are necessary for fashion leadership and store image.
	• To increase the profitability of key resources for selected classifications.
	• To cultivate executive and operational talent within the department.
	• To interact effectively with all external and internal support networks.
RESPONSIBILITIES	Planning and Buying
	• Projects and monitors the open-to-buy budgets for selected classifications.
	• Executes purchase orders for classification responsibilities.
	• Works with buyer to plan and control allocated advertising budget from store and vendor contributions.
	• Works with the current resource structure to improve profitability.
CONTROL AND ADMINISTRATION	• Maintains a store control program for selected classifications and assists buyer in implementing controls for the department. Methods include:
	(a.) Accuracy checks for invoices, transfers, price changes, and vendor returns.
	(b.) Monitors purchases journal transcriptions for timeliness and accuracy.
	• Assists in preparation for, and reconciliation of, inventory.
DEVELOPMENT OF STORE PERSONNEL	• Assists in the development of assistant buyer and trainee through exposure to all aspects of buying and merchandising. Provides informal guidelines and evaluations to encourage professional growth for junior executives.
	• Supervises clerical, sales, and stock personnel in the execution of their responsibilities.
INTERNAL RELATIONSHIPS	Assists the buyer in promoting the department through effective interaction with:
	• Fashion office.
	• Visual merchandising.
	• Advertising.
	• Sales Promotion.
	• Public Relations.
	• Store Operations.
EXTERNAL RELATIONSHIPS	Assists the buyer in:
	• Developing and maintaining a fair, equitable, and professional working relationship with all vendors.
	• Participating in and supporting RBO functions and requests.
	• Striving to ensure good customer relations.
	• Regularly shopping major local competition to be familiar with the activities of similar departments in comparable RBO stores and other major stores.
	• Maintaining communications with domestic and foreign RBO, and gaining familiarity with trade journals, periodicals, and other merchandise information publications.

**THE PROBLEM —
THE BUYING GAME**

George Johnson then explained: "Nicole, as you know, Jarrod & Young enjoys an unsurpassed reputation as a retail organization of integrity and fashion know-how, which is a position we intend to maintain. Also, we are in a highly competitive business, and nothing is to be assumed. You should never stop worrying about your customer or your competition, for that matter. Unfortunately, looking behind to see who is catching up will often stop you from going forward. And once you stop moving your business forward, you lose market share.

"Management has been researching methods for our store to maintain its pre-eminent fashion leadership in our trading area. We also want to keep a cap on expenses to avoid any of the financial pitfalls some stores experienced in the 1980s. We believe that our store is in the very enviable position of having low debt and a history of good customer service without excessive operating overhead. Also, we have some very positive demographics in our favor. Polk County, where most of our business is done, is the county with the largest population in the state, and has the highest per capita income. 54% of our total population is young and in their prime career years. The demographic breakdown by age is 17% total population between the ages of 27 to 35, 16% ages 36 to 45, 11% from 46 to 55, and 10% between 22 and 26. This is a wonderful age mix for selling female ready-to-wear. Also, Iowa State University at Ames, is expanding the Schools of Nursing, Education, and Computer Science — all of which will provide us with more potential customers.

"Imagine, Nicole, what these facts can mean to us! Some of these people will be newcomers and seeking stores to patronize that can satisfy their needs.We know of two national chains that are also negotiating for local store sites. But let them have the popular-priced business, that is not our target. If there is a race for customers, we want the battle to be in our area of strength, which is from the medium to better price ranges. And that is where you come in. Our strategy is to consolidate our entire store's fashion position and add another dimension, a more fashion forward look, that will put us far out in front of any other large scale retailer in the region. And it is not beyond probability that we can capture catalog business from the entire state.

"Your part of this fashion uplift program will be as buyer of "The Gallery" — a new advanced/bridge sportswear department — which will focus on the fashion-conscious woman of today. We think "The Gallery" is a term that can be developed to mean good taste for the discriminating customer who is fashion conscious and is willing to pay the right price. It encompasses both the younger customer with some budget restraints and the trend-conscious bridge customer. We've laid out a plan, and it will be formalized in a detailed memorandum that will suggest the logical steps you should take to reach our store goal. Take two or three days, go to each department in the store — particularly ready-to-wear — and inspect the merchandise from the customer's viewpoint. Then examine the stocks of our competition, especially those of better local specialty shops. Get an overview of our position and our competition.

"Naturally, you are relieved of your present position. Your new duties are outlined in the BUYER'S JOB DESCRIPTION (see Figure 1-8, pages 14-15). As far as salary is concerned, starting April 25, it will be increased by $10,000 a year. You will receive a note with the details, as I said, and the time of an appointment to discuss the matter more fully. So, for the next few days you are on your own to assess the store, the customers, the competition, and any ideas in a general way that you think can help our strategy."

Nicole thanked Mr. Johnson and dashed out to make the first phone call with her big news.

JARROD & YOUNG

JOB TITLE: Buyer

REPORTS TO: Group/Divisional merchandise manager, Divisional vice president

SUPERVISES: Assistant buyer, special assistants, trainees, clerical personnel, sales associates; oversees associate buyers

OBJECTIVES

- To implement all activities necessary to achieve departmental profitability goals.
- To operate the department in accordance with the store policies and procedures.
- To identify and support new resources necessary for fashion leadership and store image.
- To increase the profitability of key resources.
- To guide and oversee the responsibilities of the associate buyer.
- To identify, evaluate, and develop executive talent within the department.
- To effectively interact with all external and internal support network.

RESPONSIBILITIES

Planning and Buying

- Works with the DMM/DVP in the development of six-month plans for sales, markups, stock levels, turnover, etc.; revises the approved seasonal plan as business conditions indicate.
- Projects and monitors the open-to-buy budget.
- Selects merchandise that is timely and in keeping with the store's fashion projection and pricing structure.
- Executes purchase orders clearly and thoroughly to avoid misinterpretations.
- Controls allocated advertising budget from store and vendor contributions.

PROMOTION AND MERCHANDISING

- Develops a thorough knowledge of the market and stays abreast of fashion trends and new developments.
- Plans advertising, signing and other promotional activities, such as department demonstrations, trunk shows, videos, displays, and credit listings.
- Coordinates activities with sales promotion departments and fashion coordinators to accomplish promotional events.
- Maintains a balanced stock level for the department in each branch. Allocates and monitors distribution of initial orders of merchandise to the stores; transfers merchandise between locations in response to merchandise trends to maximize corporate sales. Identifies and maintains seasonal in-stock position of basic merchandise.
- Communicates advertising, sales promotion plans, and merchandise information to merchandise coordinators, divisional sales managers, department managers and other concerned store personnel.
- Advises and trains store personnel at regular meetings on the proper presentation of both regular and promotional merchandise, including trending, department layout, merchandise display, signing, and merchandise coordination.
- Visits branch stores at least once every two weeks.

CONTROL AND ADMINISTRATION

- Maintains a shortage control program for the department. Methods include:
  - (a.) Checking to ensure the accuracy of all invoices, transfers, price changes, and vendor returns.
  - (b.) Monitoring all purchase journal transcriptions for timeliness and accuracy.
- Prepares the department for semi-annual inventory.
- Supervises inventory reconciliation for flagship and branch store.

DEVELOPMENT OF STORE PERSONNEL	• Directly coaches the development of the assistant buyer, special assistants, and trainees in the department. Methods include: (a.) On-the-job training in all functions. (b.) Communicating seasonal and long range department goals; and special storewide programs and activities. (c.) Interpreting store policies. (d.) Establishing objectives and standards of performance and monitoring accomplishment goals. • Supervises the associate buyer in the execution of all responsibilities. • Indirectly coaches the development of branch store department managers. Methods include: (a.) Communicating department goals, storewide programs and activities. (b.) Establishing merchandising goals.
INTERNAL RELATIONSHIPS	Promotion of the department through effective interaction with: • Fashion office. • Visual merchandising. • Advertising. • Sales promotion. • Public relations. • Store operations.
EXTERNAL RELATIONSHIPS	Promotion of the department and the store by: • Developing and maintaining a fair, equitable, and professional working relationship with all vendors. • Participating in and supporting RBO functions and requests. • Striving to ensure good customer relations. • Regularly shopping major local competition to be familiar with the activities of similar departments in other major stores. • Providing input and support for product development programs from RBO. • Maintaining communications with domestic and foreign RBO; maintaining familiarity with trade journals, periodicals, and other merchandise information publications.

CHAPTER TWO

The Merchandising Plan

OBJECTIVES

- *Utilize the* MOR Report *as a criterion to establish a department's potential performance.*
- *Recognize the elements and role of the merchandising plan.*
- *Determine the relationships between the elements in the merchandising plan.*
- *Apply the strategies and formulas necessary to develop an actual six-month merchandising plan.*
- *Interpret the role of the open-to-buy as a merchandising tool.*

ASSIGNMENT

Nicole received a memorandum from George Johnson as promised. Although the memo detailed all responsibilities for "The Gallery", the three duties Nicole (you) considered the most important are:

- To study the merchandising plans of an established department, Dept. 375 (better misses sportswear) for the period August through January of last year. (This can be a framework from which a plan can be drawn for the new department.)
- To prepare a six-month plan for your new department and submit it by February 10.
- To detail, on a separate sheet, the factors that influenced the estimates of sales and stock figures for your plan.

Department 375 (better misses sportswear) does an annual volume of $40.8 million, the junior department (378) does approximately $7 million, the women's department does $9.2 million, and the total store's yearly volume for sportswear is $57 million. It is your estimate that "The Gallery" — department 345 — as an advanced bridge business should be able to generate a volume of an additional $9 million in sportswear sales for the first year.[1]

---

[1]All these figures are consolidated to include the flagship store and all branches because "The Gallery" plan will encompass all seven stores.

The six-month plan (also called merchandise plan, dollar plan, or dollar control) is an estimate based on experience plus anticipation. As a flexible tool, it is adjusted based on actual or anticipated developments. The six-month plan considerations include:

- All figures are based on retail prices, known as the retail method of inventory, which is an accounting system used by most department stores. Simply stated, all transactions are at retail. Merchandise is charged into the department's stock at retail, owned at retail, marked up or down at retail, transferred at retail, and sold at retail.
- The major purposes of a plan, which are:
  (a) To insure the most efficient use of capital.
  (b) To maintain a proper balance between stock and sales.
  (c) To set merchandising standards of accomplishment for the greatest profit return, based on percentage figures or ratios for stock turnover, initial markup, stock shortage, advertising cost, discounts, and other figures management deems necessary for the six-month plan. (It should be noted that all standards are related to sales.)
- The major elements of the six-month plan, which are:
  (a) **Planned sales**, which are the estimated sales projected for the month.
  (b) **Retail stock (BOM**—beginning of the month), which is the dollar figure of the inventory necessary to achieve planned sales.
  (c) **Markdowns**, which are the dollar amount of reductions to be taken in the retail selling prices.
  (d) **Retail purchases**, which are the planned amount of stock, at retail, needed to meet the EOM[2] (end of the month) stock figure. Additional components of the six-month plan, such as stock/sales ratio, stock turnover, and percent of initial markon are tools used to measure the actual business performance versus business plan.
- The steps to be followed to arrive at a budget for the purchase of merchandise for delivery within a given period, which are:
  (1) Planned sales.
  (2) Plus planned EOM stock.
  (3) Plus planned markdowns.
  (4) Equals total merchandise requirement.
  (5) Less inventory BOM.
  (6) Equals planned retail purchases.
  (7) Plus or minus stock variations.
  (8) Equals total unadjusted open-to-buy.
  (9) Minus outstanding orders, (i.e., orders placed against anticipated budget).
  (10) Equals current open-to-buy this month.

Analysis of the Six-Month Merchandising Plan

Figure 2-1 (page 22), is a SIX-MONTH MERCHANDISE PLAN FOR DEPARTMENT 375 — AUGUST TO SEPTEMBER that contains the elements incorporated in most six-month merchandising plans. Department 375, misses sportswear, is a well-established business in the store. As previously stated, all figures on the six-month plan are based on the retail method of inventory. Although there are variations of the form, at the buyer level they must include the planned sales

---

[2] The terms beginning-of-the-month (BOM) and end-of-the-month (EOM) inventory figures can be used to describe the same stock in different time frames. For example, the BOM for February is the same as the EOM for January.

and planned stock, markdowns, and retail purchase figures. When the elements are held to this minimum, the merchandise manager adds the additional factors because they are a requirement of management.

Jarrod & Young assigns the responsibility for the entire initial planning to the buyer, who submits the plan to the divisional merchandise manager for approval. It should be understood that a buyer is evaluated by merchandising results and, consequently, all buyers should know how to plan and use all the elements of an entire plan. George Johnson has told Nicole that computerized systems are being tested throughout the store, and will eventually be used for all store information. It is important for Nicole to understand and be comfortable with a variety of report formats, both manual and computerized.

An explanation of each element of Figure 2-1, has been letter cross-referenced, (i.e., (a), (b), etc.) and are explained as follows:

(a) **Planned sales** — The initial step of a six-month merchandising plan is the estimation of sales for each month. Monthly planned sales figures are pivotal to the efficiency of the plan's use and control. Last year's figures and actual sales from the same six-month period are the department's history. Plan figures are the sales goals for this year and percent of increase is the difference between last year's actual versus the plan.

(b) **Planned stock** — After planned sales are determined, it is then necessary to establish monthly inventory (BOM) figures that adequately cover the anticipated sales for that period. Planned sales and planned retail stock are critical to establish a well-conceived plan that can be realistically achieved and provide planned profit results. Retail stock figures and BOM (beginning of the month inventory), are determined at the buyer's level by the application of this stock/sales ratio formula:

$$\text{Stock/Sales Ratio (S/S)} = \frac{\textbf{BOM Retail Stock}}{\textbf{Planned Sales}}$$

(b1) **S/S ratio** — This is determined by the consensus of the buyer's and merchandise manager's experience of the selling patterns of the department, conditions in the current market, and estimated planned economic conditions. Additionally, past history is looked at in planning the stock to sales ratio for each month. The stock/sales ratio is usually different for each month of the six-month period because monthly sales vary due to established peaks and declines in consumer buying patterns. The stock/sales ratio is of primary importance to a buyer to plan the most efficient investment of stock in dollars on a monthly basis. Use of the stock/sales ratio gives a basis for planning stocks that should be on hand at a given time rather than planning average stock, as with stock turnover.

(c) **Planned markdowns** — Markdowns are determined by considering past history and arriving at an acceptable and realistic markdown percent (of sales) for each season. Department 375's planned markdown percent for the season is 24.5% of planned sales, or $5,741,200. Monthly markdown percentages (of monthly sales) are then determined by the same process used in seasonal markdown planning — past history and reasonable expectations. First, the markdown percent of sales, by month, is determined. Second, the markdown dollar figures are established by applying the percent to the planned sales figures. The distribution of markdowns over the six-month period is based on periods during a season when seasonal changes require different emphasis in styles and types of goods desired by customers. The amount of old stock on hand at the beginning of a new season dictates the amount of dollar markdowns necessary at that time.

(d) **Planned retail purchases** — The formula to compute the planned monthly retail purchases is:

> **Planned Sales**
> **+ Planned EOM Stock**
> **+ Planned Markdowns**
>
> **Total Requirements**
> **− Planned BOM Stock**
> **= Planned Retail Purchases**

Planned retail purchases are the result of a mathematical process and only indicate the planned amount of stock at retail needed to meet the EOM stock figure. This should not be mistaken for the open-to-buy figure for the month because that figure varies depending on actual figures and commitments. Once the merchandise plan is put into effect and actual sales figures occur, the merchandising results are included in planning a budget — the open-to-buy (OTB). The buyer must obtain the approval from the divisional merchandise manager (DMM) to spend the open-to-buy dollars.

(e) **Planned percentage of initial markup**[3] — Markup is the difference between the cost price and the retail price. The formula is:

$$\textbf{\\$ Markup} = \textbf{\\$ Retail Price} - \textbf{\\$ Cost Price}$$

The initial markup is the markup that is placed on goods when first received in a retail store. The planned initial markup percentage is one figure for the six-month period and is an average initial markup to be placed on merchandise. This percentage has great significance to both the buyer and management because it reflects the need to make a sufficient gross profit to cover the cost of goods and the cost of doing business, and consequently netting a profit yield on investment. The formula for calculating initial markup percentage is:

$$\textbf{Markup \\% = } \frac{\textbf{\\$ Markup}}{\textbf{\\$ Retail Price}}$$

(f) **Planned end of month (EOM) stock** — The closing inventory of the last month of the plan that gives the seventh inventory figure, which is used for averaging the turnover in the six-month plan. Obviously, it is the BOM for the first month of the following six-month plan.

(g) **Workroom cost** — Charges incurred in running the department, (e.g., alterations, staffing, labels, utilities, housekeeping, pro-rated RBO charges, etc.)

(h) **Cash discount** — A reduction in price for prompt payment to the vendor. The cash discount is expressed as a percent to sales.

(i) **Season stock turnover** — This is a management tool used to measure the efficiency of department over a period of time. It refers to the number of times, within a period, (e.g., six months), that an average stock of merchandise has been turned into sales. Average stock (inventory) and net sales figures are required to calculate stock turnover. To arrive

---

[3] Markup and markon are sometimes used interchangably.

at the average stock figure the planned BOM retail stock figures for six months must be added, plus the EOM for the last month of the period. By including the BOM inventory—which is the result of the purchases of the previous month — the average that is reflected is more precise. This is shown in the following figures, which have been extrapolated from Figure 2-1:

	BOM Stock
August	$10,458,030
September	10,420,091
October	9,373,392
November	13,810,126
December	11,857,340
January	7,748,667
January (EOM)	6,764,550
Total Stock	**$70,432,196**

The total figure is divided by 7, which is the number of inventory figures used:

$$\text{\$ Average Inventory} = \frac{\$70,432,196}{7} = \$10,061,742$$

To determine net sales add the sales figures for the six-month period.

The stock turnover formula is:

$$\text{Stock Turnover} = \frac{\text{\$ Net Sales}}{\text{\$ Average Inventory}}$$

The stock turnover figure can be used with planned or actual figures.

Although the stock turnover and stock/sales ratio figures are related and measure the same merchandising plans or results, there is a difference. The difference is that stock turnover measures the stock average to sales for an entire period and, stock/sales ratio measures stock to sales at a specific point in time, (i.e., the beginning of a month).

(j) **Shortages** — The difference between the dollar amount of merchandise charged to a department — via a purchase journal[4] — and what is actually owned. Actual ownership is determined by taking a physical inventory count. Shortage is expressed as a percent to sales.

(k) **Average stock** — This figure is determined while calculating the season stock turnover — see the explanation for (i).

(l) **Markdown %** — This is the percent to sales representation of the dollar markdowns for the period. The formula is:

$$\text{Markdown \%} = \frac{\text{\$ Total MD}}{\text{\$ Total Net Sales}}$$

The merchandise manager has the option of using different types of six-month plan manual forms. Department 345 chose to use the form depicted in Figure 2-1, page 22. For reference use, Figures 2-2 and 2-3 (pages 23 and 24) show ALTERNATIVE SIX-MONTH MERCHANDISE PLAN FORMS. Although the formats of Figures 2-2 and 2-3 differ from each other — and from Figure 2-1 — the major planning elements of all three forms are the same.

---

[4] The purchase journal is one of the control systems covered in Chapter Eight.

JARROD & YOUNG

Department Name .... Misses Sportswear .... Department No. 375 ....

		PLAN (This Year)	ACTUAL (Last Year)
SIX-MONTH MERCHANDISING PLAN	Workroom cost	1.0	2.8
	Cash discount %	5.2	4.8
	Season stock turnover	2.25	2.22
	Shortage %	2.00	2.65
	Average stock	10,414,106	10,061,742
	Markdown %	24.5	25.8

	SPRING 19	FEB.	MAR.	APR.	MAY	JUNE	JULY	SEASON TOTAL
	FALL 19	AUG.	SEP.	OCT.	NOV.	DEC.	JAN.	
SALES $	Last Year	3,169,100	3,593,135	3,347,640	4,061,802	5,646,353	2,499,570	22,317,600
	Plan	3,354,550	3,745,790	3,538,455	4,264,894	5,940,348	2,589,443	23,433,480
	Percent of Increase	5.8	4.2	5.7	5.0	5.2	3.6	5.0
	Revised							
	Actual							
RETAIL STOCK (BOM) $	Last Year	10,458,030	10,420,091	9,373,392	13,810,126	11,857,340	7,748,667	63,667,646
	Plan	11,070,015	10,488,212	9,199,983	14,500,640	12,401,006	8,136,105	65,795,961
	Revised							
	Actual							
MARKDOWNS $	Last Year	535,600	834,900	932,700	880,500	1,151,700	1,422,500	5,757,900
	Plan (dollars)	576,100	801,700	930,100	824,800	1,196,200	1,412,300	5,741,200
	Plan (percent)	17.1	21.4	26.3	19.3	20.1	54.5	24.5
	Revised							
	Actual							
RETAIL PURCHASES	Last Year	3,666,761	3,381,336	7,904,714	2,989,516	2,689,380	2,937,953	
	Plan	3,348,847	3,259,261	9,769,212	2,990,060	2,871,647	2,968,423	
	Revised							
	Actual							
PERCENT OF INITIAL MARKON	Last Year							
	Plan							
	Revised							
	Actual							
ENDING STOCK July 31 Jan. 31	Last Year						6,764,550	
	Plan						7,102,785	
	Revised							
	Actual							

| Stock/Sales Ratio | LY | 3.3 | 2.9 | 2.8 | 3.4 | 2.1 | 3.1 | 3.0 (FEB) |
| | Plan | 3.3 | 2.8 | 2.6 | 3.4 | 2.1 | 3.1 | 3.0 (FEB) |

Comments Planned sales for the next Spring are $19,406,520. February is planned at 12.2% of the Spring season sales, or $2,367,595.

Merchandise Manager .... Buyer ....

Controller ....

FIGURE 2-2 ALTERNATE SIX-MONTH MERCHANDISING PLAN FORM

Buyer	DIV MGR	GEN MGR	DEPT

6-MONTH MERCHANDISING PLAN FOR PERIOD FROM .... TO .... YEAR ....

STORE NO.			NET SALES	FEB/AUG	MAR/SEP	APR/OCT	MAY/NOV	JUN/DEC	JUL/JAN
ACT LY	PLANNED THIS YEAR	ACT TY	LAST YEAR						
	NET SALES		PLAN						
	AV MO STOCK		THIS YEAR						
	STOCK TURN		EOM STOCK	JAN/JUL	FEB/AUG	MAR/SEP	APR/OCT	MAY/NOV	JUN/DEC	JUL/JAN
	MARK DN %		ACT LY						
	GROSS MARG		PLAN TY						
	MAINT M/U		ACT TY						
			MD LY						
			MD TY						

STORE NO.			NET SALES	FEB/AUG	MAR/SEP	APR/OCT	MAY/NOV	JUN/DEC	JUL/JAN
ACT LY	PLANNED THIS YEAR	ACT TY	LAST YEAR						
	NET SALES		PLAN						
	AV MO STOCK		THIS YEAR						
	STOCK TURN		EOM STOCK	JAN/JUL	FEB/AUG	MAR/SEP	APR/OCT	MAY/NOV	JUN/DEC	JUL/JAN
	MARK DN %		ACT LY						
	GROSS MARG		PLAN TY						
	MAINT M/U		ACT TY						
			MD LY						
			MD TY						

STORE NO.			NET SALES	FEB/AUG	MAR/SEP	APR/OCT	MAY/NOV	JUN/DEC	JUL/JAN
ACT LY	PLANNED THIS YEAR	ACT TY	LAST YEAR						
	NET SALES		PLAN						
	AV MO STOCK		THIS YEAR						
	STOCK TURN		EOM STOCK	JAN/JUL	FEB/AUG	MAR/SEP	APR/OCT	MAY/NOV	JUN/DEC	JUL/JAN
	MARK DN %		ACT LY						
	GROSS MARG		PLAN TY						
	MAINT M/U		ACT TY						
			MD LY						
			MD TY						

STORE NO.			NET SALES	FEB/AUG	MAR/SEP	APR/OCT	MAY/NOV	JUN/DEC	JUL/JAN
ACT LY	PLANNED THIS YEAR	ACT TY	LAST YEAR						
	NET SALES		PLAN						
	AV MO STOCK		THIS YEAR						
	STOCK TURN		EOM STOCK	JAN/JUL	FEB/AUG	MAR/SEP	APR/OCT	MAY/NOV	JUN/DEC	JUL/JAN
	MARK DN %		ACT LY						
	GROSS MARG		PLAN TY						
	MAINT M/U		ACT TY						
			MD LY						
			MD TY						

STORE NO.			NET SALES	FEB/AUG	MAR/SEP	APR/OCT	MAY/NOV	JUN/DEC	JUL/JAN
ACT LY	PLANNED THIS YEAR	ACT TY	LAST YEAR						
	NET SALES		PLAN						
	AV MO STOCK		THIS YEAR						
	STOCK TURN		EOM STOCK	JAN/JUL	FEB/AUG	MAR/SEP	APR/OCT	MAY/NOV	JUN/DEC	JUL/JAN
	MARK DN %		ACT LY						
	GROSS MARG		PLAN TY						
	MAINT M/U		ACT TY						
			MD LY						
			MD TY						

FIGURE 2-3 ALTERNATE SIX-MONTH MERCHANDISING PLAN FORM

PLANNING AND CONTROL

SIX-MONTH MERCHANDISING PLAN

DEPARTMENT NAME

DEPARTMENT NO.

PERIOD COVERED

	LAST YEAR	PLAN		LAST YEAR	PLAN
Initial Markup	....	....	Gross Margin	....	....
Reductions	....	....	Operating Expense	....	....
Maintained Markup	....	....	Operating Profit	....	....
Cash Discount	....	....	Season Turnover	....	....
Buyer	....	....	Date Prepared	....	....

Spring	Fall	Sales +			E.O.M. +			Reductions -			B.O.M. =			Retail Purchases			Cost Purchases		
		Last Year	Plan	Actual	Last Year	Plan	Actual	Last Year	Plan	Actual	Last Year	Plan	Actual	Last Year	Plan	Actual	Last Year	Plan	Actual
Feb.	Aug.																		
Mar.	Sept.																		
Apr.	Oct.																		
May	Nov.																		
June	Dec.																		
July	Jan.																		
	Total																		

Computerized Six-Month Merchandising Plan

Figure 2-4 on page 26, is a sample of the COMPUTER GENERATED SIX-MONTH MERCHANDISING PLAN PROTOTYPE being considered by Jarrod & Young's management for future use. Information from a fictitious department was used to generate this prototype print-out for the Spring 1995 season. This six-month plan shows — by month and by store — the projected sales, beginning of period stocks, markdown dollars, and stock/sales ratio. In addition to a column for the calculation of the open-to-receive figure, an explanation of the elements in Figure 2-4 is cross referenced by letter — (a), (b), etc.[5], and reads:

(a) **Sales** — planned sales for spring 1995 and actual past season figures.

(b) **BOP stock** — Inventory at the beginning of the period, for four years: one year projected, three years actual.

(c) **Markdowns** — The planned markdown dollar figure is arrived at by applying a pre-determined markdown percentage to the planned sales. Actual figures are from the three previous years.

(d) **Open-to-receive** — The amount of stock dollars that can be brought in during a given month. This is closely related to the retail purchases element on Figure 2-1, page 22.

(e) **Stock/sales ratio** — The number of months of stock on hand for the period. As previously noted, department history is looked at in planning the stock/sales ratio for each store and each month.

(f) **Six-month totals** — A summary, for the season, by store, which is divided into the following subcategories:
(f1) *Total dollar sales.*
(f2) *Percent change in sales compared to previous year*, example: the planned sales for Spring '95 represent a .4% increase compared to '94 actual sales. Actual sales for Spring '93 were 45.1% below Spring '92.
(f3) *Total season markdowns in dollars.*
(f4) *Total season markdowns, as a percent to sales.*
(f5) *Stock turn.*

(g) **First period of the next season** — This figure is needed for the BOP stock figure, which is the EOM stock for the previous month.

Open-to-Buy and Open-to-Receive

Open-to-buy (OTB) and open-to-receive (OTR) are control tools that give the buyer a reading of actual department performance versus plan. OTB and OTR provide a means for allocating purchases to meet planned levels. Open-to-buy (OTB) is a budget for purchase of merchandise that may be bought for delivery within the balance of a period to achieve the planned closing stock. This is expressed as:

$$OTB = OTR - On\ Order$$

At the beginning of a period — if no reorders have been placed — it is expressed as:

$$OTB = OTR$$

---

[5] Figures for elements of the six-month merchandising plan print-out are quoted for four years—projections for the planned year (1995), plus actual figures for the previous three years (1994, 1993, 1992). This gives the buyer a better grasp of the history of the department. The elements of this format are largely identical to the elements of the six-month plan on Figure 2-1, page 22.

━ JARROD & YOUNG ━

SIX-MONTH MERCHANDISE PLAN SPRING 1994   VP   DMM   DEPT

MO YR	Cedar Rapids (a.) SALES	(b.) BOP STK	(c.) MKDN $	(d.) O-T-R	(e.) S/S	Ames SALES	BOP STK	MKDN $	O-T-R	S/S	Des Moines SALES	BOP STK	MKDN $	O-T-R	S/S	Davenport SALES	BOP STK	MK
FEB-01 ACT																		
PL	8.1	44.9	0.5		5.5	6.5	52.4	0.9		8.1	9.9	53.4	0.5		5.4	1.6	11.8	
94	8.1	50.0	1.8		6.7	6.5	58.4	3.1		9.0	9.9	59.5	1.7		6.0	1.6	13.1	
93	10.1	36.4	1.4		3.6	8.6	37.1	0.5		4.3	15.8	52.3	0.8		3.3	1.6	16.4	
92	11.0	29.1	-		2.6	6.7	-2.1	-		NM	13.0	41.8	0.2		3.2	1.3	8.7	
MAR-02 ACT																		
PL	15.3	48.8	0.9		3.2	14.3	56.7	1.2		4.0	22.0	65.1	1.0		3.0	3.2	14.9	
94	15.0	61.0	2.9		4.1	14.0	70.8	3.8		5.1	21.6	81.3	3.3		3.8	3.1	18.6	1
93	16.7	61.5	-		3.7	13.8	45.9	0.7		3.3	22.8	63.0	0.9		2.8	3.4	19.1	
92	26.9	31.2	0.6		1.2	14.2	39.8	-		2.8	26.7	49.8	-		1.9	2.6	7.4	
APR-03 ACT																		
PL	12.2	47.9	1.7		3.9	11.5	59.8	1.2		5.2	17.9	67.8	0.8		3.8	2.7	15.2	
94	12.2	53.5	1.9		4.4	11.5	66.8	1.4		5.8	17.9	75.7	0.9		4.2	2.7	17.0	
93	13.0	66.0	2.4		5.1	11.3	46.8	1.6		4.1	23.6	77.4	2.3		3.3	2.2	21.0	
92	30.8	70.2	0.7		2.3	16.6	81.0	1.9		4.9	36.0	84.7	1.0		2.4	5.0	23.0	1
MAY-04 ACT																		
PL	12.2	51.7	-		4.2	9.0	56.4	-		6.3	13.8	70.0	1.5		5.1	1.8	18.0	
94	12.2	52.0	-		4.3	9.0	56.8	-		6.3	13.8	70.4	0.4		5.1	1.8	18.1	
93	10.9	64.3	2.6		5.9	10.8	49.1	-0.3		4.5	21.8	76.4	0.5		3.5	3.3	22.5	
92	26.2	60.4	-		2.3	12.4	53.1	-		4.3	27.6	79.9	3.7		2.9	3.7	21.5	
JUN-05 ACT																		
PL	23.9	53.9	2.8		2.3	23.2	61.6	3.1		2.7	33.8	76.0	3.8		2.2	5.2	23.6	1
94	24.1	51.7	9.1		2.1	23.4	59.0	10.3		2.5	34.0	72.8	12.6		2.1	5.2	22.6	4
93	19.1	55.8	1.9		2.9	14.7	48.9	2.2		3.3	26.4	81.4	2.3		3.1	3.4	21.6	
92	35.2	42.0	1.1		1.2	19.8	49.7	1.0		2.5	36.9	72.2	1.3		2.0	5.0	16.7	
JUL-06 ACT																		
PL	9.1	47.3	1.1		5.1	9.6	54.5	2.7		5.6	13.8	64.4	2.7		4.7	4.2	19.6	1
94	9.0	35.2	1.5		3.9	9.5	40.5	3.8		4.3	13.5	47.9	3.8		3.5	4.1	14.6	1
93	9.3	45.9	4.0		4.9	10.7	42.2	3.9		3.9	18.6	75.0	5.4		4.0	1.8	21.2	1
92	14.1	41.7	3.3		3.0	11.0	42.3	4.0		3.8	17.8	63.3	3.3		3.6	2.5	10.8	

SIX MO TOT	$-SALES (f1.)	%LY (f2.)	$-MKDN (f3.)	% (f4.)	STKTN (f5.)	$-SALES	%LY	$-MKDN	%	STKTN	$-SALES	%LY	$-MKDN	%	STKTN	$-SALES	%LY	$
(f.) ACT																		
PL	80.9	0.4	7.0	8.7	1.6	74.2	0.4	9.1	12.3	1.3	111.2	0.5	10.3	9.3	1.7	18.7	1.1	3
94	80.6	1.9	17.3	21.5	1.7	73.9	5.7	22.4	30.3	1.3	110.7	-14.2	22.7	20.5	1.7	18.5	17.8	7
93	79.1	-45.1	12.3	15.5	1.4	69.9	-13.4	8.6	12.3	1.6	129.0	-18.4	12.2	9.5	1.8	15.7	-21.9	4
92	144.2	-	5.7	4.0	3.1	80.7	-	6.9	8.6	1.9	158.0	-	9.5	6.0	2.4	20.1	-	1
AUG-07 ACT																		
(g.) PL	-	63.7	-		-	-	53.4	-		-	-	68.4	-		-	-	22.5	
94	14.8	37.7	0.4		2.5	11.5	31.6	0.2		2.7	21.3	40.5	2.8		1.9	2.9	13.3	
93	8.4	53.1	-		6.3	10.3	40.1	0.9		3.9	27.0	68.3	-0.2		2.5	1.4	11.7	
92	25.6	53.3	-		2.1	15.5	34.9	-		2.3	32.7	70.4	0.1		2.2	3.8	19.0	

SIX-MONTH MERCHANDISE PLAN SPRING 1994   VP   DMM   DEPT

Open-to-receive (OTR) is the amount of merchandise that may be received — regardless of what is "on order" — during the period to achieve the planned closing stock. Open-to-buy is used as a purchase planning tool; open-to-receive is a real indicator of a department's ability to meet its end-of-month stock requirements. Factors that affect OTB and OTR are:
(Please note that + means increase, − means decrease, and 0 means no effect.)

	OTB	OTR
Sales	+	+
Markdowns	+	+
Return to vendors[6]	+	+
Shortage	+	+
Increased sales plan	+	+
Increased markdown plan	+	+
Increased EOM stock plan	+	+
Canceling orders	+	0
Postponing orders	+	0
Writing orders	−	0
Receiving Merchandise	−	−

The Open-to-Buy Report

Each Monday, the buyer receives an open-to-buy report. This report gives current information about how the department is performing against the six-month plan. The major element of open-to-buy reports are the same as six-month plans: sales, stock, markdowns, and purchases (open-to-buy).

Figure 2-5, page 31, is a COMPUTER GENERATED OPEN-TO-BUY REPORT prototype that is being tested by another department at Jarrod & Young. An explanation of each element of Figure 2-5 is letter cross-referenced — (a), (b), etc. The elements of this OTB report are:

(a) **Sales**, which is divided into such subcategories as:
(a1) *Current period plan* — Planned sales for the month taken from the six-month plan, or as revised to reflect current business performance. At the end of the month, this line shows next month's planned sales.
(a2) *Period to date — this year* — Actual sales for this month. This will be flash sales early in the month, and a combination of audit and flash mid-month. Last OTB strip of the period includes an adjustment for audit up/down through Tuesday of prior week.
(a3) *Period to date — last year* — Last year's audited sales for the same period. This is included for comparison purposes.
(a4) *% Change* — Percent increase, or, if followed by − (minus) percent decrease, this year versus last year.
(a5) *Sales: year to beginning of period — this year* — Audited sales for this year up to but not including this month.
(a6) *Sales: year to beginning of period — last year* — Audited sales for the same period last year.
(a7) *% Change* — Percent increase/decrease of audited sales compared to last year.

---

[6] Merchandise damaged, not ordered, or merchandise shipped not as ordered.

(b) **Stocks**, which is divided into such subcategories as:

(b1) *Audited stock beginning of period* — Dollar amount of stock on hand at beginning of month. This is an audited figure and includes bills not journalized.

(b2) *Bills not journalized (BNJ)* — A memo figure, from previous period.

(b3) *Net receipts — period to date* — Merchandise received into stock this period, minus returns to vendor, plus OTB corrections. Totals for additions to stock are taken from purchase journals and flash receipts reports. For merchandise received but not yet journalized, the prior month maintained markup is used to compute approximate retails from actual or estimated costs.

(b4) *Transfers in* — Additions to stock, incoming merchandise transfers, as of previous Wednesday noon.

(b5) *Transfers out* — Reductions from stock, that is merchandise transferred to other stores. As in *Transfers in*, white copies of transfers received in statistics the previous Wednesday noon will appear in these totals. The sum of the two transfer lines will be "0".

(b6) *Last week on hand — this year* — Estimated stock (flash) in each store as reported on last week's OTB strip.

(b7) *Beginning of period stock plan* — From the six-month plan, this appears on first report of month only.

(b8) *This week on hand — this year* — Estimated stock (flash) in each store on date of report, which may be checked against department's physical stock. Large discrepancies should be investigated. The stock on hand figure is computed by adding BOP Stock, flash receipts, transfers. The sales and markdowns to date are then subtracted from this total. No adjustments are made for inventory shortage except when inventory is being taken.

(b9) *This week on hand — last year* — Estimated stock on hand this week last year, included for comparison.

(b10) *TY-LY $ Change* — Dollar increase/decrease compared to last year.

(b11) *Beginning of period stock plan* — Planned stock of beginning of the next period, from six-month plan.

(c) **Outstanding orders** — These are listed by month for the next three months. This sample shows report for end-of-month and is divided into the following subcategories:

(c1) *Current period* — Merchandise on order expected this month, which is taken from yellow copies of orders on file in order checking.

(c2) *After — outstanding* — Merchandise ordered for delivery after this three-month period.

(d) **Open-to-buy balance** — The amount of money available for purchases this month, or, at the end of the month, the amount available for purchases next month. This is computed by adding planned sales and planned end of month stocks, then subtracting from this total the sales to date, current stock on hand, current outstanding orders, and planned markdowns not yet taken.

(e) **Markup %** — The difference between the cost of goods sold and the retail price, divided by the retail price. This is divided into the following subcategories:

(e1) *Last period — actual* — Markup % for last month, from purchase journal.

(e2) *Last period — plan* — Planned markup, from six-month plan.

(e3) *Season to BOP — this year* — Maintained markup for season to beginning of this month.

(e4) *Season to BOP — last year* — Last year's maintained markup for the same period, for comparison.

(f) **Markdowns** — which are divided into the following subcategories:

(f1) *Period to date* — Actual markdowns in dollars for this month by store. Taken from price change documents received in the statistical department by previous Thursday noon.

(f2) *This period plan* — Planned markdowns by store, from six-month plan.

(f3) *Year to beginning of period* — Actual markdowns taken in dollars to the beginning of the period. Also shown is percent to sales for year to beginning of period.

Open-to-Buy Reconciliation

Figure 2-6, JARROD & YOUNG'S BUYER'S INVENTORY RECONCILIATION SHEET, page 32, contains information from the open-to-buy report and is used to adjust projections on the six-month plan. These adjustments to projections are calculated every week on the open-to-buy reconciliation sheet, after receipt of the OTB report. Reconciliation allows the buyer to reassess continuously the department's actual performance versus planned performance, and to realistically modify future projections.

Most open-to-buy (or inventory) reconciliation sheets cover a three-month period: the current month, first future (the month after the current month), and second future (the month after the first future). The designated "current month" changes at the start of the new month. The weekly columns in each month allow the buyer to progressively make adjustments, (i.e., plus or minus) to sales, stock, on-hand, on-order, open-to-buy, and open-to-receive figures.

APPLICATION

As part of Nicole's research, she must analyze the most current *Merchandising and Operating Results Reports (MOR)*. This trade publication is published annually and is a compilation of actual departmental and classification merchandising results. Figure 2-7, pages 33-52, represents selected pages from the *MOR*. Nicole (you) should study these carefully because they provide the most pertinent comprehensive retail information for your purpose, which is:

- The pattern of sportswear growth.
- Stock turnover.
- Contribution of sportswear to the division and total store.
- Other pertinent statistical information that includes markup, stock/sales ratio, markdowns, and shortages.

After examining these figures, you are now ready to evaluate the performance and plan of department 375, misses sportswear (see Figure 2-1, page 22), as a basis for forming a six-month merchandising plan for "The Gallery", department 345. You consider the following:

- Evidence supports the premise that sportswear represents an area of continued growth potential for Jarrod & Young compared with the *MOR* figures.

- Jarrod & Young's total sportswear volume is currently $57 million, or 19% of the total store sales, which is below the industry record stated in the *MOR*. This was concluded on the following basis:

  (a) Female Apparel (*MOR*, Dept. No 1000, page 42), constitutes approximately 36.2% (median) of the net sales of the total store.

  (b) Total Sportswear (*MOR*, Dept. No. 1040, page 49), is approximately 21.4% (median) to 23.8% (superior) of the net sales of the total store. A reasonable percentage goal for total sportswear would be approximately 22% of the net sales of the total store.

  (c) Using Jarrod & Young's current total store volume of $300,000,000 × 22% = $66,000,000, or $9,000,000 more that could be generated as compared to the current actual total sportswear volume of $57,000,000.

You conclude that there is a potential to increase the store's sportswear business by $9,000,000.

On the basis of a planned volume of $9,000,000 for the first year of department 345, "The Gallery", prepare a six-month merchandise plan for the period August 1 to January 31. Refer to the CONVENTIONAL DEPARTMENT STORES MONTHLY SALES DISTRIBUTION chart in the *MOR* section (Figure 2-7, page 47), for the total percent to the business done during these six months.

Complete and submit Figure 2-8, SIX-MONTH MERCHANDISING PLAN FORM, page 53, to Mr. Johnson (Instructor) for approval. Use Figures 2-9 and 2-10, (pages 55, 57) as worksheets.

In compliance with your divisional merchandise manager's (DMM) request, also prepare an ANALYSIS OF FIGURES report (Figures 2-11 through 2-14, pages 59-62) that shows how you gathered and analyzed the factors that led to your conclusions. Be prepared to justify:

- The total estimated sales for the six-month period.
- The sales estimates for each month.
- The planned BOM stock for each month.
- The stock turnover for the period.
- The planned markdowns for the period.
- The planned monthly retail purchases.

Mr. Johnson has advised that you are to "keystone" to calculate your initial markup figure, which should be shown in its proper place on the plan. Keystoning will give you a 50% initial markup%. Remember:

$$\text{Markup \%} = \frac{\$ \text{ Retail price} - \$ \text{ Cost price}}{\$ \text{ Retail price}}$$

For example, if $35.00 is the cost price and your markup is based on keystone, $70.00 is the retail price.

$$\text{Markup \%} = \frac{\$70.00 - \$35.00}{\$70.00}$$

$$= \frac{\$35.00}{\$70.00}$$

$$= 50\%[7]$$

---

[7] Or a dollar retail price that is double your cost price.

FIGURE 2-5   JARROD & YOUNG'S COMPUTER GENERATED OPEN-TO-BUY REPORT

JARROD & YOUNG

		(a.) SALES	-SALES	-SALES	-SALES	-SALES	-SALES	-SALES	-SALES	-SALES
(a1.)	APR	PERIOD PLN	13.9	10.6	21.6	27.9	12.2	11.5	17.9	2.7
(a2.)	MAR	PTD TY	17.4	13.0	32.3	27.3	18.9	14.6	19.8	3.0
(a3.)		LY	19.4	14.9	25.3	29.0	15.0	14.0	21.6	3.1
(a4.)	MAR TY-LY	%CHG	-7.7	-12.8	58.6	-5.9	26.0	4.3	-8.3	-3.2
(a5.)	YR TD BOP	MAR TY	12.3	12.0	23.1	19.1	10.2	9.8	13.9	2.3
(a6.)		LY	12.4	9.5	8.5	15.0	8.1	6.5	9.9	1.6
(a7.)	YR TY-LY	%CHG	-0.5	26.3	171.8	27.3	25.9	50.8	40.4	43.8
(b.)		STOCK	STK	STK	STK	STK	STK	STK	STK	STK
(b1.)	MAR AUDIT	OH BOP	62.6	65.0	74.8	80.2	58.4	47.6	71.0	23.5
(b2.)	MAR -MEMO-BNJ	BOP	23.1	5.9	17.0	14.9	4.9	7.2	10.0	1.1
(b3.)	MAR NET RCPTS	PTD	37.5	34.2	60.0	76.8	50.1	36.3	53.1	14.3
(b4.)	MAR TRANSFERS	IN	0.2	0.8	12.1	2.4	0.3	1.0	3.1	0.2
(b5.)		OUT	-3.2	-5.4	-0.7	-2.4	-5.8	-2.6	-5.6	-0.2
(b6.)	LAST WK ON HND	TY	81.8	82.4	105.1	126.3	72.1	64.8	92.4	32.9
(b7.)	APR BOP STOCK	PLN	95.3	49.4	86.0	77.0	47.9	59.8	67.8	15.2
(b8.)	THIS WK ON HND	TY	88.0	81.6	114.0	129.7	84.1	67.7	101.8	34.8
(b9.)		LY	108.7	57.8	104.3	89.2	54.9	67.5	79.8	17.3
(b10.)	TY-LY	%CHG	-20.7	23.8	9.7	40.5	29.2	0.2	22.0	17.5
(b11.)	MAY BOP STOCK	PLN	105.5	51.4	91.2	77.2	51.7	56.4	70.0	18.0
(c.)	OUTSTANDING	OTB	OUTST	OUTST	OUTST	OUTST	OUTST	OUTST	OUTST	OUTST
	MAR	OUTST	1.6	6.3	19.3	12.1	4.8	11.7	15.8	8.6
	APR	OUTST	34.9	16.8	22.7	21.3	5.1	17.1	20.0	9.4
	MAY	OUTST	14.0	11.5	17.5	17.5	13.0	10.1	14.7	7.0
(c1.)	JUN	OUTST								
(c2.)	AFTER JUN	OUTST								
(d.)	APR OP-TO-BUY	BAL	-3.6	-42.1	-41.5	-54.7	-28.4	-27.4	-43.9	-32.1
(e.)		MARKUP								
(e1.)	FEB	ACT %	47.2	47.1	48.4	51.1	47.1	46.9	47.1	47.3
(e2.)	FEB	PLAN %								
(e3.)	MMU—SEAS TD	TY								
(e4.)	BOP MAR	LY								
(f.)		MARKDOWNS	MKD	MKD	MKD	MKD	MKD	MKD	MKD	MKD
(f1.)	MAR	PTD								
(f2.)	MAR	PLN	0.9	0.8	1.3	1.0	0.9	1.2	1.0	0.4
(f3.)	YR TD BOP MAR	TY$	0.2	0.2	1.0	0.4	0.4	0.5	0.4	0.1
		TY%	1.6	1.7	4.3	2.1	3.9	5.1	2.9	4.3
			DEPT	DEPT	DEPT	DEPT	DEPT	DEPT	DEPT	DEPT
			04-02-	04-02-	04-02-	04-02-	04-02-	04-02-	04-02-	04-02-

FIGURE 2-6 JARROD AND YOUNG'S BUYER'S INVENTORY RECONCILIATION SHEET

JARROD & YOUNG
BUYER'S INVENTORY RECONCILIATION SHEET

Department No. ....

Current Month ....

Current Month ( )	BOP	2nd Wk	3rd Wk	4th Wk	5th Wk
1. On Hand on OTB this week					
2. Plus or minus adjustments*					
3. Adjusted on hand					
4. Actual on order					
5. Total liabilities					
6. Planned sales					
7. Revised planned sales					
8. Planned BOM stock (6-month plan)					
9. Current estimated BOM stock					
10. Balance OTR for month					
11. OTR Reserve					
12. Adjusted on order					

Second Month ( )					
1. EST BOP stock					
2. Plus or minus adjustments*					
3. Adjusted on hand					
4. Actual on order					
5. Total liabilities					
6. Planned sales					
7. Revised planned sales					
8. Planned BOM stock (6-month plan)					
9. Current estimated BOM stock					
10. Balance OTR for month					
11. OTR Reserve					
12. Adjusted on order					

Third Month ( )					
1. EST BOP stock					
2. Plus or minus adjustments*					
3. Adjusted on hand					
4. Actual on order					
5. Total liabilities					
6. Planned sales					
7. Revised planned sales					
8. Planned BOM stock (6-month plan)					
9. Current estimated BOM stock					
10. Balance OTR for month					
11. OTR Reserve					
12. Adjusted on order					

*Explanation of Adjustments (RTV's, etc.)

FIGURE 2-7   MOR REPORT

```
┌─────────────────────────────┐
│   M O R -- R E F E R E N C E │
└─────────────────────────────┘
```

Usage and Definitions

Uses Of The MOR

Data in the MOR have three major uses: strategic, merchandising and public. For different firms and over time these uses will vary in importance.

Strategically, data which convey sales, productivity, gross margin, and selected expense information for various kinds of retailers selling the same category of merchandise have several important purposes. Data can serve as benchmarks for firms assessing whether to introduce a category of merchandise into new or existing stores. They can also help when considering whether to change the merchandise thrust of an existing merchandise line. Conversely, the data may also be of assistance when contemplating whether to discontinue a particular merchandise design. Still, another strategic use is to help establish feasible goals for long-range operational improvements.

The merchandising uses of these data are mainly for long-range purposes. For example, the data can be used to appraise how, over a several year period, a firm's own operation in a particular merchandising area fares compared with industry performance. Because of lack of precise comparability and unavoidable delays in

availability, use caution when comparing the MOR data with your current operations.

Suppliers will find the data useful as well. The MOR data can be used to help ascertain what retailers require from suppliers for participation in the marketing of a specific product line.

The public uses of the data include providing information for labor and lease negotiations and for government investigations into the industry. Should circumstances ever warrant a return to price controls, the MOR information could be important in the administration of such controls. Also, of course, the information is useful both to the academic and financial communities and to the media in their assessment of the retail industry.

In summary, the purposes of publishing the MOR data is to help make retailing, government, and industry analysts aware of actual operating results in the industry and to reinforce the industry's competitive climate.

Meaning and Source of MOR Ratios

Source of the MOR Information

All the information presented in this report is based upon actual departmental and classification merchandising information reported to the NRF for incorporation in this survey.

Cooperating companies converted their department and classifications to the corresponding MOR merchandising groups. They then provided actual dollar information which was translated into MOR ratio format in accordance with the computer programs written expressly for this purpose. Similarly, as will be explained below, this computer program also provides for the automatic determination and print-out of the results published herein. It also provides each contributor with a print-out of his own performance data. The tables

presented are photo reproductions of the output reports generated by the computer pursuant to this program.

The data continued in this report comes from companies which reported information for the total fiscal year end only...i.e., after the conclusion of the fiscal year as soon as this source information had been compiled on their books. Here, dollar data was converted to MOR ratio format and incorporated into the aggregate samples from which the information presented in this book was derived.

Median Performance

A median is determined by listing the various ratios in order of magnitude. The ratio situated at the mid-point of the list is the median.

For example, assume a range of markdowns from 4.5 percent to 5.7 percent exist among the 17 reporting companies as shown below:

Number of Companies	Markdown Ratio Reported
1	4.5%
4	4.8%
1	5.1%
3	5.2%
3	5.6%
5	5.7%

The median is determined by selecting the ratio at the mid-point when all of the results are listed from low to high. In this example (see below), the median is 5.2 percent. There are eight stores above and eight stores below this median.

Superior Performance

A superior ratio is determined using the same listing as in the selection of the median. The listing is divided into four quarters or "quartiles." The superior figure published represents a performance level superior to that achieved by 75 percent of all companies in the sample. (see illustration.)

For ratios where a low result is desirable, the superior would be the lower quartile figure (in the above example the fourth ratio, 4.8 percent). Where a high result is desirable, the superior would be the higher quartile (referring to the preceding example, the fourth from the bottom 5.7 percent). Users of this report should exercise caution when interpreting "Superior" performance. Superior performance is defined merely as the lower quartile for expense related measures and upper quartile for productivity measures. It is not necessarily indicative of *superior company profitability*.

Minimum Sample Size

To insure meaningful information, all published data was obtained from a sample of at least six stores, except when indicated otherwise.

MOR Merchandise Classifications

Participating companies matched their selling departments and classifications with the merchandise groupings detailed in the instruction booklets entitled "MOR Merchandise Classifications."

The numbering system used to identify the merchandising groups was designed to reflect primarily two different reporting levels within each major merchandise group:

1. Merchandise Division or Category
2. Demand Center or Department

Net Sales Percent Change Over Last Year

Net sales are gross sales less customer returns and allowances. The ratio of net sales this year to those of the same period last year was calculated using last year's net sales as the base (100 percent).

Net Sales—Percent of Total Store

These ratios represent the percentage of total store net sales (owned plus leased departments), accounted for by each cost, retail and leased selling departments.

Cumulative Markon

Cumulative markon is the percentage of markon applicable to all goods available for sale since the beginning of the current period (i.e., beginning inventory plus all merchandise received and recorded to date).

The cumulative markon in dollars is the difference between the delivered cost of the merchandise and the cumulative selling prices originally set.

a) Beginning of the year inventory at *retail* plus additions to date. = Cumulative (i.e., total) merchandise available at retail.

b) Beginning of the year inventory at cost plus net merchandise purchases at *cost* to date. = Cumulative (i.e., total) merchandise available at cost.

c) Cumulative retail (line a) minus cumulative cost (line b). = Cumulative markon dollars.

d) Cumulative markon dollars (line c) divided by cumulative retail (line a). = Cumulative markon percentage.

The delivered cost of the merchandise consists of beginning inventory at cost plus the gross invoice cost of merchandise purchased (adjusted for returns to vendors and transfers between departments at cost) and including transportation charges.

The gross invoice cost represents the invoice cost before cash discounts have been deducted. For the purpose of computing cumulative markon, stores were instructed not to deduct cash discounts.

Markdowns

Markdowns are the dollar reduction from the originally set retail prices of merchandise and are net of markdown cancellations.

Markdowns include allowances granted to customers and discounts to employees but do not include inventory shortages. Markdown ratios are computed by dividing the dollars of markdowns by net sales.

Stock Shortage

Stock shortage is also sometimes referred to as inventory shortage or inventory shrinkage.

Stock shortage is the difference between book inventory, at retail (as derived under the retail inventory method), and the physical inventory in terms of retail values.

This difference is divided by the net sales and yields the stock shortage as a percent of net sales.

Gross Margin—Percent of Net Sales

Gross margin is the excess of sales over the cost of sales. Cost of sales includes cost of merchandise sold plus alteration or workroom costs and cash discounts earned under the retail method of inventory.

The method of computing gross margin is as follows:

	Cost	Retail	% of Sales	Cumulative Markon %
1. Beginning Inventory plus additions	$6,000	$10,000		40.0%
2. Net Sales		2,000	100.0%	
3. Markdowns		200	10.0	
4. Inventory Shortage		40	2.0	
5. Total (Lines 2, 3 and 4)		2,240		
6. Closing Retail Inventory (Line 1 minus Line 5)		$7,760		
7. Closing Inventory at Cost ($7,760 x 60%; i.e., 100%—Cum. Markon %	$4,656			
8. Merchandise Cost of Sales (Line 1 minus Line 7)	$1,344			
9. Merchandise Margin (Line 2 Minus Line 8)	656		32.8	
10. Plus: Cash Discounts	80		4.0	
11. (Line 9 plus Line 10)	734		36.8	
12. Less: Net Workroom Cost	-20		-1.0	
13. Gross Margin	$716		35.8%	

Gross Margin Return per Dollar of Cost Inventory

This ratio is a measure of the efficiency of the investment of inventory. It is computed by dividing gross margin by average cost of inventory. Average cost inventory is the sum of the cost inventories at the end of each month added to the opening inventory at the beginning of the year and divided by thirteen, i.e., the number of inventories used.

This is a most significant ratio which identifies the degree of efficiency in the utilization of funds invested in inventory. A dollar invested into inventory can be thought of as being similar to a share of stock. This ratio of the productivity of each dollar invested in inventory represents an equivalent corresponding, to a degree, to earnings per share of stock.

The most significant factor influencing and affecting this result is the rate of inventory turnover. The more times a year the money invested in inventory is converted into sales and gross margin, re-invested in inventory and reconverted into sales, the greater will be the return per dollar of inventory. The frequency of this "re-use or re-investment" is a more significant factor than differences in a department's rate of markon or gross margin.

No store can afford to tie up working capital in inventory that is not producing the maximum amount of gross margin dollars on the minimum investment.

Stock Turns (Times) at Retail

Stock turnover is calculated by dividing average inventory at retail into the net sales for the year. Average inventory is the sum of the retail inventories at the end of each month added to the initial opening inventory and divided by thirteen, the number of inventories used. Year-end and monthly book inventories include all merchandise received but not yet charged to the departmental inventories. Merchandise in transit, i.e., not yet physically received by the store, is not included in calculating monthly and year-end inventories. Total store turnover is based on total owned retail department results only. Cost department sales and inventory are excluded.

Selling Salaries—Percent of Sales

To provide a uniform basis of comparison among the various forms of selling organizations, the selling function, for accounting purposes, includes salespeople, zone and central check-out cashiers and personnel performing stock keeping and stock replenishment on the selling floor.

Salespeople's salaries consist of wages, commissions, premium monies and bonuses paid to the regular and extra salespeople, and include other direct or indirect compensation of salespersons charged directly to selling departments; i.e., vacations, sick leave, separation and military pay, are included here.

Although many stores require buyers to spend some time on selling floor, for the purpose of consistency in accounting and expense control, no part of the buyer's time should have been charged to selling. Assistant buyers, however, may spend a lot of time on the selling floor. It is recommended that payroll transfers to selling departments be kept at a minimum or avoided entirely.

Buying Salaries

This represents the expenses associated with the buying function. It includes the salary and expenses of the buyer as well as support personnel such as assistant buyer, clerical and others who generally assist in the discharge of the buyers responsibilities.

Advertising Expense

This includes all expenses associated with media advertising including institutional advertising, i.e., newspapers, magazines, TV, radio, direct mail and any other form of direct mass media advertising.

Total Direct Expense

For MOR purposes, this is the sum of selling, advertising and buying expense expressed as a percent of net sales. It does not include interest on inventory at cost.

Contribution Dollar Return per Dollar Average Cost Inventory

This ratio is a refinement of the Gross Margin Return per Average Dollar of Cost Inventory ratio by going one step further.

It is computed by dividing contribution dollars (gross margin dollars less total direct expense dollars) by average cost inventory.

Net Sales per Square Foot of Selling Space

This ratio reflects the sales volume productivity of each square foot of selling space. Departmental results are derived by dividing each department's net sales by the average number of square feet of selling space occupied by the department. Selling space includes the total space occupied by the selling department, fitting rooms, forward stock area adjacent to the selling department, clerk aisles and customer aisles between selling department. Only the space immediately contiguous to stairways, elevators, escalators and store entrances is included in the departmental selling area.

Gross Margin per Square Foot of Selling Space

Gross margin dollars are divided by the number of square feet of selling space.

Contribution per Square Foot of Selling Space

Gross margin dollars less total direct expense dollars produces contribution dollars. Contribution dollars divided by the square feet of selling space produces contribution dollars per square foot of selling space.

Average Inventory (at Retail) per Square Foot of Selling Space

Average inventory is the sum of the retail inventories at the end of each month added to the initial opening inventory and divided by thirteen, the number of inventories used. The result is then divided by the number of square feet in the department or division. Year-end and monthly book inventories include all merchandise received but not yet charged to the departmental inventories. Merchandise in transit, not physically received by the store, is not included in calculating monthly and year-end inventories.

Merchandise Classification Description

MOR MERCHANDISE CLASSIFICATIONS
BY DIVISION, DEPARTMENT, AND CLASS
DEPARTMENT AND SPECIALTY STORES

1000--FEMALE APPAREL

1010--Coats, Dresses, and Suits--Summary

1011--Women's, Misses, and Junior Coats
1012--Women's, Misses, and Junior Suits
1015--Fur and Fur Garments
1017--Women's and Misses Dresses
1019--Junior Dresses

1040--Sportswear and Casualwear--Summary

1041--Women's and Misses Sportswear
1045--Junior Sportswear

1070--Intimate Apparel--Summary

1071--Intimate Daywear
1075--Intimate Nightwear
1076--Loungewear and Robes
1091--All Other Apparel

2000--ADULT FEMALE ACCESSORIES

2011--Fine Jewelry and Watches
2012--Costume Jewelry
2015--Hosiery
2017--Gloves
2019--Handbags

2021--Small Leather Goods
2023--Millinery
2025--Neckwear, Rainwear, Belts, Handerchiefs
2091--All Other Accessories

3000--MEN'S AND BOY'S APPAREL AND ACCESSORIES

3011--Men's and Boy's Clothing
3021--Men's and Boy's Furnishings
3031--Men's and Boy's Accessories

3041--Men's and Boy's Sportswear
3091--All Other Men's and Boy's Apparel and
Accessories

4000--INFANT'S AND CHILDREN'S CLOTHING AND ACCESSORIES

4011--Infant's and Toddler's Apparel and
Furniture (Baby World)
4021--Girl's (4-6x, 7-14) Clothing, Underwear,
and Accessories

4031--Little Boy's (4-7) Wear
4091--All Other Infant's and Children's
Clothing and Accessories

4500--SHOES

4511--Women's, Misses, and Junior Shoes
4521--Men's Footwear

4531--Children's Footwear
4541--Athletic Footwear
4591--All Other Footwear

5000--COSMETICS AND DRUGS

5011--Cosmetics, Toiletries, and Fragrances

5021--Drugs & Sundry (Beauty Aids)

All Department Store Results by Merchandise Category

All Specialty Store Results by Merchandise Category

All Department Stores

Summary by Merchandise Category	Female Apparel (1000)	Adult Female Accessories (2000)	Men's & Boys Apparel & Accessories (3000)	Infants & Children's Clothing & Accessories (4000)
Sales Data				
Net Sales % Change over Last Year	5.7%	3.1%	5.3%	7.3%
Net Sales - % of Total Store	36.2	8.4	16.2	6.2
Merchandising & Inventory				
Cumulative Markon %	53.3%	54.8%	53.2%	52.4%
Markdown % (Including Employee Discount)	30.8	16.3	25.7	26.4
Stock Shortage %	2.4	2.9	2.1	1.5
Gross Margin (Including Workroom Cost & Cash Discounts)	41.1	45.9	39.1	40.7
Inventory Productivity				
Gross Margin $ Return Per $ Average Cost Inventory	$2.80	$2.10	$1.80	$2.40
Stock Turns (Times) at Retail	3.1x	2.2x	2.2x	2.8x
Contribution $ Return Per $ Cost Inventory	$2.00	$1.70	$1.20	$1.70
Expense Data - % Net Sales				
Selling Salaries	7.3%	9.3%	7.2%	7.7%
Buying Salaries	2.2	2.7	2.3	2.3
Advertising	3.4	3.1	3.3	3.3
Total Direct Expense	13.6	15.1	12.8	15.3
Space Productivity ($ per Square Foot of Selling Space)				
Net Sales	$164.00	$185.00	$142.00	$111.00
Gross Margin	63.40	86.90	55.60	41.70
Contribution	50.00	66.90	53.10	31.50
Average Inventory (At Retail $)	46.10	81.50	58.30	36.80

Footnote: **All Department Stores Leased & Cost Departments**

	Adult Female Accessories (2000)	Shoes (4500)	Service Departments (9600)	Other Leased Departments (9900)	Cost Departments
Net Sales % Change over Last Year	9.0%	9.9%	2.5	(0.8)	3.4
Net Sales - % of Total Store	2.3	4.4	2.0	3.4	1.1

Owned Departments

	Shoes (4500)	Cosmetics & Drugs (5000)	Recreation (6000)	Home Furnishings (7000)	Other Hard Lines (8000)	All Other Merchandise (9000)
	5.3%	9.2%	3.6%	1.5%	7.9%	(2.6%)
	6.9	7.0	2.8	11.9	6.7	0.7
	52.0%	40.5%	47.3%	47.0%	34.8%	41.8%
	23.3	2.0	13.5	16.7	7.7	12.3
	1.1	1.1	2.1	1.4	1.5	2.6
	39.9	38.9	39.0	38.0	29.9	34.4
	$1.40	$1.30	$1.30	$1.20	$1.20	$2.30
	1.6x	2.1x	2.1x	1.7x	3.1x	4.3x
	--	$1.20	$0.90	$0.70	--	2.00
	11.5%	7.9%	10.1%	9.7%	--	10.0%
	3.5	1.9	3.5	2.8	--	2.4
	3.6	2.7	2.7	4.1	--	1.5
	17.7	11.7	17.3	15.9	--	17.5
	162.00	327.00	$125.50	$78.00	--	$222.50
	53.60	116.30	49.90	31.80	--	94.90
	--	89.60	35.80	18.10	--	66.50
	--	176.80	57.20	47.30	--	46.60

Since medians are used, component figures of an item may not necessarily total. Additionally, the same retailers may not participate each year, so year-to-year comparisons may not be completely valid

Performance Trends/Tables

Department Store Inventory Price Indexes--January 1990
National basis, January 1941 = 100, unless otherwise noted

			Indexes		Percent Change to Jan 1990 from	
		Jan 1989	Jul 1989	Jan 1990	Jan 1989	Jul 1989
1.	Piece Goods	409.8	418.5	452.0	10.3	8.0
2.	Domestics and Draperies	591.2	595.5	594.8	0.6	-0.1
3.	Women's and Children's Shoes	570.7	580.5	570.1	-0.1	-1.8
4.	Men's Shoes	832.4	822.1	841.4	1.1	2.3
5.	Infants' Wear	553.0	565.8	549.8	-0.6	-2.8
6.	Women's Underwear	466.2	462.4	470.7	1.0	1.8
7.	Women's Hosiery[1]	246.4	247.4	250.9	1.8	1.4
8.	Women's and Girls' Accessories	504.2	520.2	520.7	3.3	0.1
9.	Women's Outerwear and Girls' Wear	367.9	359.7	364.9	-0.8	1.4
10.	Men's Clothing	527.0	526.2	534.9	1.5	1.7
11.	Men's Furnishings	517.9	522.3	525.5	1.5	0.6
12.	Boy's Clothing and Furnishings	457.8	436.5	445.8	-2.6	2.1
13.	Jewelry	785.3	816.7	819.7	4.4	0.4
14.	Notions	522.3	522.9	540.7	3.5	3.4
15.	Toilet Articles and Drugs	724.0	733.6	747.7	3.3	1.9
16.	Furniture and Bedding	586.8	583.4	584.7	-0.4	0.2
17.	Floor Coverings	508.7	504.5	508.2	-0.1	0.7
18.	Housewares	735.6	726.4	735.4	0.0	1.2
19.	Major Appliances	248.8	244.8	243.9	-2.0	-0.4
20.	Radio and Television	94.6	93.4	92.5	-2.2	-1.0
21.	Recreation and Education2	107.8	108.5	109.4	1.5	0.8
22.	Home Improvements[2]	105.9	109.3	112.0	5.8	2.5
23.	Automotive Accessories[2]	104.2	104.7	105.4	1.2	0.7
1-15:	Soft Goods	521.3	522.3	526.2	0.9	0.7
16-20:	Durable Goods	454.1	448.8	450.2	-0.9	0.3
21-23:	Miscellaneous Goods[2]	106.7	107.8	109.0	2.2	1.1
	Store Total[3]	500.6	500.7	504.3	0.7	0.7

Source: Department of Labor, Bureau of Labor Statistics

---

[1]Title reflects change in item sampling structure made during the 1978 CPI Revision whereby Girls' Hosiery was included in Group 8, Women's and Girls' Accessories, not Group 7.
[2]Indexed on a January 1986 = 100 base.
[3]The store total index covers all departments, with the following exceptions: Candy, foods, liquor, tobacco, as well as contract departments.

Note: Indexes for previous periods and a brief description of the methods used in calculating the indexes may be obtained by contacting the Bureau of Labor Statistics at (202) 272-5064.

The application of these indexes in the preparation of tax returns is solely within the jurisdiction of the Internal Revenue Service. Treasury Decision No. 5605 accords the use of the elective inventory method by taxpayers employing the retail inventory method.

DEPARTMENT STORES

Monthly Sales Distribution
For Fiscal Year Ended January 1990

Store Volume	Feb	Mar	Apr	May	Jun	Jul	Aug	Sep	Oct	Nov	Dec	Jan
Under $50MM	5.35	7.63	7.29	7.03	8.05	6.34	7.05	8.98	7.86	9.94	18.07	6.40
$50-$100MM						Insufficient Data						
$100-$300MM						Insufficient Data						
Over $300MM	5.80	8.61	6.83	7.13	8.10	6.85	7.64	8.65	8.02	9.20	16.92	6.25

Monthly Markdowns
% of Monthly Total
Company Net Owned Sales
For Fiscal Year Ended January 1990

Store Volume	Feb	Mar	Apr	May	Jun	Jul	Aug	Sep	Oct	Nov	Dec	Jan
Under $50MM	22.24	14.36	17.15	18.27	22.07	30.92	19.49	14.87	16.82	17.37	17.72	39.24
$50-$100MM						Insufficient Data						
$100-$300MM						Insufficient Data						
Over $300MM	8.10	6.40	5.49	5.84	12.66	12.57	7.44	5.33	7.45	7.75	12.74	15.06

Stock Sales Ratios
For Fiscal Year Ended January 1990

Store Volume	Feb	Mar	Apr	May	Jun	Jul	Aug	Sep	Oct	Nov	Dec	Jan
Under $50MM	6.41	5.50	6.27	6.96	5.45	6.09	5.94	5.46	6.56	8.72	3.29	6.09
$50-$100MM						Insufficient Data						
$100-$300MM						Insufficient Data						
Over $300MM	5.05	3.77	5.01	4.99	4.30	5.05	4.62	4.24	5.05	4.73	2.65	5.47

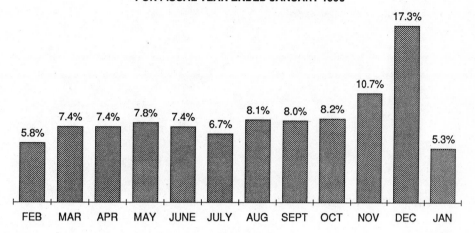

**CONVENTIONAL DEPARTMENT STORES
MONTHLY SALES DISTRIBUTION
FOR FISCAL YEAR ENDED JANUARY 1990**

5.8%	7.4%	7.4%	7.8%	7.4%	6.7%	8.1%	8.0%	8.2%	10.7%	17.3%	5.3%
FEB	MAR	APR	MAY	JUNE	JULY	AUG	SEPT	OCT	NOV	DEC	JAN

Source: U.S. Department of Commerce, Revised Monthly
Sales and Inventories (BR 13-875)

Results of All Department Stores by Merchandise Department Detail

Departmental Merchandising and Operating Results of 1989
Summary of All Department Stores

DEPT. NO.	DESCRIPTION	NO. RPTG. CO'S.	SALES DATA				
			NET SALES % CHANGE OVER LAST YEAR		NET SALES % OF TOTAL STORE		
			MEDIAN	SUPERIOR	MEDIAN	SUPERIOR	
1000	FEMALE APPAREL	64	5.7	14.3	36.2	39.7	
1010	Summary Coats, Dresses, and Suits	63	6.3	17.7	8.0	9.3	
1011	Womens, Misses, and Junior Coats	59	9.8	22.9	2.5	3.1	
1012	Womens, Misses and Junior Suits	36	23.8	41.2	0.3	0.5	
1015	Fur and Fur Garments	22	-20.3	21.8	0.4	0.7	
1017	Womens and Misses Dresses	64	11.1	22.3	3.7	4.9	
1019	Junior Dresses	36	15.6	27.0	1.0	1.5	
1040	Summary Sportswear	63	8.4	14.5	21.4	23.8	
1041	Womens and Misses Sportswear	61	10.3	23.7	15.9	18.5	
1045	Junior Sportswear	60	10.7	18.9	4.0	5.8	
1070	Summary Intimate Apparel	64	1.6	9.2	4.5	6.1	
1071	Intimate Daywear	60	3.1	10.3	2.0	3.2	
1075	Intimate Nightwear	61	1.2	12.5	1.1	1.6	
1076	Loungewear and Robes	57	3.3	10.6	0.5	0.8	
1091	All Other Female Apparel	49	6.6	29.3	1.9	2.4	
2000	ADULT FEMALE ACCESSORIES	64	3.1	12.7	8.4	9.4	
2011	Fine Jewelry and Watches	40	-3.4	5.3	0.9	1.7	
2012	Costume Jewelry	62	9.4	17.7	2.2	2.6	
2015	Hosiery	63	4.5	15.9	1.7	1.9	
2017	Gloves	48	5.6	13.4	0.5	0.7	
2019	Handbags	61	5.9	16.0	1.8	2.1	
2021	Small Leather Goods	48	4.4	18.0	0.4	0.5	
2023	Millinery	11	9.4	26.9	0.2	0.4	

Departmental Merchandising and Operating Results of 1989
Summary of All Department Stores

DEPT. NO.	MERCHANDISING & INVENTORY								INVENTORY PRODUCTIVITY			
	CUMULATIVE MARKON %		MARKDOWN % (INCLUDING EMPLOYEE DISCOUNTS)		STOCK SHORTAGE %		GROSS MARGIN (INCL. WORKROOM COST AND CASH DISCOUNTS)		GROSS MARGIN $ RETURN PER $ AVERAGE COST INVENTORY		STOCK TURNS (TIMES) AT RETAIL	
	MEDIAN	SUPERIOR	MEDIAN	SUPERIOR	MEDIAN	SUPERIOR	MEDIAN	SUPERIOR	MEDIAN	SUPERIOR	MEDIAN	SUPERIOR
1000	53.3	55.4	30.8	27.4	2.4	1.7	41.1	42.4	2.8	3.2	3.1	3.5
1010	53.2	55.6	34.2	28.1	2.3	1.8	39.7	40.8	2.6	3.1	3.2	3.7
1011	55.3	59.2	33.2	23.9	1.7	0.9	41.9	43.9	3.0	3.5	3.5	3.8
1012	54.7	56.8	39.2	30.6	3.5	2.2	38.7	41.3	1.9	2.8	2.8	3.5
1015	50.7	58.2	19.6	12.9	-0.6	-2.7	38.5	42.6	1.2	1.5	1.5	2.0
1017	52.9	54.3	37.4	32.5	3.0	2.1	37.8	39.9	2.6	3.0	3.2	3.6
1019	53.3	54.8	32.8	23.9	3.8	2.4	40.1	42.6	3.4	4.2	3.6	4.7
1040	53.4	55.9	32.3	27.4	2.7	1.7	40.1	43.0	3.1	3.3	3.4	3.7
1041	53.4	55.8	35.4	30.7	2.7	1.8	39.9	41.7	3.0	3.2	3.3	3.7
1045	54.0	56.0	33.4	27.3	3.8	2.8	41.0	44.0	3.2	3.7	3.5	4.1
1070	53.7	55.6	17.5	12.5	1.7	0.9	48.0	50.3	2.5	2.9	2.5	2.6
1071	53.7	55.2	14.6	10.3	2.0	0.8	50.2	52.0	2.2	2.5	2.0	2.4
1075	54.0	56.6	25.3	18.2	2.3	1.4	46.6	49.3	3.0	3.6	3.1	3.6
1076	53.7	56.4	31.1	20.0	0.9	0.3	44.7	46.8	3.2	4.7	3.4	3.9
1091	50.7	53.5	22.8	15.4	2.2	1.4	45.9	48.9	1.5	2.2	2.0	2.5
2000	54.8	55.4	16.3	12.5	2.9	2.1	45.9	47.1	2.1	2.5	2.2	2.6
2011	51.4	56.9	12.0	9.1	4.8	2.2	43.7	48.2	1.5	1.8	1.5	2.1
2012	55.7	56.9	16.2	10.8	4.8	3.2	47.8	49.5	2.3	2.8	2.3	2.5
2015	50.7	52.1	9.8	7.7	1.2	0.7	45.6	47.6	2.2	2.5	2.4	2.6
2017	55.2	56.8	18.4	12.4	3.5	2.8	46.9	48.5	3.3	3.6	3.3	3.5
2019	54.9	56.8	20.8	15.6	1.8	1.0	45.2	46.5	2.6	3.2	2.5	3.1
2021	54.3	55.7	13.1	10.8	5.7	4.7	46.6	48.5	2.2	2.5	2.4	2.7
2023	56.5	60.1	18.8	14.1	1.1	-1.0	49.7	54.7	4.2	6.6	3.2	5.0

Departmental Merchandising and Operating Results of 1989
Summary of All Department Stores

DEPT. NO.	DESCRIPTION	NO. RPTG. CO'S.	EXPENSE DATA % NET SALES					
			SELLING SALARIES		BUYING SALARIES		ADVERTISING	
			MEDIAN	SUPERIOR	MEDIAN	SUPERIOR	MEDIAN	SUPERIOR
1000	FEMALE APPAREL	64	7.3	6.6	2.2	1.9	3.4	2.3
1010	Summary Coats, Dresses, and Suits	63	7.6	7.0	2.7	1.9	3.4	2.5
1011	Womens, Misses, and Junior Coats	59	7.2	6.0	2.2	1.7	3.7	2.8
1012	Womens, Misses and Junior Suits	36						
1015	Fur and Fur Garments	22						
1017	Womens and Misses Dresses	64	7.9	7.4	2.7	2.0	3.1	2.2
1019	Junior Dresses	36	7.6	5.4	2.6	1.7	3.1	1.9
1040	Summary Sportswear	63	6.9	6.2	1.8	1.6	3.5	2.2
1041	Womens and Misses Sportswear	61	6.9	6.2	1.6	1.5	3.2	1.7
1045	Junior Sportswear	60	6.8	5.4	2.2	1.6	3.4	2.3
1070	Summary Intimate Apparel	64	8.1	6.8	3.3	2.8	3.2	2.2
1071	Intimate Daywear	60	8.2	6.7	3.4	2.3	2.5	2.1
1075	Intimate Nightwear	61	8.0	6.8	4.0	1.7	3.4	2.1
1076	Loungewear and Robes	57	8.1	6.7	3.6	2.7	3.1	2.1
1091	All Other Female Apparel	49	7.7	6.7	4.1	1.8	2.2	2.1
2000	ADULT FEMALE ACCESSORIES	64	9.3	8.2	2.7	2.1	3.1	2.1
2011	Fine Jewelry and Watches	40	8.5	6.4	2.3	1.7	5.9	0.7
2012	Costume Jewelry	62	9.7	7.7	3.0	2.3	3.2	2.0
2015	Hosiery	63	8.6	7.8	2.8	1.6	2.7	1.9
2017	Gloves	48	8.5	7.1	2.5	1.6	2.2	1.5
2019	Handbags	61	8.4	7.8	2.7	1.7	3.1	1.9
2021	Small Leather Goods	48	8.3	6.4	1.7	1.7	3.2	1.1
2023	Millinery	11						

Departmental Merchandising and Operating Results of 1989
Summary of All Department Stores

DEPT. NO.	EXPENSE DATA % OF NET SALES		INVENTORY PRODUCTIVITY		SPACE PRODUCTIVITY $ PER SQUARE FOOT OF SELLING SPACE							
	TOTAL DIRECT EXPENSE		CONTRIBUTION $ RETURN PER $ COST INVENTORY		NET SALES		GROSS MARGIN		CONTRIBUTION		AVERAGE INVENTORY (AT RETAIL) $	
	MEDIAN	SUPERIOR	MEDIAN	SUPERIOR	MEDIAN	SUPERIOR	MEDIAN	SUPERIOR	MEDIAN	SUPERIOR	MEDIAN	SUPERIOR
1000	13.6	11.1	2.0	2.3	164.0	196.0	63.4	73.5	50.0	59.3	46.1	38.2
1010	13.9	11.9	1.9	2.1	148.0	186.5	53.7	73.6	41.5	91.0	44.2	38.0
1011	14.2	11.2	2.3	2.5	191.0	231.0	76.9	87.0	54.1	135.8	60.8	46.1
1012												
1015												
1017	14.4	12.0	1.8	1.8	138.5	186.0	48.3	70.8	37.6	80.1	45.8	33.2
1019	14.7	9.2	2.1	3.3	110.0	156.0	33.1	64.8	27.7	64.5	33.0	30.4
1040	12.9	10.4	2.3	2.6	177.0	221.0	71.2	77.8	53.2	94.8	49.8	40.9
1041	12.1	10.4	2.4	2.8	171.0	206.0	71.6	80.1	51.8	269.5	49.4	41.7
1045	15.2	9.5	2.0	2.8	156.0	190.0	60.1	93.3	46.0	66.6	45.1	29.2
1070	16.2	12.2	1.9	2.1	129.5	169.0	62.1	83.0	49.9	54.9	54.3	38.9
1071	16.2	13.1	1.8	1.9	138.0	158.0	65.6	75.3	52.7	64.9	65.3	45.6
1075	15.1	13.1	2.3	3.2	136.0	148.0	65.9	71.0	47.8	65.3	44.5	38.2
1076	16.2	11.9	2.1	3.1	119.0	148.5	51.5	63.8	41.2	65.4	40.3	29.3
1091	17.1	12.3	1.2	1.9	126.0	150.5	47.0	71.7	34.8	54.7	68.0	57.5
2000	15.1	14.3	1.7	1.9	185.0	243.0	86.9	97.5	66.9	77.0	81.5	50.6
2011	16.0	13.3			359.5	562.0	147.3	228.0			146.9	86.2
2012	16.4	13.2	2.0	2.1	196.0	342.0	93.5	128.3	85.8	173.3	96.0	72.1
2015	15.9	14.1	1.7	1.8	190.0	220.0	85.5	95.2	57.2	75.8	94.9	62.8
2017	13.6	9.1	2.3	2.8	197.0	241.0	92.0	102.7	64.3	175.3	64.2	42.5
2019	14.8	13.3	2.1	2.7	192.0	213.0	79.6	91.6	49.7	73.6	76.4	42.9
2021	14.3	13.8			208.0	259.0	94.2	119.4			134.2	95.0
2023												

FIGURE 2-8 SIX-MONTH MERCHANDISING PLAN FORM FOR DEPT. 345, "THE GALLERY" AUGUST TO JANUARY

JARROD & YOUNG

Department Name .... Department No. ....

SIX-MONTH MERCHANDISING PLAN

	PLAN (This Year)	ACTUAL (Last Year)
Workroom cost		
Cash discount %		
Season stock turnover		
Shortage %		
Average stock		
Markdown %		

SPRING 19		FEB.	MAR.	APR.	MAY	JUNE	JULY	SEASON TOTAL
FALL 19		AUG.	SEP.	OCT.	NOV.	DEC.	JAN.	
SALES $	Last Year							
	Plan							
	Percent of Increase							
	Revised							
	Actual							
RETAIL STOCK (BOM) $	Last Year							
	Plan							
	Revised							
	Actual							
MARKDOWNS $	Last Year							
	Plan (dollars)							
	Plan (percent)							
	Revised							
	Actual							
RETAIL PURCHASES	Last Year							
	Plan							
	Revised							
	Actual							
PERCENT OF INITIAL MARKON	Last Year							
	Plan							
	Revised							
	Actual							
ENDING STOCK July 31 Jan. 31	Last Year							
	Plan							
	Revised							
	Actual							

Stock/Sales   LY
Ratio   Plan

Comments

Merchandise Manager .... Buyer ....

Controller ....

FIGURE 2-9 SIX-MONTH MERCHANDISING PLAN FORM FOR DEPT. 345, "THE GALLERY" AUGUST TO JANUARY (WORKSHEET)

JARROD & YOUNG

Department Name .... Department No. ....

		PLAN (This Year)	ACTUAL (Last Year)
	Workroom cost		
SIX-MONTH MERCHANDISING PLAN	Cash discount %		
	Season stock turnover		
	Shortage %		
	Average stock		
	Markdown %		

	SPRING 19	FEB.	MAR.	APR.	MAY	JUNE	JULY	SEASON TOTAL
	FALL 19	AUG.	SEP.	OCT.	NOV.	DEC.	JAN.	
SALES $	Last Year							
	Plan							
	Percent of Increase							
	Revised							
	Actual							
RETAIL STOCK (BOM) $	Last Year							
	Plan							
	Revised							
	Actual							
MARKDOWNS $	Last Year							
	Plan (dollars)							
	Plan (percent)							
	Revised							
	Actual							
RETAIL PURCHASES	Last Year							
	Plan							
	Revised							
	Actual							
PERCENT OF INITIAL MARKON	Last Year							
	Plan							
	Revised							
	Actual							
ENDING STOCK July 31 Jan. 31	Last Year							
	Plan							
	Revised							
	Actual							

Stock/Sales   LY
Ratio   Plan

Comments

Merchandise Manager .... Buyer ....

Controller ....

JARROD & YOUNG

SIX-MONTH MERCHANDISING PLAN

Department Name .... Department No. ....

	PLAN (This Year)	ACTUAL (Last Year)
Workroom cost		
Cash discount %		
Season stock turnover		
Shortage %		
Average stock		
Markdown %		

	SPRING 19	FEB.	MAR.	APR.	MAY	JUNE	JULY	SEASON TOTAL
	FALL 19	AUG.	SEP.	OCT.	NOV.	DEC.	JAN.	
SALES $	Last Year							
	Plan							
	Percent of Increase							
	Revised							
	Actual							
RETAIL STOCK (BOM) $	Last Year							
	Plan							
	Revised							
	Actual							
MARKDOWNS $	Last Year							
	Plan (dollars)							
	Plan (percent)							
	Revised							
	Actual							
RETAIL PURCHASES	Last Year							
	Plan							
	Revised							
	Actual							
PERCENT OF INITIAL MARKON	Last Year							
	Plan							
	Revised							
	Actual							
ENDING STOCK July 31 Jan. 31	Last Year							
	Plan							
	Revised							
	Actual							

Stock/Sales   LY
Ratio   Plan

Comments

Merchandise Manager .... Buyer ....

Controller ....

FIGURE 2-11 ANALYSIS OF FIGURES TO ACCOMPANY SIX-MONTH MERCHANDISING PLAN FOR DEPT. 345, "THE GALLERY" — AUGUST TO JANUARY — PLANNED SALES

JARROD & YOUNG

(1.) PLANNED SALES

JARROD & YOUNG

(2.) PLANNED BOM STOCK

JARROD & YOUNG

(3.) PLANNED MARKDOWNS

JARROD & YOUNG

(4.) OTHER FACTORS OR COMMENTS

CHAPTER THREE

Gross Margin Return on Inventory

OBJECTIVES

- *Clarify the factors that precipitated the need for GMROI in today's retail environment.*
- *Understand the most recent method being used by major retailers to improve their merchandising profits.*
- *Master the formulas necessary to use this new merchandising tool.*
- *Evaluate various retail strategies for improving profitability currently used by buyers.*

ASSIGNMENT

Nicole was called into the office of her merchandise manager and was given a packet of printed material marked GMROI, (i.e., G (Gross) M (Margin) R (Return) O (On) I (Inventory)). Mr. Johnson stated enthusiastically, "This is the newest and most efficient way that forward thinking retailers are looking at their operations. I would like you to read it over very carefully and then analyze your newly developed six-month plan to see how you can use GMROI to create more profit for "The Gallery" and for Jarrod & Young.

"If, after reading the material and reviewing your merchandising plan, you see the need to make any changes, or if there are other factors you need to look into, please come back to me to discuss it further before you go into New York on your buying trip."

STUDENT REVIEW

The economic emphasis of the 1990s in all industries has been and will continue to be how to make every segment of a company's operation more productive and, consequently, more profitable. To achieve these goals of more productivity and profitability, retailers have examined the factors involved in achieving these goals — mark-up, gross margin, and turnover, and have recognized that the element that had been least changed in the recent past was turnover. Additionally, they have recognized that this element could be used in a way to make it the keystone of these goals, thus GMROI.

GMROI is a way to measure how much cash a business is producing and how well it is using its investment in inventory. GMROI is a shorthand way of dealing with an easy, basic business concept: if a dollar is spent for inventory, how much of this dollar must be returned to the business to remain profitable? If that dollar is needed to buy more new goods, then that dollar has to earn enough to pay for expenses, (i.e., taxes, payroll, rent, etc.) and must make a reasonable profit so that the business will grow. The traditional methods of emphasizing mark-up and gross margin continue, but the additional new emphasis is now on turnover. Faster turnover can offset lower mark-up or margin. In other words, by speeding up turnover, more sales dollars can be produced without increasing the inventory. GMROI is dependent on three factors that can be manipulated to increase profit, which are:

- **Markup percent** — A 10% increase in markup may increase GMROI by 10%.
- **Gross margin rate** — A 10% increase in margin rate will increase GMROI by 10%.
- **Turnover rate** — A 10% increase in turnover will increase GMROI by 10%.

Here are the formulas to use to accomplish these financial aims:

$$\frac{GM\% \times TURN}{1 - MU\%} = GMROI$$

$$\frac{GM\% \times TURN}{1 - MU\%} = GMROI = \frac{\text{How much is made on a sale} \times \text{How long it takes to sell it}}{\text{How much is paid for it.}}$$

$$\frac{1 - GM\% \times TURN}{GMROI} = MU\%$$

$$\frac{GMROI \times (1 - MU\%)}{TURN} = GM\%$$

$$GMROI \times (1 - MU\%) = TURN$$

Another factor is turnover — sell through. This is expressed as WOS, (i.e., weeks of supply)

Strategies to Improve GMROI

Markup can be used to improve GMROI by:

- Basing retail prices on what customers are willing to pay for merchandise, not on vendor cost.
- Negotiating with vendors for:
    - (a) Lower costs.
    - (b) Better discounts.
    - (c) Prepaid freight.
    - (d) Exclusive merchandise.
    - (e) Volume rebates on a quarterly basis.
    - (f) Cost adjustments on late shipments.
    - (g) Special pricing on promotional goods.
- Taking advantage of additional markup opportunities.
- Considering change in the mix of vendors and brand assortment and by buying more private label merchandise.
- Searching out hot new resources in advance of the competition.
- Considering the competition's pricing strategy when deciding whether to purchase an item.

Margin can be used to improve GMROI by:

- Growing profitable sales.
- Developing a seasonal plan that supports gross margin objectives. Plan receipts closer to time of need to ensure that retailers can achieve planned inventory standards by using turnover and weeks of supply as a guide (see Figure 3-1, GMROI WEEKS OF SUPPLY (WOS) TURNOVER — SELL THROUGH, page 66), and by developing and adhering to a realistic markdown plan.
- Focussing vendor structure and building strong partnerships with important vendors who deliver high gross margin. Negotiating agreements upfront with vendors with whom growth is planned. Evaluate vendors according to:
  (a) Markdown money in season.
  (b) Quick RTV's on slow selling goods and fast re-orders of highly desirable merchandise.
  (c) Willingness to provide exclusive merchandise.
- Focussing assortments, both for total department and by location and by making a meaningful presentation to the customer.
- Developing a pricing strategy to deliver margin goal, which can include:
  (a) Price point congruency across the department.
  (b) Correct mix of pricing — regular, off-price, special value.
  (c) Goods that are priced to sell.
- Taking timely markdowns and ensuring that first reduction is large enough to liquidate slow selling merchandise. Additionally, markdowns should be merchandised with appropriate fixtures, signing, and advertising.
- Managing promotional prices and reducing or eliminating "blanket" clearance events. Permanent markdowns can be used for clearance merchandise, not point of sale (POS). POS events can be shortened and proper POS % off should be determined.
- Reducing transfers between locations.
- Resolving any purchase journal discrepancies.

Turnover can be used to improve GMROI by:

- Increasing profitable sales.
- Making merchandise available when customers want it and planning receipts close to sales to keep merchandise fresh and in complete size runs. Receipts can be flowed by week to get merchandise to stores faster and to avoid overloading early in the month.
- Eliminating fringe vendors and styles from the assortments. Stocks can be edited with a more critical eye.
- Planning vendor turnover and negotiating with vendors to set narrow windows for delivery. Receipts can be flowed in two orders where possible, instead of one large delivery of merchandise. Problems should be returned early.
- Using a test/reorder strategy for fashion goods, where possible.
- Ensuring that key items and basics are in stock at all times. A marketing plan can be developed for key items, (i.e., quick response, advertising campaigns, etc.) Model stocks should be evaluated and refined to reduce overstocks.
- Monitoring stock plan and actual results by store.

FIGURE 3-1   GMROI WEEKS OF SUPPLY (WOS) TURNOVER — SELL THROUGH

TURNOVER - SELL THROUGH				
Turnover Season	Turnover Year	Sell Through	Weeks of Supply	Average Days on Selling Floor
0.26	0.52	1.0	100.0	700
0.52	1.04	2.0	50.0	350
0.78	1.56	3.0	33.3	233
1.04	2.08	4.0	25.0	175
1.30	2.60	5.0	20.0	140
1.56	3.12	6.0	16.6	116
1.82	3.64	7.0	14.3	100
2.08	4.16	8.0	12.5	88
2.34	4.68	9.0	11.1	78
2.60	5.20	10.0	10.0	70
2.86	5.72	11.0	9.1	64
3.12	6.24	12.0	8.3	58
3.38	6.76	13.0	7.7	54
3.64	7.28	14.0	7.1	50
3.90	7.80	15.0	6.7	47
4.16	8.32	16.0	6.3	44
4.42	8.84	17.0	5.9	41
4.68	9.36	18.0	5.6	39
4.94	9.88	19.0	5.3	37
5.20	10.40	20.0	5.0	35

CHAPTER FOUR

Merchandise Classifications

OBJECTIVES

- *Appraise the stock of a department and/or specialty store.*
- *Evaluate stock assortments in relation to perceived consumer demand.*
- *Turn open-to-buy dollars into desired units of merchandise using classifications and sub-classifications.*
- *Understand the merchandiser's need and use of classifications and sub-classifications.*

ASSIGNMENT

The six-month merchandising plan — in dollars, of course — was presented to George Johnson at the scheduled merchandising meeting. The figures and the analysis were approved.

Mr. Johnson then said, "You must now work up a merchandise classification plan, which I would like to review and approve. Let us set a date for one week from today for you to submit this plan."

STUDENT REVIEW

A classification is a grouping of merchandise items that are interchangeable for one another from the customer's point of view. A sub-classification is a narrower grouping of merchandise aimed at a more specific segment of consumer demand. The difference between the two concepts is the range of choice within the groupings. For example, within the broad classification of skirts, a pleated skirt is a sub-classification.

A classification analysis achieves the following basic merchandising objectives, which are to:

- Turn OTB dollars into needed units of sub-classifications of merchandise, with reasonable accuracy.
- Develop a practical OTB position in units.
- Evaluate the performance of these narrow segments of merchandise, (i.e., markdowns, stock peak requirements, etc.).
- Recognize and address trends in relation to customer preference.
- Avoid the duplication of goods.
- Provide a means of better planning and control of merchandise.

Classifications are flexible — they can be added, increased, reduced, or eliminated. In a fashion department, the essential criterion is always consumer demand. During the pre-season planning, classifications are established. During market weeks, however, after a thorough analysis of market offerings and estimates of probable consumer demand, classifications, particularly sub-classifications, are reviewed and adjusted. Non-essential classifications can be eliminated and those that are new and not represented are added.

APPLICATION

Because Jarrod & Young does not as yet have a department comparable to "The Gallery" and because you are not familiar with the merchandise classifications that will be carried in the department, you decide to survey the competitive stores that stock most closely the merchandise suitable for your department.

Mr. Johnson's secretary has supplied forms for you to use to document your research as well as a form for your proposed classification plan. The forms were accompanied by a note from Mr. Johnson, which read:

> "Nicole, please remember that classifications and sub-classifications should be groupings of merchandise that are clearly defined. A classification system enables a buyer to pinpoint customer buying patterns by simply analyzing a selling report. Optimally, the report can help to show trends as well as to provide clues to developing trends and to assist in quickly identifying slow sellers and trends on the decline.
>
> "On the other hand, sub-classifications should indicate the identifiable merchandise characteristics that make them desirable or undesirable to consumers."

Use Figures 4-1 and 4-2, pages 69 and 71, COMPETITIVE STORE SURVEYS and Figure 4-3, page 73, PROPOSED CLASSIFICATION PLAN for "The Gallery."

FIGURE 4-1 COMPETITIVE STORE SURVEY

JARROD & YOUNG

Store Surveyed   Date Surveyed

Name of Department   Department #

Classification(s)	% to Total Sportswear Stock	Comments

100%

FIGURE 4-2 COMPETITIVE STORE SURVEY

JARROD & YOUNG

Store Surveyed .... Date Surveyed

Name of Department   Department #

Classification(s)	% to Total Sportswear Stock	Comments

100%

FIGURE 4-3 PROPOSED CLASSIFICATION PLAN FOR DEPT. 345, "THE GALLERY"

JARROD & YOUNG

Classification(s)	% to Total Sportswear Stock	Comments

100%

CHAPTER FIVE

Market Trip Preparation— The Steps for Planning a Balanced Stock

OBJECTIVES

- *Examine the elements that comprise a balanced stock.*
- *Develop individual plans to achieve a balanced stock in a department.*
- *Shop any store and analyze the existing stock to determine stock balance by major classifications.*
- *Prove by actual computation, (i.e., stock counts and stock count analysis) their conclusion as to stock balance.*

ASSIGNMENT

You have completed your competitive store survey and have received approval of your merchandise classification plan.

At yesterday's meeting, Mr. Johnson said, "Now that you have completed the initial planning steps, you are ready to go to the New York market and buy for the opening of your department. Your plan will help you achieve a balanced assortment of merchandise, which should include colors, sizes, fabrics, silhouettes, and prices based on your opinion of "The Gallery's" consumer preferences. Your over-riding responsibility is, of course, to achieve the stock at the right prices, and to have the stock in the store at the right time.

"Before you to go to New York, however, you must detail a purchase plan based on your research of our store and its competition."

STUDENT REVIEW

The fundamental goal of a balanced stock plan is to meet consumer demand. The market offers a wide variety of salable merchandise, but it is the buyer's function to be selective and to confine purchases to the most desirable merchandise for the store's consumer that also is in character with the store image. Consequently, price lines, assortments, and stock depth should be confined to merchandise that can be expected reasonably to be in demand. Additionally, a plan also should be predicated on the knowledge that every department has the inhibiting elements of space, money, and time.

The steps to be taken in proper order of the planning sequence are:

- The six-month plan (see Chapter Two).
- A merchandise classification plan (see Chapter Three).
- An estimation of the percentage importance of each fabric.
- An estimation of how sizes will be stocked, (i.e., percentage by size or designated size range assortment).
- An estimation of the colors to be stocked, by percentage or units.
- A breakdown of classifications into sub-classifications, including estimations as detailed in Chapter Three.

As discussed in Chapter Three, classifications and sub-classifications can be added, deleted, and changed to conform to current fashion trends, usually after a market trip. Similarly, planned units and colors are subject to change when and if more current and up-to-date market information is obtained.

In planning sizes covered in stock composition, a buyer knows that the size demand factor remains almost constant season after season. It is the one planning factor that varies least from season to season. In some cases, there is an area or regional pattern of size selling. For example, in the Midwest, large-sized sweaters have the greatest demand, and some stores buy few small sizes. Sometimes a particular size or style trend can upset an established pattern of size selling, (e.g., when coats become voluminous, a size 14 person can easily wear a size 12).

A carefully planned and proper assortment of colors, sizes, styles, sub-classifications, and stock depths puts the department in the best position to buy and stock merchandise that is consistent with probable consumer demand. Consequently, the store's potential is thus best able to achieve merchandising goals, continued consumer patronage, and the best return on investment.

Figure 5-1 on page 78, is a SAMPLE PLAN FOR PURCHASING A SKIRT CLASSIFICATION. **DO NOT USE THESE FIGURES AS THE BASIS FOR "THE GALLERY" PLAN.** Even though there is a breakdown of a major classification into sub-classifications, each sub-classification does not have details of units for price lines, colors, and sizes. The procedure of planning full details for each sub-classification is a fairly common practice. However, for the purposes of this text, the plan will be devised on a broader basis and with limited details.

To ensure a balanced stock, all orders that are written after the market trip — but before being sent to the manufacturers[8] — will be analyzed by your merchandise manager for proper sub-classifications. A paper inventory will be prepared to guarantee coverage within each sub-classification by units for price levels, colors, fabrics, and sizes.

Consequently, the application of the problem will be on a broad basis initially, but the post-market trip analysis will ensure a well-balanced stock commitment for the new season because of greater detail.

In summary, the planning process listed on Figure 5-1, page 78 ensures:

- A realistic budget and the best use of capital.
- A calculated estimate of consumer needs within narrowed units of consumer demand, (i.e., classifications and sub-classifications).
- A proper coverage of price lines.
- An ample quantity of fashion colors.
- A stock composition that contains the important sizes in sufficient depth.

---

[8] Not an uncommon practice.

These discussions and applications concerning a buyer's market trip are for the purpose of purchasing merchandise for a new season. A buyer, however, visits markets for other stock requirements, and trips are made as often as the department's needs require. Different departmental needs, therefore, vary with the type of merchandise, store locations, rate of sales, and store policies.

APPLICATION

The objective of this assignment is to demonstrate mastery of classification analysis and planning. For the purpose of developing this expertise, the assignment is confined to one classification of your own choice. When you have proven that you can complete this assignment, you will know that you can handle any classification, because the principles always remain the same.

The advantages of concentrating on one classification are that the time and effort to make an in-depth analysis and plan is used more efficiently, and the study of the contents of this plan in relation to the current stock of a local retailer is more focussed. Additionally, familiarization with current style trends of a narrow unit of consumer demand will enable you to handle the assignment more completely and skillfully.

Sportswear, as a department, carries a variety of classifications, which must be planned and bought to encourage multiple sales. "The Gallery" will offer a full assortment of sportswear classifications, as will the departments that you will be examining. The assignment is to select a complete sportswear department of your choice, to narrow your focus to one specific classification, (i.e., bottoms, jackets, skirts, sweaters, blouses) and then analyze this chosen classification by sub-classification, fabric, price, size, and color. You will then use this analysis as a basis for planning a comparable classification for your new department based on gathered data for the new, up-coming season.

Remember that "The Gallery" ultimately will offer pants, skirts, blouses, sweaters, jackets, coordinates, and knit tops.

The forms (Figures 5-2 through 5-6, Plan for Purchasing a _____ Classification, for Dept. 345, "The Gallery", pages 79-83), were given to you by your merchandise manager's secretary to record your classification research. Complete the forms within two days and be prepared to explain all aspects to your boss.

FIGURE 5-1   SAMPLE PLAN FOR PURCHASING A SKIRT CLASSIFICATION

JARROD & YOUNG

	Sub-Classification	% to Stock	Open-to-Buy in $
	Straight line	20	20,000
	Side pleat	20	20,000
	A-line	15	15,000
A. SUB-CLASSIFICATION	Wrap	15	15,000
	Trouser	15	15,000
	Full	5	5,000
	Dirndl	10	10,000
		100%	$100,000
			(OTB share)

	Price Range	% to Stock	
	$130.00	5	
	120.00	10	
	100.00	30	
B. PRICES	80.00	30	
	75.00	15	
	65.00	10	
		100%	

	Colors	% to Stock	
	Gray heather	10	
	Navy	10	
	Black	25	
C. COLORS	Brown	10	
	Red	10	
	Taupe	15	
	Novelty	20	
		100%	

	Sizes	% to Stock	
	4	8	
	6	16	
	8	25	
	10	25	
	12	18	
D. SIZES	14	8	
	16	–	
	18	–	
	20	–	
		100%	

	Fabrics	% to Stock	
	Wool/gabardine and/or crepe	25	
	Wool/flannel	40	
E. FABRICS	Wool/silk	10	
	Poly/wool	20	
	Acrylic/rayon	5	
		100%	

JARROD & YOUNG

A. SUB-CLASSIFICATION

Sub-Classification	% to Classification	Open-to-Buy in $
	100%	$
		(OTB share)

FIGURE 5-3 PLAN FOR PURCHASING A _____ CLASSIFICATION FOR DEPT. 345, "THE GALLERY" — PRICES

JARROD & YOUNG

B. PRICES

Price Range	% of Classification

100%

JARROD & YOUNG

C. COLORS

Colors	% of Classification

100%

JARROD & YOUNG

D. Sizes

Sizes	% of Classification
4	
6	
8	
10	
12	
14	
S	
M	
L	
	100%

JARROD & YOUNG

E. FABRICS

Fabrics	% of Classification

100%

CHAPTER SIX

Shopping The Market for a New Season

OBJECTIVES

- *Understand the objective of a buyer's need to thoroughly shop the market.*
- *Evaluate various resources to determine criteria for selection of "key resources."*
- *Discuss considerations to be used in selecting vendors and how to best implement these factors.*
- *Demonstrate the ability to fully detail and write orders in a professional manner.*
- *Demonstrate the ability to select merchandise to fulfill previously established criteria for a balanced stock by preparing a complete recap of orders written.*

ASSIGNMENT

Your dollar and assortment plans, with minor adjustments, have been approved and you are about to leave for New York City, the major market, on your first market trip. This is certainly a challenging and exciting time for you!

During the final briefing session with George Johnson you were given the following instructions:

- Detail orders to the extent of 75% of the OTB for the months of July, August, and September.
- All orders are to be written in Des Moines after returning from the market trip.
- Every order must be countersigned by George Johnson.
- Every order should be marked "**For New Department**."
- Resources must be shopped carefully, and your responsibility is to seek and cultivate manufacturers and vendors who have a pattern of success and an ability to fill the needs of the customers of Jarrod & Young. Strong efforts should be made to select key resources that will help develop the character of the department.
- Because the department is new, every effort should be made to peak the stock by August 1.

- Establish a good relationship with your resident buying office—Worldwide Buying Offices (WWBO)—particularly with your resident market representative.
- The planned commitments should include stock to support three newspaper advertisements, the first, an image ad, and the others volume producing ads (to be discussed in Chapter Seven).

Mr. Johnson's final words to Nicole were, "The merchandising team, (i.e., the six buyers and Mr. Johnson) will stay at the Gotham Hotel. I have set up a conference time each evening from 6 pm. to 7:30 pm. Any questions or problems that arise can be discussed during this time. Additionally, I'll work in the market on two days with you, but we'll agree on the specific days once we're in New York. Because this trip is to last two weeks, our joint review of resources can be made during the second week, and should be confined to the resources that you believe could be key manufacturers for your department. One last word of advice — don't be reluctant to tell manufacturers that this is your first buying job. You'll find that most vendors want to help you to succeed and will extend themselves to gain a competitive advantage in a new department. What you want and should request are:

(1) Their opinions of styles that represent the "heart" of their lines.
(2) Preferred initial and re-order delivery.
(3) Information about who they sell to in our trading area, (i.e., distribution policy), specifics on delivery dates, clearance policies, and any promotional effort on their part that will support your merchandising goals.
(4) Possible exclusives or early deliveries for "The Gallery's" opening.

"Good luck. I'll see you at WWBO Monday morning."

Merchandise Selection Considerations In Shopping the Market

A buyer shops the market for several purposes. One major objective is to get a clear visual picture of what important vendors are presenting for sale for the new season. Then, as the buyer writes the specific styles, colors, etc., it is with an understanding of what the market considers important and in trend.

Another major objective is the selection of "key"[9] vendors in the classification. The most important vendors are those that help to establish the character of the department and that the customer reasonably can expect to find represented continually in the stock. The buyer is responsible for finding, developing, and editing the vendor list. This list should focus on the department's most important sources of merchandise — branded and private labels.

When selecting vendors, keep in mind such considerations as:

- Building strong partnerships with key vendors who will provide markdown money in season, who can offer exclusive merchandise, who will provide quick RTV (return to vendor) stickers on slow selling goods and who offer reorders on wanted merchandise.
- Planning a continuous flow of new merchandise on the floor. This will keep your floor exciting and ensure a steady flow of the market's most recent shipments.
- Negotiating with your vendors for lower costs, better discount, prepaid freight, cost adjustments on late shipment, and special pricing on promotional goods.

---

[9] A resource that is stocked season after season and contributes character and profit to the department.

- Eliminating fringe resources and styles from your assortment.
- Planning merchandise turnover, negotiating with vendors to establish clearly defined delivery dates to meet your department's needs, and writing orders for specific delivery periods whenever possible.
- Discussing the style assortment of each vendor's line — which styles are the "must haves" of the line.
- Discussing the distribution policies of each vendor. You should know those competitors that are supplied within your trading area.

A major planning factor now used widely by large retailers is GMROI, which is explained fully in Chapter Three. The traditional emphasis on sales growth and mark-up does not change, but is simply supplemented with the added ingredient of turnover.

STUDENT REVIEW

Upon a buyer's arrival in the New York market, the first order of business is to visit the resident buying office (RBO) and sign the registry book. The first day of a market trip is a day of preparation. It is usually concluded by an office-prepared fashion and/or merchandise showing, often held at a hotel (or in the resident buying office if space permits). Usually Monday morning is the time to:

- Discuss with the RBO representative fashion trends and resource developments.
- Review the samples culled by the RBO representative.
- Attend merchandising meetings with other store buyers (and members of the same RBO).
- Discuss trends and merchandising activities with the office fashion director and divisional merchandise manager.

Following the meetings, an orderly sequence for shopping the market most comprehensively is planned. The technique of shopping a market varies: some buyers prefer to concentrate on one classification at a time while others prefer a more general approach and shop across classification lines. Whatever the procedure, the buyer's first objective is to determine the major fashion trends.

After shopping the major fashion trend resources, the balance of the market analysis falls into place. The store has had a record of success with certain vendors (key and preferred manufacturers) whose merchandise will be purchased, unless unusual circumstances have developed. Based on market research, additional resources will be shopped and evaluated for possible stock inclusion.

Figures 6-1 through 6-4, pages 88-94, are typical of the information that a resident representative prepares for visiting member store buyers for a new season. This information is the result of weeks of premarket research and represents the market specialist's views of the market's important trends, manufacturers, and details that support them.

APPLICATION

You have been in the market one week and have shopped fifty manufacturers. At each stop you reviewed the line carefully, using showroom order blanks to make note of the styles that impressed you most. Your order of style importance was based on a check (✓) system: one check (✓) for possible purchase, two checks (✓✓) for a style of more importance, and three checks (✓✓✓) for possible advertisement.

FIGURE 6-1 WORLDWIDE BUYING OFFICE FALL MARKET OVERVIEW

WWBO

Save It, Don't Flaunt It!

Economic news predicts consumer thinking. "If I don't need it, I'm not going to buy it." Therefore, save, save, save and make do. Consumers are worried about the economy, so they are bullish on caution.

What's Your Customer's Mind-Set?

The consumer's mind set is on the "here and now." Informational programming is what's selling on networks and in advertising across the world. Baby boomers have reshaped and redefined social attitudes and as they mature they are facing a different reality in their wants and needs.

What's Old?

Age parameters are being redefined. People are in better physical condition, living longer, living "younger." For the 90s decade, we can make a strong case for saying: "You're only as old as you look!"

Consumer-Oriented Marketing.

Find out what the consumer really thinks, not what you think she thinks! It's a fact that investment dressing and quality consciousness are replacing fads and trendiness dressing.

Niche Marketing.

This new buzzword for the 90's is supported by the "new wave" retailers (i.e., The Gap, Express, Episode, etc.) are so successful because they understand their customers and develop looks, products, and product extensions that fill their customer's needs. Get into the head of your consumer and her lifestyle and give her what she wants.

TOP OF THE LINE TRENDS ....

It Was The Vest Of Times On Seventh Avenue.

Christian Francis Roth who characterizes the season as a matter of masculinity and femininity fighting to control the body, combines the two influences in one-piece dresses that look like vests and skirts. Lauren shows vests with fobs for daytime; and for evening vests are encrusted with silver jewels. Donna Karan's vests are leather, long, and jacket- like, cinched with belts with dangling gold coins.

Pants For All Occasions.

Calvin Klein gives them a new twist by tucking them into ample boots for a sweater/pant look. Kors prefers the sleek, taut line of stirrups. Geoffrey Beene, who loves jumpsuits, shows them again, now with short jackets. Donna Karan has her pants wide and flowing.

Jeans Are Hot Everywhere.

Kamali shows them in blue denim, Perry Ellis and Michael Kors in leather. Yes, the five-pocket, zip front jean is seen in every collection. The shape is the same, the look changes with the fabric from denim, stretch, menswear fabrics, leather. Also strong are riding pants from Anne Klein.

His Shirt On Her Curves.

Byron Lars does bra seaming and waistline draping on white striped shirtings. Christian Francis Roth shows oversized shirts as tunics, belted with matching color neckties worn over matching tights. Ralph Lauren puts the menswear tie around the neck, Calvin Klein shows his shirt inside and out, but hanging straight.

Animal Magnetism.

This is the season's print attraction on both sides of the Atlantic. Adrienne Vittadini changes its stripes. Bill Blass still loves leopards, and Geoffrey Beene embroiders tigers, storks, and rhinos on short evening jackets.

Skins Keep Getting Tanned.

Leather-bound looks include Donna Karan's leather trench coat. Calvin Klein has long leather tunic/vests, vested leather suits are at Anne Klein, and Michael Kors covers the whole skin game with both leathers and suedes.

Hem And Haw As You Please.

Beene stays short, Calvin Klein goes long, Anne Klein goes both ways and so will the customers. Upscale retailers consensus....about 40% of Fall stocks will be long. The shortest skirts will be 20 inches or less.

Throughout The Designer Market — Sportswear.

This American innovation, so much admired and copied the world over, is finally getting the recognition it so richly deserves at home. Luxe on luxe layering as seen at Calvin Klein where cardigans slip over jackets, at Anne Klein where Tyler ties cardigans at the waist over silk shirts. Donna Karan ties all her pieces together with color stories and Ralph Lauren starts with separate menswear jackets and then adds and adds one separate piece after another.

Hide That Curve.

The newest shoes all cover the instep. At Calvin Klein it's the ankle-high, flat oxford, at Michael Kors it's the heeled oxford. Donna Karan focuses on the ankle, where laced-up heels combine with rich-colored knit cuffs. Another major shoe is one with criss-crossed ankle or instep straps.

Karl Lagerfeld's American Kissing Cousins.

Everything from Chanel-like link and chain belts to see-through skirts, handkerchief hemlines, trailing neck scarves, and on to back-zipped, curve enhancing jackets. No trace of menswear here.

TEN MOST IMPORTANT CONCEPTS FOR FALL ....

Silhouette News:

Both long and short work...the fundamental silhouette is waisted...an uplifted bosom, rounded hipline...sexy yet controlled.

Grown-Up Looks Work:

Customers want to look sophisticated, with an elegant edge... well put together... clearly members of the "Silent Majority"...no extremes please.

Menswear's Influence On Womenswear:

Not androgyny...but a powerful and important statement about women's influence and individuality.

Skirts:

Long, lean silhouettes are most important... skirts slasned/zipped/open-button detailing...gathered/paper-bag waist lines, high waist lines....clean masculine details (i.e., narrow belt loops, watch packets.) Soft, full skirts remain an important grace note to watch.

Pants:

More important as women straddle the skirt length fence. The basic menswear-influenced trouser will be wider at the bottom and cuffed...jeans in satin, velvets, and flannel...wildly printed leggings...zipper trims and details...self belts...watch for soft, flared pant legs.

Knitwear:

Sheer, lacy lingerie influenced knits...rib knits...tunic shapes...belled sleeves...twin sets...chenille/mohair... chunky, slubby knits...popcorn stitch...smooth...fine-guage and slinky.

Blouses:

Frilly "dandy" shirts...zipper detailing and trims...print mixes...sexy, off-the-shoulder looks...shirts are a must for layering... soft wrap/body blouses... engineered/scarf prints...wide, romantic, poetic collars and flowing sleeves and cuffs.

Head To Toe Dressing:

Practical, easy care dressing, economical...tonality, an important key to success.

Colors:

A very strong optical black and white story...black, black, and more black, with grey not far behind...browns will be used often in tonal combinations from warm ecru to mahogany and chestnut brown...the rich foliage of autumn inspires berry bright working in tandem with more traditional forest greens, apple reds, currant oranges and ochres...tones have a rich, jewelled brilliance that work well with black and traditional silhouettes.

Fabrications:

We all know we are in a retailing period when need and practicality mean as much to many consumers as fashion, meaning there will be a renewed consumer demand for classic, basic fabrics with qualities that endure, (i.e., denim, corduroy, flannel, plaids)...finishing techniques and the incorporation of performance stretch can make this trend work for you.

WWBO

RTW = 100% (For past year)

Dresses	=	15.4%
Coats	=	6.8%
Suits	=	2.1%
Sportswear	=	60.2%
Juniors	=	15.5%
Total		100.0%
Sportswear Better	=	55%
Sportswear Moderate	=	45%

OTB Percentage and Classification Breakdown	**Better Town and Country Sportswear**
Blazers/jackets	15%
Skirts (all lengths)	18%
Pants	22%
Blouses	20%
Sweaters	21%
Vests	3%

The following is a guide to the present fashion calendar as represented by approximate dates of seasonal showings and seasonal deliveries. Please keep in mind that all major resources give preferential deliveries (i.e., earliest deliveries) to their most important accounts.

Seasons	**Show Date**	**Deliveries**
Spring	Aug. 1	Dec./Jan./Feb. 25 Complete
Summer	Nov. 1.	March/April 30 Complete
Fall I or Transition	Jan. 2	May/June 30 Complete
Fall II	Mar. 1	July/Aug/Sept. 30 Complete
Holiday/Early Spring	June 15	Oct./Nov./Dec. 30 Complete

FIGURE 6-3 FASHION LEADERSHIP DEPARTMENTS FOR FALL

WWBO

Bridge, Contemporary Sportswear

This area in sportswear remains among the fastest growing and one that has newness in the business all the time. This is a market that deserves more extension and concentration. If you haven't been getting your share of these consumer dollars, hurry up and get into it — the water is still fine for snagging consumer market share.

What is the *Bridge Contemporary Sportswear Market* all about? Its for your fashion-forward customer who wants her clothes with a slightly more fashion-forward look at a slightly "pricier" level. This is the consumer who reads the fashion pages, appreciates the newest looks, knows quality and fashion newness when she sees it, but cannot pay the high price tags of designer sportswear. She is really a "dream" to stock your department for, because she's savvy enough to appreciate your efforts to buy the best of the new fashions at the most realistic prices for the high quality and good looks she demands.

Important Contemporary/Bridge Fashion Looks for Fall

- Vests, vests, and more vests...the longer the better. They pull everything together and can go on top of everything.

- Prints, top and bottom...printed jeans, tops, knitwear and jackets.

- Long skirts...just so they have slit, whether in the front, back, or side.

- Fringes...primarily in leathers and suede, but also on skirts, pants and vests.

- Body dressing...body shirts that hug the waist and never pull out, stretch leggings to wear alone with an oversized top or under a slit skirt, or as a foundation for a tonal outfit.

- Pants...man-tailored and trim trousers, indications of widening legs that hint the return of the bell bottoms...and full, flared legs...tight stirrup pants...when in "length doubt" wear pants.

- Chunky sweaters...self-patterned knits, bulky missoni type, multi-colored patterns that are 3/4–coat–length or ribbed, fitted, and waist-length.

- Return of the Poor Boy sweater...ribbed cotton or wool...long or short sleeve...crew neck or turtle neck...a must as a first layer.

- Fall colors...black, bright red, bright yellow, plus traditional Fall colors and lots of white tops.

Most important lines here at top of the line prices include Anne Klein II, DKNY, DKNY Jeans, A Line, Company Ellen Tracy, Ellen Tracy, Adrienne Vittadini, Vittadini Sport, CK Calvin Klein, Anne Lauren, Potpourri, and Elan.

Also be sure to shop Kenar, Henry Cottons, Ereg, Emanuel, Hue, and Uptight — new for suede and lycra spandex leggings.

FIGURE 6-4   SPORTSWEAR RESOURCE LIST — CONTEMPORARY/BRIDGE

WWBO

RESOURCE	ADDRESS	PHONE	COMMENTS
A-Line Anne Klein	530 7th Ave 17 Fl	852-5800	
Andrea Jovine	1441 Bway	382-2320	
Anne Lauren	512 7th Ave 42nd Fl	555-1876	
Adrienne Vittadini	1441 Bway	921-2510	
AKA Designs Los Angeles	499 7th Ave 3N	629-8410	
American Beauty Sportswear	466 Bway 707	302-0101	
Anne Klein II	530 7th Ave 18th Fl	626-6100	
Argenti	512 7th Ave 2nd Fl	221-1840	
Axo	1411 Bway 3rd Fl	944-6633	
Bernardo	499 7th Ave 906	268-5157	
Beverly Hills Clothing Co.	1411 Bway 1612	869-3021	
Brinkworth Deisgns	1400 Bway 919	221-8422	
Bronx Clothiers	499 7th Ave 3N	629-8410	
Celia Tejada	1466 Bway 418	719-0094	
Cherry Lane	499 7th Ave	947-8500	
CK Calvin Klein	205 W. 39 St.	575-0800	
Claude Z	485 7th Ave 211	967-0606	
Cordic	499 7th Ave 1106N	967-9848	
Cristina Maxx	1411 Bway 401	869-4888	
De Crespi	1411 Bway 421	221-6520	
Dianne Beaudry	512 7th Ave 27th Fl	354-6474	
DKNY/DKNY Jeans	240 W. 40th St.	869-3569	
Eileen Fisher	214 W 39th St.	944-0808	
Elan	1411 Bway 2201	555-0016	
Ellen Tracy	1441 Bway	944-6999	
Emanuel	65 W. 37th St.	944-2091	
Erez	525 7th Ave	869-2980	
Eric Martin	488 7th Ave 6K	695-0684	
Episode	1410 Bway 501	768-7566	
Fauust	149 W. 36 St 2nd Fl	239-6535	
Gilbert Gear	1441 Bway 1475	302-4130	
Giuseppe	512 7th Ave 36th Fl	382-1780	
Globetrotters	1402 Bway 3901	391-8486	
Go Silk	530 7th Ave 23 Fl	382-3303	
Granite	1466 Bway 1406	398-2887	
Gruppo Americano	512 7th Ave 36th Fl	382-1780	
Guess ?	1385 Bway 22nd Fl	221-1199	
Hino & Malee II	214 W. 39th St. 205	944-7980	

RESOURCE	ADDRESS	PHONE	COMMENTS
I.B. Diffusion Sports	1410 Bway 6th Fl	921-2350	
In-Wear/Martinique	485 7th Ave 900	563-3285	
Info U.S.S.	1441 Bway 1450	921-0724	
Jane Tise	499 7th Ave 3N	629-8410	
Jennie's Rainbow	209 W 38th St 603	944-2410	
JM by Shelli Segal	1411 Bway 603	575-2221	
Joan Geddes	499 7th Ave 3N	629-8410	
Joan Vass USA	485 7th Ave	947-3417	
Kei Okada	488 7th Ave 6K	695-0684	
Kenar	530 7th Ave 25th Fl	948-2760	
Kors by Michael Kors	630 5th Ave 16th Fl	581-5100	
L. Bates	499 7th Ave 3N	629-8410	
L.A. Design Group	1411 Bway 1159	764-5087	
LA Young Designers	488 7th Ave 6K	695-0684	
Laura Kieffer	1441 Bway 2303	391-2992	
Laurel	1412 Bway 8th Fl	852-5300	
Leon Max	495 7th Ave. 605	714-1730	
Liz Ashley	1400 Bway 3rd Fl	354-2120	
Marithe & Francois Girbaud	214 W. 39th St.	398-8500	
Michii Moon for Sanyo	512 7th Ave 7th Fl	869-2990	
Moska	1412 Bway	302-2055	
Odessa	488 7th Ave. 6K	695-0684	
Point to Point	1411 Bway 423	719-4810	
Portfolio	1441 Bway	921-8500	
Potpourri	209 W 38th St 56 Fl	555-3910	
Ralph Lauren Classics, Roughwear, Active	550 7th Ave 3rd Fl	221-0675	
Semplice	530 7th Ave.	575-1190	
S.P.Y.	498 7th 15B-10	563-6250	
Several Fine Lines	1466 Bway 608C	944-6930	
Spring Street	1411 Bway 1117	869-5244	
Street Buzz	1431 Bway 11 Fl	221-7690	
Street Life	1466 Bway 430	869-0300	
Terry B	498 7th Ave. 15th Fl	947-8811	
The Collection Agency	209 W 38th	354-6530	
Wers	499 7th 18N	947-8500	
Westonwear	499 7th 1106N	967-9848	
Willis & Cleo	1466 Bway 1109	764-4333	
Wisdom, Madness & Folly	80 W 40th St 3rd Fl	354-2255	

Your conclusions are:

- To hold key resource commitments down to three.
- 75% of your blouse budget will be spent with three manufacturers, who are now offering selected groups of bottoms. Because they are important resources to your department, you plan to buy a sampling of these goods (20-25% of your bottoms total).
- By concentrating your investment, you can stock the major themes of the season, achieve resource cooperation, and start building department character.

Your merchandise manager agrees to shop three of the major resources with you.

The sixty styles in Figures 6-5, ANNE LAUREN COLLECTION, 6-6, POTPOURRI COLLECTION, and 6-7, ELAN COLLECTION, pages 96-122, represent those of the three manufacturers from which you will select styles for stock inclusion. Because you are the buyer, Mr. Johnson has instructed you to make the commitments as you see fit, but only after he reviews the lines with you.

It is standard practice today for major multi-store retailers to have at least two separate types of order forms. One form is simplified to be used when ordering merchandise for a single store, (e.g., special goods for the flagship store at highest prices, reorders for one of the stores, or any other special reason for purchasing goods for one store only). A sample of a SINGLE STORE PURCHASE ORDER is included because it is still used under certain circumstances (see Figure 6-8, page 123).

The second form (MULTI-STORE PURCHASE ORDER) is used more widely because most large multi-store retailers today are writing orders in bulk and having the merchandise shipped to their store's warehouse. The warehouse personnel then assorts the goods for each store according to the buyer's specific instructions (see Figure 6-9, pages 125-126).

Review the merchandise, and use one BUYER'S WORKSHEET (Figures 6-10, 6-11, and 6-12, pages 127-132) for each vendor to select the styles. Detail the orders as you think they should be written. Remember to include: style numbers, colors, sizes, delivery dates, quantities that will give your stock the best representation, and any necessary instructions to the vendors on the face of the orders.[10] When you are satisfied with your worksheet, you are ready to write the purchase orders. Use the MULTI-STORE PURCHASE ORDERS (Figures 6-13, 6-14, and 6-15, pages 133-138), for your finalized quantities. You will write the orders when you return to Iowa. They will be analyzed, and then given to Mr. Johnson for his countersignature.

The orders that are submitted to George Johnson for his signature are to be accompanied by a memorandum that includes an analysis proving that the commitments add up to a balanced stock.

Classifications are noted under "class" (you will have to establish your own classifications); a duplicate copy of each order is "retailed", (i.e., the house number[11], the retail price of each style, and the total retail of each order.) One copy (the original) will be sent to the manufacturer, the second copy to the receiving room for receiving and marking, the third copy to unit control, and the fourth to the buyer.

---

[10] Make sure that orders are written with a start ship date of 7/20; merchandise shipped before this date will not be accepted. Jarrod & Young's warehouse is prepared to start receiving merchandise for "The Gallery" on 7/22.

[11] The house numbers for the three manufacturers represented in this text are: Anne Lauren 550; Potpourri, 505; Elan, 525.

FIGURE 6-5 ANNE LAUREN COLLECTION

STYLES	COLOR	DESCRIPTION	UNIT PRICE	SIZES
100% Cotton/100% Cotton Lace – Machine Washable				
24679	02 White 11 Chablis 41 Night	Long sleeve blouse, collar, no pockets, fly front, with vertical lace inserts	$53.50/$110	4-14
100% Cotton/100% Cotton Lace – Machine Washable				
24437	02 White	Edwardian ruffled lace front and lace cuff blouse	$59.50/$120	4-14
100% Cotton Batiste – Hand Washable				
55377	02 White 11 Chablis 36 Lipstick 41 Night 46 Mallard 28 Cognac	Spread collar blouse with two flap pockets	$61.50/$124	4-14

STYLES	COLOR	DESCRIPTION	UNIT PRICE	SIZES

100% Silk Charmeuse – Dry Clean Only

STYLES	COLOR	DESCRIPTION	UNIT PRICE	SIZES
55221	02 White 28 Cognac	Wide lapel blouse, picture frame neck, no cuffs	$59.50/$120	4-14

100% Silk Charmeuse – Dry Clean Only

STYLES	COLOR	DESCRIPTION	UNIT PRICE	SIZES
72661	11 Chablis 41 Night 70 Chrysanthemum	Ruffle collar blouse, poet sleeves, large front buttons	$61.50/$124	4-14

100% Silk Charmeuse – Dry Clean Only

STYLES	COLOR	DESCRIPTION	UNIT PRICE	SIZES
53571	02 White 11 Chablis	Pleat/ruffle front and sleeve blouse, with pleat ruffle mandarin collar and cuff	$68.50/$139	4-14

STYLES	COLOR	DESCRIPTION	UNIT PRICE	SIZES

100% Silk Charmeuse – Dry Clean Only

STYLES	COLOR	DESCRIPTION	UNIT PRICE	SIZES
53751	70 White/black 90 White/lipstick	Ruffled/edged jabot blouse, tuxedo collar, gold-tone buttons	$63.50/$128	4-14

100% Silk Charmeuse – Dry Clean Only

STYLES	COLOR	DESCRIPTION	UNIT PRICE	SIZES
55331	02 White 46 Mallard 36 Lipstick 28 Cognac	Button front, poet sleeve blouse with collar	$68.50/$139	4-14

100% Silk Charmeuse – Dry Clean Only

STYLES	COLOR	DESCRIPTION	UNIT PRICE	SIZES
55301	02 White 28 Cognac 03 Coal 36 Lipstick	Neck draped blouse, jewel neckline	$63.50/$128	4-14

STYLES	COLOR	DESCRIPTION	UNIT PRICE	SIZES

100% Silk Charmeuse – Dry Clean Only

| 55530 | 02 White
41 Night | Ruffle trim blouse,
button front, fitted
waist, pullover | $63.50/$128 | 4-14 |

100% Silk Tissue Faille – Dry Clean Only

| 70331 | 02 White
11 Chablis
03 Coal | Pin tuck front blouse,
ruffle cuff, gold-tone
button, fly front | $63.50/$128 | 4-14 |

100% Silk Tissue Faille – Dry Clean Only

| 44272 | 02 White
11 Chablis
41 Night
36 Lipstick | Pointed shawl collar,
blouse, protrait neck,
surplice front, french cuffs | $61.50/$124 | 4-14 |

STYLES	COLOR	DESCRIPTION	UNIT PRICE	SIZES

100% Silk Tissue Faille – Dry Clean Only

| 44363 | 02 White
11 Chablis
36 Lipstick
03 Coal
28 Cognac | V-neck blouse, button front, no collar | $59.50/$120 | 4-14 |

100% Silk Tissue Faille – Dry Clean Only

| 42462 | 11 Chablis
84 Bittersweet
46 Mallard
36 Lipstick | Wide fly front blouse, two pockets, tailored | $68.50/$139 | 4-14 |

100% Silk Tissue Faille – Dry Clean Only

| 52441 | 02 White
84 Bittersweet
11 Chablis
41 Night | Soft pleat blouse, notched collar, button front | $68.50/$139 | 4-14 |

STYLES	COLOR	DESCRIPTION	UNIT PRICE	SIZES

100% Silk Tissue Faille – Dry Clean Only

STYLES	COLOR	DESCRIPTION	UNIT PRICE	SIZES
52351	02 White 11 Chablis 28 Cognac 36 Lipstick 03 Coal	High cowl neck blouse, pleated waist, french cuffs	$61.50/$124	4-14

100% Silk Tissue Faille – Dry Clean Only

STYLES	COLOR	DESCRIPTION	UNIT PRICE	SIZES
52391	02 White 11 Chablis 41 Night	Criss-cross draped front blouse, button back	$62.50/$126	4-14

100% Silk Crepe de Chine – Dry Clean Only

STYLES	COLOR	DESCRIPTION	UNIT PRICE	SIZES
72421	02 White 11 Chablis 41 Night 46 Mallard 84 Bittersweet	Notched collar blouse, french cuffs, tailored	$59.50/$120	4-14

STYLES	COLOR	DESCRIPTION	UNIT PRICE	SIZES

100% Silk Crepe de Chine – Dry Clean Only

STYLES	COLOR	DESCRIPTION	UNIT PRICE	SIZES
70321	02 White 11 Chablis 36 Lipstick 70 Chrysanthemum	Box pleat blouse, crew neck, french cuffs	$53.50/$110	4-14

100% Sueded Silk – Hand Washable

STYLES	COLOR	DESCRIPTION	UNIT PRICE	SIZES
55341	02 White 11 Chablis 41 Night 36 Lipstick 28 Cognac 03 Coal 70 Chrysanthemum	High neck blouse, plain front, button back	$53.50/$110	4-14

100% Wool Flannel – Dry Clean Only

STYLES	COLOR	DESCRIPTION	UNIT PRICE	SIZES
21011	41 Night 03 Coal 11 Chablis	Long wrap skirt, no waistband, 30"	$65.50/$132	4-14

STYLES	COLOR	DESCRIPTION	UNIT PRICE	SIZES

100% Wool Flannel – Dry Clean Only

STYLES	COLOR	DESCRIPTION	UNIT PRICE	SIZES
21016	41 Night 03 Coal 11 Chablis	Classic trouser, zipper front, side-slit pockets, button waistband	$59.50/$120	4-14

100% Wool Gabardine – Dry Clean Only

STYLES	COLOR	DESCRIPTION	UNIT PRICE	SIZES
21012	41 Night 36 Lipstick 28 Cognac	Draped front pant, side button, side pockets	$69.50/$140	4-14

STYLES	COLOR	DESCRIPTION	UNIT PRICE	SIZES

100% Wool Gabardine – Dry Clean Only

21010	41 Night 36 Lipstick 28 Cognac	Short draped front skirt, button back, 20"	$58.50/$118	4-14

100% Wool Gabardine – Dry Clean Only

21071	11 Chablis 03 Coal 41 Night	Full swing skirt, side pocket, button back, 30"	$69.50/$140	4-14

FIGURE 6-6   POTPOURRI COLLECTION

STYLES	COLOR	DESCRIPTION	UNIT PRICE	SIZES
100% Silk Georgette – Dry Clean Only				
3006602	01 White 04 Écru 18 Sapphire 44 Onyx	Draped crossover collar blouse, covered buttons, paisley print	$43.50/$90	4-14
100% Silk Georgette – Dry Clean Only				
3006604	18 Sapphire 50 Emerald 32 Claret 44 Onyx 04 Écru	Lace trimmed notch collar, front, and cuff blouse	$43.50/$90	4-14
100% Silk Georgette – Dry Clean Only				
3006603	04 Écru 01 White 44 Onyx 32 Claret	Pleat front blouse, lace trimmed bow, french cuffs	$48.00/$100	4-14

STYLES	COLOR	DESCRIPTION	UNIT PRICE	SIZES

100% Silk Georgette – Dry Clean Only

| 3006601 | 01 White
04 Écru
50 Emerald
44 Onyx
32 Claret
18 Sapphire | Asymmetric ruffle
collar blouse,
fly front | $43.50/$90 | 4-14 |

100% Silk Georgette – Dry Clean Only

| 3006605 | 01 White
18 Sapphire
44 Onyx
32 Claret | Shirred shoulder
surplice front
blouse, two button
unfitted sleeves | $44.50/$92 | 4-14 |

100% Silk Georgette – Dry Clean Only

| 3006606 | 01 White
44 Onyx
32 Claret
50 Emerald
04 Écru
18 Sapphire | High three button
collar blouse,
three button cuffs,
fly front | $43.50/$90 | 4-14 |

Microfiber Crepe de Chine – Hand Washable

| 3006432 | 01 White
05 Ivory
07 Steel
79 Mustard
39 Red Dragon
44 Onyx
48 Teal | Double breasted blouse,
two flap pockets,
notch collar, pleats | $42.50/$86 | 4-14 |

Microfiber Crepe de Chine – Hand Washable

| 3006442 | 05 Ivory
44 Onyx
39 Red Dragon
48 Teal | Draped yoke blouse,
fly front, soft | $41.50/$84 | 4-14 |

Microfiber Crepe de Chine – Hand Washable

| 3006452 | 05 Ivory
01 White
07 Steel
79 Mustard
39 Red Dragon
48 Teal
44 Onyx | Two patch/flap
pocket blouse,
shirttail bottom,
placket front | $41.50/$84 | 4-14 |

STYLES	COLOR	DESCRIPTION	UNIT PRICE	SIZES

Microfiber Crepe de Chine – Hand Washable

| 3006462 | 01 White
44 Onyx
79 Mustard
39 Red Dragon | Pointed collar blouse,
dropped armhole, large
buttons | $39.50/$82 | 4-14 |

Microfiber Crepe de Chine – Hand Washable

| 3006472 | 01 White
05 Ivory
44 Onyx
79 Mustard | High collar, plain
front blouse, soft
wide sleeves, button
back | $39.50/$82 | 4-14 |

Microfiber Crepe de Chine – Hand Washable

| 3006482 | 01 White
05 Ivory
48 Teal
44 Onyx
79 Mustard
39 Red Dragon | High collar, pleat
front blouse,
ascot bow | $42.50/$86 | 4-14 |

STYLES	COLOR	DESCRIPTION	UNIT PRICE	SIZES

100% Silk Charmeuse – Dry Clean Only

| 3006501 | 01 White
05 Ivory
52 Platinum
44 Onyx
37 Fire | Banded scoop neck
blouse, pleat front,
button back | $47.50/$98 | 4-14 |

100% Silk Charmeuse – Dry Clean Only

| 3006502 | 01 White
05 Ivory
52 Platinum
44 Onyx
37 Fire | Two button high collar
blouse, pleat/fly front | $48.00/$100 | 4-14 |

100% Silk Charmeuse – Dry Clean Only

| 3006503 | 89 Peach
52 Platinum
44 Onyx
05 Ivory
01 White | Double breasted shawl
collar blouse | $45.50/$95 | 4-14 |

STYLES	COLOR	DESCRIPTION	UNIT PRICE	SIZES

100% Silk Charmeuse – Dry Clean Only

| 3006505 | 01 White
44 Onyx
37 Fire
05 Ivory | Criss cross pointed collar blouse, "purse" print on body, sleeves, cuffs | $44.50/$92 | 4-14 |

100% Silk Charmeuse – Dry Clean Only

| 3006506 | 01 White
44 Onyx
05 Ivory
52 Platinum
37 Fire | Jewel-neck blouse, two pockets with gold-tone buttons, chain-link print | $44.50/$92 | 4-14 |

100% Silk Charmeuse – Dry Clean Only

| 3006004 | 01 White
52 Platinum
05 Ivory
44 Onyx
89 Peach | Low notch collar blouse, french cuffs, tailored | $45.50/$95 | 4-14 |

STYLES	COLOR	DESCRIPTION	UNIT PRICE	SIZES
100% Washed Silk – Hand Washable				
3006723	01 White 05 Ivory 79 Mustard 44 Onyx 39 Red Dragon 07 Steel 18 Sapphire 06 Khaki	Placket front blouse, plain edged collar and cuffs	$42.50/$86	4-14
100% Washed Silk – Hand Washable				
3006724	01 White 05 Ivory 44 Onyx 39 Red Dragon 18 Sapphire	Jewel-neck blouse, single pleat front, french cuffs	$41.50/$84	4-14
100% Washed Silk – Hand Washable				
3008702	06 Khaki 44 Onyx 07 Steel	Side classic, triple pleated pant, side pockets	$42.50/$86	4-14

STYLES	COLOR	DESCRIPTION	UNIT PRICE	SIZES

100% Washed Silk – Hand Washable

| 3008602 | 06 Khaki
44 Onyx
18 Sapphire
79 Mustard | Softly gathered flare skirt, 30" | $42.50/$86 | 4-14 |

100% Wool Flannel – Dry Clean Only

| 3009701 | 23 Camel
07 Steel
44 Onyx
06 Khaki | Back zipper, clean front pant, on-seam pockets | $47.50/$98 | 4-14 |

STYLES	COLOR	DESCRIPTION	UNIT PRICE	SIZES

100% Wool Flannel – Dry Clean Only

| 3009601 | 23 Camel
07 Steel
44 Onyx
06 Khaki
79 Mustard
39 Red Dragon | Soft pleat front wrap skirt, 30" | $48.00/$100 | 4-14 |

100% Wool Flannel – Dry Clean Only

| 3009602 | 23 Camel
44 Onyx
06 Khaki
07 Steel | Short wrap skirt, 20" | $45.50/$95 | 4-14 |

FIGURE 6-7   ELAN COLLECTION

STYLES	COLOR	DESCRIPTION	UNIT PRICE	SIZES
100% Pure Silk Broadcloth – Dry Clean Only				
43599	13 White 21 Creme 16 Black	Tucked neck and front double breasted blouse, shawl collar	$38.50/$80	4-14
100% Pure Silk Broadcloth – Dry Clean Only				
43443	21 Creme 13 White 19 Taupe	Draped/buttoned yoke blouse, notch collar	$42.00/$85	4-14
100% Pure Silk Broadcloth – Dry Clean Only				
43421	21 Creme 10 Vermillion 16 Black	Ruffle fly front blouse	$42.00/$85	4-14

STYLES	COLOR	DESCRIPTION	UNIT PRICE	SIZES

100% Pure Silk Broadcloth – Dry Clean Only

| 43579 | 13 White
21 Creme
16 Black | Notch collar blouse, french cuffs, single gold button front | $43.50/$90 | 4-14 |

100% Pure Washed Silk – Hand Washable

| 26154 | 11 Red
21 Creme
16 Black
13 Royal | Jewel-neck, double breasted blouse | $38.50/$80 | 4-14 |

100% Pure Washed Silk – Hand Washable

| 26124 | 21 Creme
16 Black
13 White | Jewel-neck fly front blouse, two pleats | $48.00/$100 | 4-14 |

STYLES	COLOR	DESCRIPTION	UNIT PRICE	SIZES

100% Pure Washed Silk – Hand Washable

| 26003 | 13 White
21 Creme
13 Royal
16 Black | Three button draped shawl collar blouse | $45/$92 | 4-14 |

100% Pure Washed Silk – Hand Washable

| 26095 | 13 White
21 Creme
11 Red
16 Black | Two flap pocket, fly front blouse | $45.00/$92 | 4-14 |

100% Pure Washed Silk – Hand Washable

| 23048 | 13 White
21 Creme
19 Taupe
13 Royal
25 Charcoal | Fly front soft pleat blouse | $42.00/$85 | 4-14 |

STYLES	COLOR	DESCRIPTION	UNIT PRICE	SIZES

100% Polyester Crepe de Chine – Hand Washable

| 30031 | 13 White
21 Creme
61 Blush
16 Black | Pleated front blouse with high neck lace collar | $34.50/$70 | 4-14 |

100% Polyester Crepe de Chine – Hand Washable

| 30039 | 13 White
21 Creme
25 Charcoal
13 Royal | Tucked front blouse with pleated ascot bow | $36.50/$75 | 4-14 |

100% Polyester Crepe de Chine – Hand Washable

| 30315 | 13 White
21 Creme
11 Red
13 Royal
16 Black | Jewel-neck, tucked front, covered buttons | $34.50/$70 | 4-14 |

STYLES	COLOR	DESCRIPTION	UNIT PRICE	SIZES

100% Polyester Crepe de Chine – Hand Washable

| 30155 | 11 Red
13 White
13 Royal
16 Black | V-neck collared blouse,
fly front, french cuffs | $28.50/$60 | 4-14 |

100% Polyester Crepe de Chine – Hand Washable

| 33001 | 77 Paisley
(Red/Purple/Black) | Single button front
blouse, french cuffs | $28.50/$60 | 4-14 |

100% Polyester Crepe de Chine – Hand Washable

| 33054 | 99 Block Print
(White/Red/Black) | Single button front
blouse, block print | $31.50/$64 | 4-14 |

STYLES	COLOR	DESCRIPTION	UNIT PRICE	SIZES

100% Polyester Crepe de Chine – Hand Washable

| 30119 | 13 Royal
11 Red
16 Black | Embroidered fly front blouse (scroll motif) | $35.50/$75 | 4-14 |

100% Polyester Crepe de Chine – Hand Washable

| 31198 | 13 White
21 Creme | Embroidered buttoned front blouse (leaf motif) | $35.50/$75 | 4-14 |

100% Polyester Crepe de Chine – Hand Washable

| 30124 | 21 Creme
13 White
16 Black | Soft draped bow blouse, covered buttons, french cuffs | $31.50/$64 | 4-14 |

STYLES	COLOR	DESCRIPTION	UNIT PRICE	SIZES

100% Polyester Crepe de Chine – Hand Washable

30054	13 White 21 Creme 16 Black	Pleated "basket" design blouse, gold-tone buttons	$34.50/$70	4-14

100% Polyester Crepe de Chine – Hand Washable

30314	13 White 21 Creme 10 Pink 16 Black	Pleat front, pleat pocket blouse, jewel-neck	$34.50/$70	4-14

50/50 Polyester/Wool Blend – Dry Clean Only

23063	19 Taupe 16 Black 14 Gray Heather	Soft inverted pleat front skirt, 23"	$38.50/$80	4-14

STYLES	COLOR	DESCRIPTION	UNIT PRICE	SIZES

50/50 Polyester/Wool Blend – Dry Clean Only

| 23062 | 19 Taupe
16 Black
14 Gray Heather | Double pleated slim skirt, 30" | $42.00/$85 | 4-14 |

50/50 Polyester/Wool Blend – Dry Clean Only

| 23061 | 19 Taupe
16 Black
14 Gray Heather | Hip-stitched knife pleat skirt, 30" | $46.50/$95 | 4-14 |

STYLES	COLOR	DESCRIPTION	UNIT PRICE	SIZES

50/50 Polyester/Wool Blend – Dry Clean Only

23064	19 Taupe 16 Black 14 Gray Heather	Soft inverted pleat pant, wide leg, side pockets	$45.00/$92	4-14

50/50 Polyester/Wool Blend – Dry Clean Only

23065	19 Taupe 16 Black 14 Gray Heather	Clean front pant, tapered leg, on-seam pockets	$42.00/$85	4-14

FIGURE 6-8 JARROD & YOUNG'S SINGLE STORE PURCHASE ORDER

FIGURE 6-9 JARROD & YOUNG'S MULTI-STORE PURCHASE ORDER

JARROD & YOUNG PURCHASE ORDER

Buyer .... DMM .... Date .... Page .... Of ....

DEPT. NO.	ORDER NO.		CONTINUATION NO.	CHARGE MONTH	DELIVERY DATE	CANCEL IF NOT REC'D BY	MFR. NO.	ORDER DATE
	5858075							

SPECIAL INSTRUCTIONS

MARK ALL PACKAGES & INVOICES WITH OUR ORDER NO. AND CONTINUATION NO.

☐
☐
☐ OTHER

FOR ACCOUNTS PAYABLE USE ONLY

NAME ....

VENDOR DUNS NUMBER

ADDRESS ....

DISCOUNT

FREIGHT TERMS
☐ Vendor Pays
☐ Special _____ Pays

CITY .... STATE .... ZIP CODE

FOB

TICKETING INSTRUCTIONS

SHIPPED FROM

☐ CONFIRMATION OF ORDER–DO NOT DUPLICATE

SHIP TO: ☐ (Drop Ship) Individual Stores ☐ J&Y Warehs. Route 89E DM, Iowa

LINE	MANUFAC- TURER'S STYLE NO.	STYLE NO.	CLASS	DESCRIPTION	COLOR NAME	COLOR NO.	SIZE	TOTAL QUANTITY	UNIT COST	UNIT RETAIL	DM	CR	Am	CB	IC	SC	Dv	Wh	TOTAL COST	TOTAL RETAIL
1																				
2																				
3																				
4																				
5																				
6																				
7																				
8																				
9																				
10																				
11																				
12																				
13																				
14																				
15																				
16																				
17																				
18																				
19																				
20																				
21																				
22																				
23																				
24																				
25																				
26																				
27																				

MU%
RETAIL
COST

RETAIL
COST

REPRODUCTION

TERMS All terms begin on date of receipt of goods and invoice by Jarrod & Young. Under EOM terms merchandise received on or after the 25th of any month will be paid for as though received on the first of the following month. This order is 1) subject to all of the terms and conditions stated on both sides of this order, please note particularly conditions appearing on reverse side, 2) not valid unless counter signed by a divisional merchandise manager or an officer. (over)

BILLING & SHIPPING INSTRUCTIONS

BILLING
To assure prompt payment
1. Prepare a separate invoice for each department and location within a shipment.
2. Enclose each location's invoice with shipment in a clearly marked "lead" carton. If this is not possible, send your invoices, no later than the shipment date to Jarrod & Young.
3. The invoice must cover only the merchandise shipped, and show:
  a) Vendor name
  b) Vendor DUNS number
  c) J & Y Purchase Order number
  d) J & Y Department number
  e) Location name and number
  f) Complete description of merchandise by style, color, size and unit cost, with line extensions.
Address all inquiries about invoices to the Box 741 address, above.

PACKING & SHIPPING
4. Shipment must be packed, labeled and segregated by Store, Department, and Order number.
5. The Packing List must be enclosed in a clearly marked "lead" carton and must show, by location:
  a) Vendor name
  b) Purchase Order number
  c) Invoice number, when feasible
  d) Department number
  e) Location name and number
6. Merchandise quantities should not differ from the original order.
7. Partial shipments are not permitted unless stipulated on the face of this Purchase Order.
8. The label on each carton must show:
  a) Vendor name
  b) Purchase Order number
  c) Department number
  d) Location name and number
Failure to comply with the above instructions may subject you to a charge to offset the additional costs incurred in processing your invoice and merchandise.

ROUTING
9. Based upon the freight terms on the face of this order, when J & Y is responsible for freight:
  a) Route shipments according to our "STANDARD ROUTING LETTER"
  b) Multi-store shipments consigned to the same bill of lading destination on one day must be combined and shipped on a single bill of lading. The piece count and weight by store should be shown on that bill of lading.
  c) When air freight is authorized, an air freight authorization number (supplied by buyer) must be shown on all shipping documents.
Failure to follow our routing instructions, with or without incurring higher transportation charges, shall be considered as your agreement to PAY ALL TRANSPORTATION CHARGES. Authority to deviate must be obtained from the J & Y Traffic Manager or his authorized representative prior to shipment.
If you have any questions on the above labeling, packing or shipping instructions and/or require a routing letter address your inquiries to J & Y traffic manager, Des Moines, Iowa

SHIPPING TERMS AND INSTRUCTIONS (ANY DEVIATIONS AT VENDOR'S RISK AND EXPENSE).

1. Follow all routing instructions. Note routing guide referred to on face of order.
2. An unextended packing list must accompany each shipment (showing breakdown of color and size where applicable).
3. Risk of loss or damage in transit to PARCEL POST shipments shall be upon the Vendor, notwithstanding who pays shipping costs.
4. Do not ship before or after dates on face of order. Violation of this requirement will subject Vendor to (a) storage and handling charges of 5% of the gross value of the invoice or (b) merchandise will be returned to Vendor with charge-back of inbound and outbound transportation and handling charges incurred by J & Y.

The following applies where Purchaser pays transportation charges in absence of different instructions in Routing Guide:

5. If there is sufficient volume available and freight charges will be less, ship as carload or truckload.
6. Two or more shipments being forwarded to the same delivery point on the same day must be combined and shipped on the single bill of lading irrespective of departmental variance.
7. Merchandise must be packed, shipped and described on bills of lading in accordance with applicable freight tariffs. Differently rated commodities must be in separate containers and be separately described on the bill of lading.
8. In absence of contrary instructions, do not insure shipments, and do not declare value on express shipments for benefit of J & Y.

GENERAL TERMS

1. Vendor warrants and represents that it has the right to sell the merchandise purchased hereunder and agrees to indemnify and save the Purchaser harmless from and against any and all suits, actions, claims or demands that may be brought against Purchaser and from and against all liability, loss, damages, costs and expenses, including attorney's fees, incurred by Purchaser by reason thereof, on the grounds that the purchase or sale of any of the merchandise covered by this order constitutes unfair competition or infringement of patent, copyright or trademark or an invasion of the rights of any person or corporation, and Vendor further agrees at its own cost and expense to defend, upon the request of Purchaser, any such suits, action, claims and demands.
2. In addition to the warranties set forth in Sections 2-312 (1) and (3), Section 2-313 (1), Section 2-314 of the Uniform Commercial Code, Vendor warrants that the goods are fit for the purpose of retail sale, and Vendor represents that it is a merchant with respect to the merchandise, and that no express or implied warranties have been excluded by examination of the goods or otherwise.
3. All electrical appliances and devices must comply with the requirements and bear the seal of Underwriters' Laboratories, Inc.
4. The time stated for delivery hereunder is of the essence hereof.
5. Purchaser reserves the right to cancel this order if the terms and conditions hereof are not fully complied with. Purchaser further reserves the right to refuse any merchandise and to cancel all or any part of this order if Vendor fails to deliver all or any part of the merchandise in accordance with the terms of this order. Acceptance of any part of the order shall not bind Purchaser to accept future shipments, nor deprive it of the right to return merchandise already accepted. Payment of all or any part of the purchase price shall not be construed as a waiver of any claims of the Purchaser for defects or delay in delivery or for breach of the contract, and any and all such claims shall survive payment.
6. Vendor represents that the merchandise covered by this order has been manufactured and labeled in accordance with the requirements of all applicable Federal, State and Municipal laws, rules and regulations, including but not limited to the Fair Labor Standards Act, the Wool Products Labeling Act, the Fur Products Labeling Act, the Textile Fiber Products Identification Act, the Flammable Fabrics Act, the Federal Hazardous Substance Labeling Act, and the Federal Food, Drug and Cosmetic Act. Vendor's invoice shall bear the separate guarantees provided for under any of such acts or shall contain the appropriate statement that a continuing guarantee has been filed in accordance with such acts and applicable rules and regulations of the Federal Trade Commission and other governmental agencies with jurisdiction in the premises.
7. Vendor agrees to deliver the merchandise at prices stated herein or at ceiling or prevailing price at the time of delivery, whichever is lower, and Vendor warrants that no other purchaser from Vendor is receiving more favorable terms than J & Y.
8. Purchaser's failure to insist in any one or more instances upon the strict or timely performance of any of the terms, provisions or conditions of this instrument shall not be considered as a waiver or a relinquishment in the future of the requirements of such terms, provisions and conditions, or of Purchaser's rights based upon Vendor's failure to perform any of such terms, provisions or conditions, but the same shall continue in full force and effect. This Agreement may not be modified or terminated orally, and no modification or termination nor any claimed waiver of any of the provisions hereof shall be binding unless in writing and signed by the party against whom such modifications, termination or waiver is sought to be enforced. ADDITIONAL OR DIFFERENT TERMS IN ANY INVOICE OR OTHER DOCUMENT ISSUED BY VENDOR SHALL NOT BE BINDING ON PURCHASER.
9. All costs incurred by Purchaser because of non-compliance with the terms and conditions of this order (including Shipping and Billing Instructions) will be charged to Vendor.
10. By signing a copy of this order or making any shipments, Vendor shall be deemed to have accepted this order. FAILURE OF VENDOR TO GIVE NOTICE OR REJECTION WITHIN REASONABLE TIME SHALL CONSTITUTE ACCEPTANCE OF THIS ORDER.
11. INDEMNITY AND INSURANCE

    Vendor shall protect, defend, indemnify and save Purchaser harmless against any and all claims, demands or causes of action of every nature whatsoever arising in favor of any person, including both Vendor's and Purchaser's employees on account of personal injuries or death or damages to property occurring, growing out of, incident to, or resulting directly or indirectly from the performance by Vendor hereunder, whether such loss, damage, injury or liability is contributed to by the negligence of the Purchaser or its employees, or by the premises themselves or any equipment thereon whether latent or patent, or from other causes whatsoever, except that the Vendor shall have no liability for damages or costs incident thereto caused by the sole negligence of Purchaser.

    Vendor agrees to obtain and maintain, at its expense, a policy or policies of products liability insurance, with a limit of liability of not less than One Million Dollars, and with broad form Vendor's endorsement naming Purchaser, in such companies and containing such other provisions which shall be satisfactory to Purchaser covering merchandise sold to Purchaser hereunder. All such policies shall provide that the coverage thereunder shall not be terminated without at least thirty (30) days prior written notice to Purchaser. Vendor agrees to promptly supply Purchaser with evidence satisfactory to Purchaser, upon demand by Purchaser, of the existence of said aforementioned policy or policies.

FIGURE 6-10 JARROD & YOUNG'S BUYER'S WORKSHEET

JARROD & YOUNG

BUYER'S WORKSHEET

PO #		Page	of

DEPT #	VENDOR #	SHIP DATE MM/DD/YY	REFERENCE #	VENDOR NAME/ADDRESS

DISTRO TYPES	V=VENDOR PACK/MAIL W=VENDOR PACK/DO NOT MAIL D=DROP SHIP TO STORE I=IMPORT ORDER

CANCEL DATE MM/DD/YY	ALLOCATION %	SPECIAL TERMS

(FOR SPECIAL TERMS YOU MUST ADD AN A/P NOTE)

EVENT #	GROUP

VENDOR STYLE								
CLASS/SUBCLASS								
MARK STYLE								
MASTER STYLE								
DESCRIPTION								
MASTER DIVISION								
COST $								
UM/C DESCRIPTION UM/C COUNT								
OWNED RETAIL $								
UM/R DESCRIPTION UM/R COUNT								
TICKET RETAIL $								
UM/R DESCRIPTION UM/R COUNT								
2ND TICKET RETAIL/ COMP/2 FOR $								
UM/C COUNT								
PO TKT NAME								
OUTDATE (MONTH) REORDER THRU (MONTH)								
SIZE PACK # ORD 01 01	01 01	01 01	01 01	01 01	01 01	01 01	01 01	

COLOR CODE	COLOR NAME	Store CODE	NAME					
		1	DM					
		2	CR					
		3	Am					
		4	CB					
		5	IC					
		6	SC					
		7	Dv					
		0	Wh					

NOTES: 01=TRAFFIC 02=GENERAL 03=VENDOR 04=WAREHOUSE 05=AP 07=IMPORT OFFICE

Prepared by .... Date ...../...../.................

Keyed by .... Date ...../...../......... TOTAL COST $ .... TOTAL RETAIL $ ....

FIGURE 6-11 JARROD & YOUNG'S BUYER'S WORKSHEET

─ **JARROD & YOUNG** ─

BUYER'S WORKSHEET

				PO #		Page	of

DEPT #	VENDOR #	SHIP DATE MM/DD/YY	REFERENCE #	VENDOR NAME/ADDRESS

DISTRO TYPES	V=VENDOR PACK/MAIL W=VENDOR PACK/DO NOT MAIL D=DROP SHIP TO STORE I=IMPORT ORDER

CANCEL DATE MM/DD/YY	ALLOCATION %	SPECIAL TERMS
		(FOR SPECIAL TERMS YOU MUST ADD AN A/P NOTE)
		EVENT # GROUP

VENDOR STYLE							
CLASS/SUBCLASS							
MARK STYLE							
MASTER STYLE							
DESCRIPTION							
MASTER DIVISION							
COST $							
UM/C DESCRIPTION UM/C COUNT							
OWNED RETAIL $							
UM/R DESCRIPTION UM/R COUNT							
TICKET RETAIL $							
UM/R DESCRIPTION UM/R COUNT							
2ND TICKET RETAIL/ COMP/2 FOR $							
UM/C COUNT							
PO TKT NAME							
OUTDATE (MONTH) REORDER THRU (MONTH)							
SIZE PACK # ORD 01 01	01 01	01 01	01 01	01 01	01 01	01 01	01 01

COLOR CODE	COLOR NAME	Store CODE	NAME						
		1	DM						
		2	CR						
		3	Am						
		4	CB						
		5	IC						
		6	SC						
		7	Dv						
		0	Wh						

NOTES: 01=TRAFFIC 02=GENERAL 03=VENDOR 04=WAREHOUSE 05=AP 07=IMPORT OFFICE

Prepared by .... Date / / ....

Keyed by .... Date / / TOTAL COST $ .... TOTAL RETAIL $ ....

FIGURE 6-12 JARROD & YOUNG'S BUYER'S WORKSHEET

JARROD & YOUNG

BUYER'S WORKSHEET

| | | | | PO # | | Page | of |

| DEPT # | VENDOR # | SHIP DATE MM/DD/YY | REFERENCE # | VENDOR NAME/ADDRESS |

| DISTRO TYPES | V=VENDOR PACK/MAIL W=VENDOR PACK/DO NOT MAIL D=DROP SHIP TO STORE I=IMPORT ORDER |

| CANCEL DATE MM/DD/YY | ALLOCATION % | SPECIAL TERMS |

(FOR SPECIAL TERMS YOU MUST ADD AN A/P NOTE)

EVENT #   GROUP

VENDOR STYLE

CLASS/SUBCLASS

MARK STYLE

MASTER STYLE

DESCRIPTION

MASTER DIVISION

COST $

UM/C DESCRIPTION
UM/C COUNT

OWNED RETAIL $

UM/R DESCRIPTION
UM/R COUNT

TICKET RETAIL $

UM/R DESCRIPTION
UM/R COUNT

2ND TICKET RETAIL/
COMP/2 FOR $

UM/C COUNT

PO TKT NAME

OUTDATE (MONTH)
REORDER THRU (MONTH)

SIZE PACK # ORD 01 01   01 01   01 01   01 01   01 01   01 01   01 01   01 01

COLOR CODE	COLOR NAME	Store CODE	NAME						
		1	DM						
		2	CR						
		3	Am						
		4	CB						
		5	IC						
		6	SC						
		7	Dv						
		0	Wh						

NOTES: 01=TRAFFIC   02=GENERAL   03=VENDOR   04=WAREHOUSE   05=AP   07=IMPORT OFFICE

Prepared by ....   Date   /   /

Keyed by ....   Date   /   /   TOTAL COST $ ....   TOTAL RETAIL $ ....

FIGURE 6-13 JARROD & YOUNG'S MULTI-STORE PURCHASE ORDER

JARROD & YOUNG PURCHASE ORDER

Buyer _____ DMM _____ Date _____ Page _____ Of _____

ORDER NO. **5858075**

MARK ALL PACKAGES & INVOICES WITH OUR ORDER NO. AND CONTINUATION NO.

SPECIAL INSTRUCTIONS

☐
☐
☐ OTHER

☐ CONFIRMATION OF ORDER–DO NOT DUPLICATE

DEPT. NO. | CONTINUATION NO. | CHARGE MONTH | DELIVERY DATE | CANCEL IF NOT REC'D BY | MFR. NO. | ORDER DATE

NAME

ADDRESS

CITY | STATE | ZIP CODE

VENDOR DUNS NUMBER

DISCOUNT

FOB

SHIPPED FROM

FOR ACCOUNTS PAYABLE USE ONLY

FREIGHT TERMS
☐ Vendor Pays
☐ Special _____ Pays

TICKETING INSTRUCTIONS

SHIP TO: ☐ (Drop Ship) Individual Stores ☐ J&Y Warehs. Route 89E DM, Iowa

TERMS All terms begin on date of receipt of goods and invoice by Jarrod & Young. Under EOM terms merchandise received on or after the 25th of any month will be paid for as though received on the first of the following month. This order is 11 subject to all of the terms and conditions stated on both sides of this order, please note particularly conditions appearing on reverse side, 2) not valid unless counter signed by a divisional merchandise manager or an officer. (over)

BILLING & SHIPPING INSTRUCTIONS

BILLING
To assure prompt payment
1. Prepare a separate invoice for each department and location within a shipment.
2. Enclose each location's invoice with shipment in a clearly marked "lead" carton. If this is not possible, send your invoices, no later than the shipment date to Jarrod & Young.
3. The invoice must cover only the merchandise shipped, and show:
   a) Vendor name
   b) Vendor DUNS number
   c) J & Y Purchase Order number
   d) J & Y Department number
   e) Location name and number
   f) Complete description of merchandise by style, color, size and unit cost, with line extensions.
Address all inquiries about invoices to the Box 741 address, above.

PACKING & SHIPPING
4. Shipment must be packed, labeled and segregated by Store, Department, and Order number.
5. The Packing List must be enclosed in a clearly marked "lead" carton and must show, by location:
   a) Vendor name
   b) Purchase Order number
   c) Invoice number, when feasible
   d) Department number
   e) Location name and number
6. Merchandise quantities should not differ from the original order.
7. Partial shipments are not permitted unless stipulated on the face of this Purchase Order.
8. The label on each carton must show:
   a) Vendor name
   b) Purchase Order number
   c) Department number
   d) Location name and number
Failure to comply with the above instructions may subject you to a charge to offset the additional costs incurred in processing your invoice and merchandise.

ROUTING
9. Based upon the freight terms on the face of this order, when J & Y is responsible for freight:
   a) Route shipments according to our "STANDARD ROUTING LETTER"
   b) Multi-store shipments consigned to the same bill of lading destination on one day must be combined and shipped on a single bill of lading. The piece count and weight by store should be shown on that bill of lading.
   c) When air freight is authorized, an air freight authorization number (supplied by buyer) must be shown on all shipping documents.
Failure to follow our routing instructions, with or without incurring higher transportation charges, shall be considered as your agreement to PAY ALL TRANSPORTATION CHARGES. Authority to deviate must be obtained from the J & Y Traffic Manager or his authorized representative prior to shipment.
If you have any questions on the above labeling, packing or shipping instructions and/or require a routing letter address your inquiries to J & Y traffic manager, Des Moines, Iowa.

LINE	MANUFAC-TURER'S STYLE NO.	STYLE NO.	CLASS	DESCRIPTION	COLOR NAME	NO.	SIZE	TOTAL QUANTITY	UNIT COST	UNIT RETAIL	DM	CR	Am	CB	IC	SC	Dv	Wh	TOTAL COST	TOTAL RETAIL
1																				
2																				
3																				
4																				
5																				
6																				
7																				
8																				
9																				
10																				
11																				
12																				
13																				
14																				
15																				
16																				
17																				
18																				
19																				
20																				
21																				
22																				
23																				
24																				
25																				
26																				
27																				

RETAIL | COST

MU%
RETAIL
COST

REPRODUCTION

SHIPPING TERMS AND INSTRUCTIONS (ANY DEVIATIONS AT VENDOR'S RISK AND EXPENSE).

1. Follow all routing instructions. Note routing guide referred to on face of order.
2. An unextended packing list must accompany each shipment (showing breakdown of color and size where applicable).
3. Risk of loss or damage in transit to PARCEL POST shipments shall be upon the Vendor, notwithstanding who pays shipping costs.
4. Do not ship before or after dates on face of order. Violation of this requirement will subject Vendor to (a) storage and handling charges of 5% of the gross value of the invoice or (b) merchandise will be returned to Vendor with charge-back of inbound and outbound transportation and handling charges incurred by J & Y.

The following applies where Purchaser pays transportation charges in absence of different instructions in Routing Guide:

5. If there is sufficient volume available and freight charges will be less, ship as carload or truckload.
6. Two or more shipments being forwarded to the same delivery point on the same day must be combined and shipped on the single bill of lading irrespective of departmental variance.
7. Merchandise must be packed, shipped and described on bills of lading in accordance with applicable freight tariffs. Differently rated commodities must be in separate containers and be separately described on the bill of lading.
8. In absence of contrary instructions, do not insure shipments, and do not declare value on express shipments for benefit of J & Y.

GENERAL TERMS

1. Vendor warrants and represents that it has the right to sell the merchandise purchased hereunder and agrees to indemnify and save the Purchaser harmless from and against any and all suits, actions, claims or demands that may be brought against Purchaser and from and against all liability, loss, damages, costs and expenses, including attorney's fees, incurred by Purchaser by reason thereof, on the grounds that the purchase or sale of any of the merchandise covered by this order constitutes unfair competition or infringement of patent, copyright or trademark or an invasion of the rights of any person or corporation, and Vendor further agrees at its own cost and expense to defend, upon the request of Purchaser, any such suits, action, claims and demands.
2. In addition to the warranties set forth in Sections 2-312 (1) and (3), Section 2-313 (1), Section 2-314 of the Uniform Commercial Code, Vendor warrants that the goods are fit for the purpose of retail sale, and Vendor represents that it is a merchant with respect to the merchandise, and that no express or implied warranties have been excluded by examination of the goods or otherwise.
3. All electrical appliances and devices must comply with the requirements and bear the seal of Underwriters' Laboratories, Inc.
4. The time stated for delivery hereunder is of the essence hereof.
5. Purchaser reserves the right to cancel this order if the terms and conditions hereof are not fully complied with. Purchaser further reserves the right to refuse any merchandise and to cancel all or any part of this order if Vendor fails to deliver all or any part of the merchandise in accordance with the terms of this order. Acceptance of any part of the order shall not bind Purchaser to accept future shipments, nor deprive it of the right to return merchandise already accepted. Payment of all or any part of the purchase price shall not be construed as a waiver of any claims of the Purchaser for defects or delay in delivery or for breach of the contract, and any and all such claims shall survive payment.
6. Vendor represents that the merchandise covered by this order has been manufactured and labeled in accordance with the requirements of all applicable Federal, State and Municipal laws, rules and regulations, including but not limited to the Fair Labor Standards Act, the Wool Products Labeling Act, the Fur Products Labeling Act, the Textile Fiber Products Identification Act, the Flammable Fabrics Act, the Federal Hazardous Substance Labeling Act, and the Federal Food, Drug and Cosmetic Act. Vendor's invoice shall bear the separate guarantees provided for under any of such acts or shall contain the appropriate statement that a continuing guarantee has been filed in accordance with such acts and applicable rules and regulations of the Federal Trade Commission and other governmental agencies with jurisdiction in the premises.
7. Vendor agrees to deliver the merchandise at prices stated herein or at ceiling or prevailing price at the time of delivery, whichever is lower, and Vendor warrants that no other purchaser from Vendor is receiving more favorable terms than J & Y.
8. Purchaser's failure to insist in any one or more instances upon the strict or timely performance of any of the terms, provisions or conditions of this instrument shall not be considered as a waiver or a relinquishment in the future of the requirements of such terms, provisions and conditions, or of Purchaser's rights based upon Vendor's failure to perform any of such terms, provisions or conditions, but the same shall continue in full force and effect. This Agreement may not be modified or terminated orally, and no modification or termination nor any claimed waiver of any of the provisions hereof shall be binding unless in writing and signed by the party against whom such modifications, termination or waiver is sought to be enforced. ADDITIONAL OR DIFFERENT TERMS IN ANY INVOICE OR OTHER DOCUMENT ISSUED BY VENDOR SHALL NOT BE BINDING ON PURCHASER.
9. All costs incurred by Purchaser because of non-compliance with the terms and conditions of this order (including Shipping and Billing Instructions) will be charged to Vendor.
10. By signing a copy of this order or making any shipments, Vendor shall be deemed to have accepted this order. FAILURE OF VENDOR TO GIVE NOTICE OR REJECTION WITHIN REASONABLE TIME SHALL CONSTITUTE ACCEPTANCE OF THIS ORDER.
11. INDEMNITY AND INSURANCE

    Vendor shall protect, defend, indemnify and save Purchaser harmless against any and all claims, demands or causes of action of every nature whatsoever arising in favor of any person, including both Vendor's and Purchaser's employees on account of personal injuries or death or damages to property occurring, growing out of, incident to, or resulting directly or indirectly from the performance by Vendor hereunder, whether such loss, damage, injury or liability is contributed to by the negligence of the Purchaser or its employees, or by the premises themselves or any equipment thereon whether latent or patent, or from other causes whatsoever, except that the Vendor shall have no liability for damages or costs incident thereto caused by the sole negligence of Purchaser.

    Vendor agrees to obtain and maintain, at its expense, a policy or policies of products liability insurance, with a limit of liability of not less than One Million Dollars, and with broad form Vendor's endorsement naming Purchaser, in such companies and containing such other provisions which shall be satisfactory to Purchaser covering merchandise sold to Purchaser hereunder. All such policies shall provide that the coverage thereunder shall not be terminated without at least thirty (30) days prior written notice to Purchaser. Vendor agrees to promptly supply Purchaser with evidence satisfactory to Purchaser, upon demand by Purchaser, of the existence of said aforementioned policy or policies.

FIGURE 6-14 JARROD & YOUNG'S MULTI-STORE PURCHASE ORDER

JARROD & YOUNG PURCHASE ORDER

SPECIAL INSTRUCTIONS

☐
☐
☐ OTHER

☐ CONFIRMATION OF ORDER–DO NOT DUPLICATE

MARK ALL PACKAGES & INVOICES WITH OUR ORDER NO. AND CONTINUATION NO.

ORDER NO. 5858075

DEPT. NO.

NAME

ADDRESS

CITY STATE ZIP CODE

TICKETING INSTRUCTIONS

SHIP TO: ☐ (Drop Ship) Individual Stores ☐ J&Y Warehs. Route 89E DM, Iowa

DMM .... Date .... Page .... Of ....

Buyer ....

CONTINUATION NO. CHARGE MONTH DELIVERY DATE CANCEL IF NOT REC'D BY MFR. NO. ORDER DATE

VENDOR DUNS NUMBER

FOR ACCOUNTS PAYABLE USE ONLY

DISCOUNT

FOB

SHIPPED FROM

FREIGHT TERMS
☐ Vendor Pays
☐ Special

Pays

TERMS All terms begin on date of receipt of goods and invoice by Jarrod & Young. Under EOM terms merchandise received on or after the 25th of any month will be paid for as though received on the first of the following month. This order is 1) subject to all of the terms and conditions stated on both sides of this order, please note particularly conditions appearing on reverse side, 2) not valid unless counter signed by a divisional merchandise manager or an officer. (over)

BILLING

To assure prompt payment

1. Prepare a separate invoice for each department and location within a shipment.
2. Enclose each location's invoice with shipment in a clearly marked "lead" carton. If this is not possible, send your invoices, no later than the shipment date to Jarrod & Young.
3. The invoice must cover only the merchandise shipped, and show:
   a) Vendor name
   b) Vendor DUNS number
   c) J & Y Purchase Order number
   d) J & Y Department number
   e) Location name and number
   f) Complete description of merchandise by style, color, size and unit cost, with line extensions.
   Address all inquiries about invoices to the Box 741 address, above.

PACKING & SHIPPING

4. Shipment must be packed, labeled and segregated by Store, Department, and Order number.
5. The Packing List must be enclosed in a clearly marked "lead" carton and must show, by location:
   a) Vendor name
   b) Purchase Order number
   c) Invoice number, when feasible
   d) Department number
   e) Location name and number
6. Merchandise quantities should not differ from the original order.
7. Partial shipments are not permitted unless stipulated on the face of this Purchase Order.
8. The label on each carton must show:
   a) Vendor name
   b) Purchase Order number
   c) Department number
   d) Location name and number
   Failure to comply with the above instructions may subject you to a charge to offset the additional costs incurred in processing your invoice and merchandise.

ROUTING

9. Based upon the freight terms on the face of this order, when J & Y is responsible for freight:
   a) Route shipments according to our "STANDARD ROUTING LETTER"
   b) Multi-store shipments consigned to the same bill of lading destination on one day must be combined and shipped on a single bill of lading. The piece count and weight by store should be shown on that bill of lading.
   c) When air freight is authorized, an air freight authorization number (supplied by buyer) must be shown on all shipping documents.
   Failure to follow our routing instructions, with or without incurring higher transportation charges, shall be considered as your agreement to PAY ALL TRANSPORTATION CHARGES. Authority to deviate must be obtained from the J & Y Traffic Manager or his authorized representative prior to shipment.
   If you have any questions on the above labeling, packing or shipping instructions and/or require a routing letter address your inquiries to J & Y traffic manager, Des Moines, Iowa.

LINE	MANUFAC-TURER'S STYLE NO.	STYLE NO.	CLASS	COLOR NAME NO.	SIZE	TOTAL QUANTITY	UNIT COST	UNIT RETAIL	DM	CR	Arm	CB	IC	SC	Dv	Wh	TOTAL COST	TOTAL RETAIL
1																		
2																		
3																		
4																		
5																		
6																		
7																		
8																		
9																		
10																		
11																		
12																		
13																		
14																		
15																		
16																		
17																		
18																		
19																		
20																		
21																		
22																		
23																		
24																		
25																		
26																		
27																		

REPRODUCTION

RETAIL
COST

MU%
RETAIL
COST

SHIPPING TERMS AND INSTRUCTIONS (ANY DEVIATIONS AT VENDOR'S RISK AND EXPENSE).

1. Follow all routing instructions. Note routing guide referred to on face of order.
2. An unextended packing list must accompany each shipment (showing breakdown of color and size where applicable).
3. Risk of loss or damage in transit to PARCEL POST shipments shall be upon the Vendor, notwithstanding who pays shipping costs.
4. Do not ship before or after dates on face of order. Violation of this requirement will subject Vendor to (a) storage and handling charges of 5% of the gross value of the invoice or (b) merchandise will be returned to Vendor with charge-back of inbound and outbound transportation and handling charges incurred by J & Y.

The following applies where Purchaser pays transportation charges in absence of different instructions in Routing Guide:

5. If there is sufficient volume available and freight charges will be less, ship as carload or truckload.
6. Two or more shipments being forwarded to the same delivery point on the same day must be combined and shipped on the single bill of lading irrespective of departmental variance.
7. Merchandise must be packed, shipped and described on bills of lading in accordance with applicable freight tariffs. Differently rated commodities must be in separate containers and be separately described on the bill of lading.
8. In absence of contrary instructions, do not insure shipments, and do not declare value on express shipments for benefit of J & Y.

GENERAL TERMS

1. Vendor warrants and represents that it has the right to sell the merchandise purchased hereunder and agrees to indemnify and save the Purchaser harmless from and against any and all suits, actions, claims or demands that may be brought against Purchaser and from and against all liability, loss, damages, costs and expenses, including attorney's fees, incurred by Purchaser by reason thereof, on the grounds that the purchase or sale of any of the merchandise covered by this order constitutes unfair competition or infringement of patent, copyright or trademark or an invasion of the rights of any person or corporation, and Vendor further agrees at its own cost and expense to defend, upon the request of Purchaser, any such suits, action, claims and demands.
2. In addition to the warranties set forth in Sections 2-312 (1) and (3), Section 2-313 (1), Section 2-314 of the Uniform Commercial Code, Vendor warrants that the goods are fit for the purpose of retail sale, and Vendor represents that it is a merchant with respect to the merchandise, and that no express or implied warranties have been excluded by examination of the goods or otherwise.
3. All electrical appliances and devices must comply with the requirements and bear the seal of Underwriters' Laboratories, Inc.
4. The time stated for delivery hereunder is of the essence hereof.
5. Purchaser reserves the right to cancel this order if the terms and conditions hereof are not fully complied with. Purchaser further reserves the right to refuse any merchandise and to cancel all or any part of this order if Vendor fails to deliver all or any part of the merchandise in accordance with the terms of this order. Acceptance of any part of the order shall not bind Purchaser to accept future shipments, nor deprive it of the right to return merchandise already accepted. Payment of all or any part of the purchase price shall not be construed as a waiver of any claims of the Purchaser for defects or delay in delivery or for breach of the contract, and any and all such claims shall survive payment.
6. Vendor represents that the merchandise covered by this order has been manufactured and labeled in accordance with the requirements of all applicable Federal, State and Municipal laws, rules and regulations, including but not limited to the Fair Labor Standards Act, the Wool Products Labeling Act, the Fur Products Labeling Act, the Textile Fiber Products Identification Act, the Flammable Fabrics Act, the Federal Hazardous Substance Labeling Act, and the Federal Food, Drug and Cosmetic Act. Vendor's invoice shall bear the separate guarantees provided for under any of such acts or shall contain the appropriate statement that a continuing guarantee has been filed in accordance with such acts and applicable rules and regulations of the Federal Trade Commission and other governmental agencies with jurisdiction in the premises.
7. Vendor agrees to deliver the merchandise at prices stated herein or at ceiling or prevailing price at the time of delivery, whichever is lower, and Vendor warrants that no other purchaser from Vendor is receiving more favorable terms than J & Y.
8. Purchaser's failure to insist in any one or more instances upon the strict or timely performance of any of the terms, provisions or conditions of this instrument shall not be considered as a waiver or a relinquishment in the future of the requirements of such terms, provisions and conditions, or of Purchaser's rights based upon Vendor's failure to perform any of such terms, provisions or conditions, but the same shall continue in full force and effect. This Agreement may not be modified or terminated orally, and no modification or termination nor any claimed waiver of any of the provisions hereof shall be binding unless in writing and signed by the party against whom such modifications, termination or waiver is sought to be enforced. ADDITIONAL OR DIFFERENT TERMS IN ANY INVOICE OR OTHER DOCUMENT ISSUED BY VENDOR SHALL NOT BE BINDING ON PURCHASER.
9. All costs incurred by Purchaser because of non-compliance with the terms and conditions of this order (including Shipping and Billing Instructions) will be charged to Vendor.
10. By signing a copy of this order or making any shipments, Vendor shall be deemed to have accepted this order. FAILURE OF VENDOR TO GIVE NOTICE OR REJECTION WITHIN REASONABLE TIME SHALL CONSTITUTE ACCEPTANCE OF THIS ORDER.
11. INDEMNITY AND INSURANCE

   Vendor shall protect, defend, indemnify and save Purchaser harmless against any and all claims, demands or causes of action of every nature whatsoever arising in favor of any person, including both Vendor's and Purchaser's employees on account of personal injuries or death or damages to property occurring, growing out of, incident to, or resulting directly or indirectly from the performance by Vendor hereunder, whether such loss, damage, injury or liability is contributed to by the negligence of the Purchaser or its employees, or by the premises themselves or any equipment thereon whether latent or patent, or from other causes whatsoever, except that the Vendor shall have no liability for damages or costs incident thereto caused by the sole negligence of Purchaser.

   Vendor agrees to obtain and maintain, at its expense, a policy or policies of products liability insurance, with a limit of liability of not less than One Million Dollars, and with broad form Vendor's endorsement naming Purchaser, in such companies and containing such other provisions which shall be satisfactory to Purchaser covering merchandise sold to Purchaser hereunder. All such policies shall provide that the coverage thereunder shall not be terminated without at least thirty (30) days prior written notice to Purchaser. Vendor agrees to promptly supply Purchaser with evidence satisfactory to Purchaser, upon demand by Purchaser, of the existence of said aforementioned policy or policies.

FIGURE 6-15 JARROD & YOUNG'S MULTI-STORE PURCHASE ORDER

JARROD & YOUNG PURCHASE ORDER

SPECIAL INSTRUCTIONS

☐
☐
☐ OTHER

☐ CONFIRMATION OF ORDER–DO NOT DUPLICATE

Buyer .... DMM .... Date .... Page .... Of ....

DEPT. NO.

ORDER NO. **5858075**

MARK ALL PACKAGES & INVOICES WITH OUR ORDER NO. AND CONTINUATION NO.

NAME
ADDRESS
CITY   STATE   ZIP CODE

TICKETING INSTRUCTIONS

SHIP TO: ☐ (Drop Ship) Individual Stores ☐ J&Y Warehs. Route 89E DM, Iowa

CONTINUATION NO. CHARGE MONTH DELIVERY DATE CANCEL IF NOT REC'D BY MFR. NO. ORDER DATE

VENDOR DUNS NUMBER

DISCOUNT
FOB
SHIPPED FROM

FOR ACCOUNTS PAYABLE USE ONLY

FREIGHT TERMS
☐ Vendor Pays
☐ Special

Pays

LINE	MANUFACTURER'S STYLE NO.	STYLE NO.	CLASS	DESCRIPTION	COLOR NAME	NO.	SIZE	TOTAL QUANTITY	UNIT COST	UNIT RETAIL	DM	CR	DM	CB	Am	IC	SC	Dv	Wh	TOTAL COST	TOTAL RETAIL
1																					
2																					
3																					
4																					
5																					
6																					
7																					
8																					
9																					
10																					
11																					
12																					
13																					
14																					
15																					
16																					
17																					
18																					
19																					
20																					
21																					
22																					
23																					
24																					
25																					
26																					
27																					

REPRODUCTION

RETAIL
COST

MU%
RETAIL
COST

TERMS All terms begin on date of receipt of goods and invoice by Jarrod & Young. Under EOM terms merchandise received on or after the 25th of any month will be paid for as though received on the first of the following month. This order is 1) subject to all of the terms and conditions stated on both sides of this order, please note particularly conditions appearing on reverse side, 2) not valid unless counter signed by a divisional merchandise manager or an officer. (over)

BILLING & SHIPPING INSTRUCTIONS

BILLING
To assure prompt payment
1. Prepare a separate invoice for each department and location within a shipment.
2. Enclose each location's invoice with shipment in a clearly marked "lead" carton. If this is not possible, send your invoices, no later than the shipment date to Jarrod & Young.
3. The invoice must cover only the merchandise shipped, and show:
   a) Vendor name
   b) Vendor DUNS number
   c) J & Y Purchase Order number
   d) J & Y Department number
   e) Location name and number
   f) Complete description of merchandise by style, color, size and unit cost, with line extensions.
Address all inquiries about invoices to the Box 741 address, above.

PACKING & SHIPPING
4. Shipment must be packed, labeled and segregated by Store, Department, and Order number.
5. The Packing List must be enclosed in a clearly marked "lead" carton and must show, by location:
   a) Vendor name
   b) Purchase Order number
   c) Invoice number, when feasible
   d) Department number
   e) Location name and number
6. Merchandise quantities should not differ from the original order.
7. Partial shipments are not permitted unless stipulated on the face of this Purchase Order.
8. The label on each carton must show:
   a) Vendor name
   b) Purchase Order number
   c) Department number
   d) Location name and number
Failure to comply with the above instructions may subject you to a charge to offset the additional costs incurred in processing your invoice and merchandise.

ROUTING
9. Based upon the freight terms on the face of this order, when J & Y is responsible for freight:
   a) Route shipments according to our "STANDARD ROUTING LETTER"
   b) Multi-store shipments consigned to the same bill of lading destination on one day must be combined and shipped on a single bill of lading. The piece count and weight by store should be shown on that bill of lading.
   c) When air freight is authorized, an air freight authorization number (supplied by buyer) must be shown on all shipping documents.
Failure to follow our routing instructions, with or without incurring higher transportation charges, shall be considered as your agreement to PAY ALL TRANSPORTATION CHARGES. Authority to deviate must be obtained from the J & Y Traffic Manager or his authorized representative prior to shipment.
If you have any questions on the above labeling, packing or shipping instructions and/or require a routing letter address your inquiries to J & Y traffic manager, Des Moines, Iowa.

SHIPPING TERMS AND INSTRUCTIONS (ANY DEVIATIONS AT VENDOR'S RISK AND EXPENSE).

1. Follow all routing instructions. Note routing guide referred to on face of order.
2. An unextended packing list must accompany each shipment (showing breakdown of color and size where applicable).
3. Risk of loss or damage in transit to PARCEL POST shipments shall be upon the Vendor, notwithstanding who pays shipping costs.
4. Do not ship before or after dates on face of order. Violation of this requirement will subject Vendor to (a) storage and handling charges of 5% of the gross value of the invoice or (b) merchandise will be returned to Vendor with charge-back of inbound and outbound transportation and handling charges incurred by J & Y.

The following applies where Purchaser pays transportation charges in absence of different instructions in Routing Guide:

5. If there is sufficient volume available and freight charges will be less, ship as carload or truckload.
6. Two or more shipments being forwarded to the same delivery point on the same day must be combined and shipped on the single bill of lading irrespective of departmental variance.
7. Merchandise must be packed, shipped and described on bills of lading in accordance with applicable freight tariffs. Differently rated commodities must be in separate containers and be separately described on the bill of lading.
8. In absence of contrary instructions, do not insure shipments, and do not declare value on express shipments for benefit of J & Y.

GENERAL TERMS

1. Vendor warrants and represents that it has the right to sell the merchandise purchased hereunder and agrees to indemnify and save the Purchaser harmless from and against any and all suits, actions, claims or demands that may be brought against Purchaser and from and against all liability, loss, damages, costs and expenses, including attorney's fees, incurred by Purchaser by reason thereof, on the grounds that the purchase or sale of any of the merchandise covered by this order constitutes unfair competition or infringement of patent, copyright or trademark or an invasion of the rights of any person or corporation, and Vendor further agrees at its own cost and expense to defend, upon the request of Purchaser, any such suits, action, claims and demands.
2. In addition to the warranties set forth in Sections 2-312 (1) and (3), Section 2-313 (1), Section 2-314 of the Uniform Commercial Code, Vendor warrants that the goods are fit for the purpose of retail sale, and Vendor represents that it is a merchant with respect to the merchandise, and that no express or implied warranties have been excluded by examination of the goods or otherwise.
3. All electrical appliances and devices must comply with the requirements and bear the seal of Underwriters' Laboratories, Inc.
4. The time stated for delivery hereunder is of the essence hereof.
5. Purchaser reserves the right to cancel this order if the terms and conditions hereof are not fully complied with. Purchaser further reserves the right to refuse any merchandise and to cancel all or any part of this order if Vendor fails to deliver all or any part of the merchandise in accordance with the terms of this order. Acceptance of any part of the order shall not bind Purchaser to accept future shipments, nor deprive it of the right to return merchandise already accepted. Payment of all or any part of the purchase price shall not be construed as a waiver of any claims of the Purchaser for defects or delay in delivery or for breach of the contract, and any and all such claims shall survive payment.
6. Vendor represents that the merchandise covered by this order has been manufactured and labeled in accordance with the requirements of all applicable Federal, State and Municipal laws, rules and regulations, including but not limited to the Fair Labor Standards Act, the Wool Products Labeling Act, the Fur Products Labeling Act, the Textile Fiber Products Identification Act, the Flammable Fabrics Act, the Federal Hazardous Substance Labeling Act, and the Federal Food, Drug and Cosmetic Act. Vendor's invoice shall bear the separate guarantees provided for under any of such acts or shall contain the appropriate statement that a continuing guarantee has been filed in accordance with such acts and applicable rules and regulations of the Federal Trade Commission and other governmental agencies with jurisdiction in the premises.
7. Vendor agrees to deliver the merchandise at prices stated herein or at ceiling or prevailing price at the time of delivery, whichever is lower, and Vendor warrants that no other purchaser from Vendor is receiving more favorable terms than J & Y.
8. Purchaser's failure to insist in any one or more instances upon the strict or timely performance of any of the terms, provisions or conditions of this instrument shall not be considered as a waiver or a relinquishment in the future of the requirements of such terms, provisions and conditions, or of Purchaser's rights based upon Vendor's failure to perform any of such terms, provisions or conditions, but the same shall continue in full force and effect. This Agreement may not be modified or terminated orally, and no modification or termination nor any claimed waiver of any of the provisions hereof shall be binding unless in writing and signed by the party against whom such modifications, termination or waiver is sought to be enforced. ADDITIONAL OR DIFFERENT TERMS IN ANY INVOICE OR OTHER DOCUMENT ISSUED BY VENDOR SHALL NOT BE BINDING ON PURCHASER.
9. All costs incurred by Purchaser because of non-compliance with the terms and conditions of this order (including Shipping and Billing Instructions) will be charged to Vendor.
10. By signing a copy of this order or making any shipments, Vendor shall be deemed to have accepted this order. FAILURE OF VENDOR TO GIVE NOTICE OR REJECTION WITHIN REASONABLE TIME SHALL CONSTITUTE ACCEPTANCE OF THIS ORDER.
11. INDEMNITY AND INSURANCE

    Vendor shall protect, defend, indemnify and save Purchaser harmless against any and all claims, demands or causes of action of every nature whatsoever arising in favor of any person, including both Vendor's and Purchaser's employees on account of personal injuries or death or damages to property occurring, growing out of, incident to, or resulting directly or indirectly from the performance by Vendor hereunder, whether such loss, damage, injury or liability is contributed to by the negligence of the Purchaser or its employees, or by the premises themselves or any equipment thereon whether latent or patent, or from other causes whatsoever, except that the Vendor shall have no liability for damages or costs incident thereto caused by the sole negligence of Purchaser.

    Vendor agrees to obtain and maintain, at its expense, a policy or policies of products liability insurance, with a limit of liability of not less than One Million Dollars, and with broad form Vendor's endorsement naming Purchaser, in such companies and containing such other provisions which shall be satisfactory to Purchaser covering merchandise sold to Purchaser hereunder. All such policies shall provide that the coverage thereunder shall not be terminated without at least thirty (30) days prior written notice to Purchaser. Vendor agrees to promptly supply Purchaser with evidence satisfactory to Purchaser, upon demand by Purchaser, of the existence of said aforementioned policy or policies.

CHAPTER SEVEN

Planning Sales Promotion

OBJECTIVES

- *Recognize the different types and functions of various print advertising.*
- *Understand the considerations and steps taken in ad planning and termination.*
- *To perform and follow the necessary coordination activities among store divisions involved with executing a print campaign.*
- *Research and prepare an advertising program for "The Gallery."*

ASSIGNMENT

Your market orders have been approved by your divisional merchandise manager. There is a meeting scheduled tomorrow with Mr. Johnson to discuss planned ads for "The Gallery." You must prepare for this meeting by reviewing the types, goals, and preparations of print advertisement.

STUDENT REVIEW

Jarrod & Young's promotion division is responsible for developing materials that increase store traffic and sales. The advertising department is the area within the promotion division that works closely with the merchandising division to create exciting, image-defining store promotions. The three categories of promotional materials produced by the advertising department are:

- Broadcast, (e.g., television, radio).
- Direct mail/catalogue.
- Print ads, (e.g., newspaper, magazine).

Your department is budgeted for three print ads during the fall season.

The three general types of print ads — each with a different goal are:

- **Market specific ads,** which focus on **building customer acceptance** of specific department's brands, classifications, or trends. Market specific ads encourage customer traffic in one department of the store. A co-op ad, (i.e., an ad in which expenses are shared between the department featuring the merchandise and the merchandise supplier) is an example of a market specific ad. Newspapers and magazines targeted to a specific segment of Jarrod & Young's customer base are the vehicle for these types of ads. Figure 7-1, page 144, is an example of a MARKET SPECIFIC AD. The first two print ads planned for "The Gallery" will be market specific ads to introduce the new department.

- **Action ads**, which ideally **generate high traffic and sales volume** over a short period of time. Sales events are examples of action ads. Newspapers and inserts are used to publicize these ads. The merchandising division must ensure that stock-on-hand supports the timing and anticipated public demand generated by action ads. Figure 7-2, page 145, is an example of an ACTION AD. "The Gallery" plans one action ad during the fall season.
- **Institutional ads**, which focus on **building the overall store image** and "good will". These ads encourage long-term customer loyalty and consequently, store profitability. Commemorations are examples of institutional ads. Unlike the other two ad types, institutional ads do not require any special merchandise stock. Newspapers and magazines patronized by all segments of the store's customer base are used for institutional ads. Figure 7-3, page 146, an example of an INSTITUTIONAL AD.

Merchandise Considerations in Planning an Ad

The major factors that should concern the buyer in planning an ad are:

- The goal of the ad must be clearly identified during the planning phase. This ensures the correct timing and type of ad used.
- Merchandise must be in stock in adequate quantities on the advertised date. Advertised merchandise that is unavailable results in missed sales, customer frustration, and a tarnished store image.
- The anticipated sales volume must justify the expense of the ad.
- The essential and continuous communication between the buyer and manufacturers, which ensures timely initial delivery as well as reorder coverage.

Steps in Ad Planning

Budget
Advertising money is allocated at the beginning of each season by senior store management — the president, vice president, general merchandise managers — based on the projected business plans and analysis of the profit and loss statement. Seasonal planning sheets are completed by the divisional merchandise managers (DMM), after the overall budget is finalized. The DMM then works with buyers to discuss the individual promotional needs for each department.

Monthly Meetings
Each month, DMM's meet with buyers to discuss upcoming ads for the next two months. Print ads in newspapers require 1+ month pre-planning, and broadcast and magazine ads require 2+ months advance work. During these meetings, buyers request a portion of the total division's ad budget for their department. The DMM decides the departments that will receive ad money, based on such factors as:

- *Planned sales and last year's actual sales* — in which each department's merchandising reports, (i.e., sales flash, weekly open-to-buy, net sales by store) are used to determine if the department's sales trends need advertisement, how much advertisement, and the type of merchandise to be featured.

- *Last year's advertising pattern* — in which buyers compare last year's sales of an advertised item before and after the ad was run. This helps determine the circumstances and types of merchandise that were advertised most successfully.
- *Co-op advertising dollars* — in which a supplier will often share the expense (or assume total expense) of running an ad to promote the supplier's product. This arrangement benefits the merchant and the manufacturer, and should be used as often as possible.
- *Availability of appropriate merchandise* — in which the buyer must be able to get the right merchandise in the right quantities, at the right time, for the right price. Availability of backup merchandise and special orders should also be discussed with vendors.
- *Major events* — in which the six-month calendar (a joint effort between merchandising, promotion, and the fashion office) pinpoints all major store events for the season. For example, January White Sales, Founder's Day, Back-to-School, etc., are cornerstones for promotional events.

When the advertising schedule is finalized and completed, monthly promotional plan forms are sent to the advertising department and the branches. Figure 7-4, page 147, is a sample of Jarrod & Young's Monthly Promotional Plans Form.

Additions and Changes to the Monthly Ad Schedule

Additions
All additions to the schedule must be accompanied by an Addition to Advertising Schedule Form (see Figure 7-5, page 148), signed by the vice president. This form must be completed and is accompanied by a sample of an advertising information fact sheet form. When it is completed it is taken to the promotion scheduling office.

Changes
Changes in the ad schedule, (e.g., date, publications, etc.) are submitted to the promotion scheduling office on a Change in Advertising Schedule Form (see Figure 7-6, page 149).
To guarantee that your changes are noted, make sure to:

- Make corrections in red in the margins with an arrow to indicate the proper space.
- Never write over a word, price, or other information.
- Write legibly.
- Sign the form — changes will not be made without the buyer's signature.

Killed ad
To terminate an ad, write "killed" midway on a change in advertising form, and submit it to the promotion scheduling department. The department will be charged for any production costs, (e.g., photography, models, studio rentals, etc.) already incurred. If an ad must be killed because a vendor cannot deliver merchandise, the buyer or DMM should try to negotiate payment of the kill charges to the vendor (see Figure 7-6, page 149).

Weekly Meetings
For four consecutive Mondays prior to the ad week, the advertising department meets with the DMM, buyers, and sometimes associate and/or assistant buyers to finalize the ad.

Buyers must bring an ADVERTISING INFORMATION SHEET (see Figure 7-7, page 150), samples of the merchandise, and completed VENDOR CHARGEBACK FORM (see Figure 7-8, page 151) if the vendor shares expenses.

The advertising information sheet is the preliminary ad request form that organizes the pertinent information. Once the ad is finalized, the buyer completes a NEWSPAPER FACT SHEET and distributes copies to the advertising department and merchandise manager's office (see Figure 7-9, page 152).

The advertising department is responsible for the copy (that is, the choice of words), the layout, artwork, and style of writing. It takes the advertising department approximately four weeks to produce an ad. The step-by-step description of the buyer's follow-through duties for advertised merchandise includes:

- **A merchandise check**, which comprises:
  (1) Checking the arrival of merchandise at all branches before the ad is released and allowing time to transfer merchandise to branch stores, if necessary.
  (2) Inspecting merchandise for sizes, workmanship, colors, etc., upon arrival and comparing with the information in the ad copy.
  (3) Knowing the availability of replenishment in sizes and colors.
- **An advertising communications follow-through**, which comprises:
  (1) Completing the advertising information sheets and — if applicable — vendor chargeback forms five weeks before the planned ad.
  (2) Completing the newspaper fact sheet four weeks before the ad runs.
  (3) Completing the first review three weeks before run date. Advertising will contact the buyer to proofread a rough copy of the ad. The buyer should verify all information in the ad, (e.g., price, content, the branch stores carrying the merchandise, colors, spelling of vendor's name.) The choice of words and grammar should be left up to the advertising department.
  (4) Completing the second review one week before run date. The buyer's second opportunity to review the ad to make sure the revisions have been made. The buyer signs off on the ad.[12]
- **Display and signage preparation**, which includes:
  (1) Submitting a SIGN REQUISITION (see Figure 7-10, page 153) to the sign shop in advance, checking merchandise information and spelling, and including requests for branch stores.
  (2) Initiating retail price changes, if any, to ensure that ad and merchandise prices match.
  (3) Working with display to arrange merchandise in the best possible traffic area.
  (4) Posting signs in conspicuous locations in department, elevator, etc.
- **Selling support communications**, which includes:
  (1) Giving telephone salespeople a copy of the corrected ad.
  (2) Instructing telephone salespeople to ask for a second color choice, one is available.
  (3) Arranging with stock supervisors for extra stock help or extra storage space, if necessary.
  (4) Informing receiving and marking supervisors of the large shipments.
  (5) Arranging for additional sales personnel, if possible.
  (6) Ensuring that floor sales associates know the timing and copy of the ad.

---

[12] The buyer must remove samples from the advertising department before the ad runs.

(7) Telling the salespeople of the expected and/or promised reorder date.

(8) Taking periodic counts for projections or reorders.

(9) Setting up stock space for efficient order filling floor fill-ins.

- **Branch communications**, which include:

(1) Informing department managers well in advance of ads running in Des Moines and/or branch store papers.

(2) Informing department managers of the availability of merchandise.

(3) Sending adequate assortments of merchandise and signs.

(4) Checking stock position and sales after the ad has been run.

- **Administration follow-through**, which comprises:

(1) Recording all mail and telephone orders as they come in by style, color, price; by hour; by units.

(2) Promptly informing the telephone order board if you run short of a size, color, or style and giving them the expected reorder delivery date.

(3) Recording ad results daily. Use a six-year book and/or promotional event recap for specific details. Figure 7-11, page 154, is a sample of a PROMOTIONAL EVENT RECAP FORM.

APPLICATION A

PLANNING SALES PROMOTIONS

In preparation for the advertising meeting with your DMM, you must:

- Decide on the size of the ads.
- Research costs for advertising space.
- Prepare to justify your ad requests, which will include:

(a) The total cost of ads.

(b) Merchandise selected (from the styles you selected).

(c) The quantity purchased.

APPLICATION B

PROVIDING INFORMATION FOR THE SALES PROMOTION DEPARTMENT

The advertising program is set and the three ads are scheduled. Complete and submit to your merchandise manager for approval the following forms: three NEWSPAPER FACT SHEETS, Figures 7-12, 7-13, and 7-14, pages 155-159; and three SIGN REQUISITION FORMS, Figures 7-15, 7-16, and 7-17, pages 161-165.

FIGURE 7-1 JARROD & YOUNG'S MARKET SPECIFIC AD

JARROD & YOUNG

Presents "The Gallery"

A relaxed comfortable look at a thoroughly comfortable price.

The look for versatility, comfort, simplicity and, of course, style. Our wool flannel blazer from Elan complements skirts, pants, jeans, and tights. In navy, creme, khaki, black, and gray heather, sizes 4-14. $150.00. In The Gallery at all Jarrod & Young locations.

FIGURE 7-2   JARROD & YOUNG'S ACTION AD

JARROD & YOUNG

SPECTACULAR SAVINGS SALE!

20% to 50% Off

ALSO SPECIALLY PRICED SELECTIONS

Fall and Winter Savings On Your Favorite Makers, Designers and Styles

DRESSES & SUITS

25% to 50% Off
Famous Maker Career, Dinner and
Evening Dresses
Misses • Petites • Women
Selections include silks, wools, blends
Orig. $69 to $259, **Now $34 to $194**

$69 to $159 New Fall Knits Long
& Short, 100% wool and blends, many
styles

**$79 to $169 Holiday and Special
Occasion Dresses** All lengths, styles,
many designer names

$89 to $199 Famous Maker Suits
Wools, wool blends, all new
merchandise

$19 to $69 Career Separates Many
selections from your favorite makers,
including skirts, blouses, jackets, sweaters,
vests and much more

SPORTSWEAR

**25% OFF CAREER SPORTSWEAR
SEPARATES**

**JACKETS Orig. $129 to $199,
Now $96 to $149**

**SKIRTS Orig. $59 to $129,
Now $44 to $96**

**PANTS Orig. $69 to $119,
Now $51 to $89**

**VESTS Orig. $39 to $129,
Now $29 to $96**

**BLOUSES & TOPS Orig. $49 to $99,
Now $36 to $74**

Take 30% to 40% Off Designer &
Famous Maker Sportswear
Jackets, skirts, jumpsuits and pants in
wool, wool blends, knits – all styles and
fits Orig. $29 to $399, **Now $17 to $279**

25% Off Your Favorite Silk Designer
Luxurious jackets, skirts, sweaters, dresses
All with that marvelous silk feel and easy fit –
Plus a name that you trust
Orig. $55 to $119, **Now $41 to $89**

**25% Off Weekend Wear from Many
Famous Makers** Tailored jackets, pants
and shorts, knit tops, skirts, flannel shirts,
many fabrics and styles

**50% Off Denim From Our Best Selling
Designers** Jeans, vests, jackets, skirts,
dresses Orig. $39 to $159, **Now $19 to $79**

$29 to $59 Casual Dressing Easy to
wear separates and loungewear in many
different styles, fabrics, colors

$19 to $39 Silk Blouses, Shells, Tanks
Special purchase, spectacular savings

50% TO 75% OFF ALL SUMMER STOCK!
Spectacular end-of-season savings on all
summer merchandise, but hurry,
supplies are limited!

**PLUS TAKE AN ADDITIONAL 10% for
shopping with your Jarrod & Young
Preferred Customer Charge!**

Come pick up your copy of our Spectacular Savings Catalogue today – and SAVE!

**ALL LOCATIONS OPEN LATE WEDNESDAY AND THURSDAY, 10 AM TO 8:30 PM. AND NOW SHOP LATER MONDAY, TUESDAY, FRIDAY
AND SATURDAY, 10 AM TO 7 PM, SUNDAY, 12 PM TO 6 PM.**

Our regular and original prices are offering prices only and may or may not have resulted in sales. Advertised merchandise may be available at sale prices in upcoming sale events.

FIGURE 7-3   JARROD & YOUNG'S INSTITUTIONAL AD

FROM ALL OF US AT THE GALLERY,
WE WISH YOU THE MERRIEST
AND BRIGHTEST
HOLIDAY SEASON EVER.

AT
JARROD & YOUNG'S
EXCITING NEW DEPARTMENT,
THE GALLERY,
YOU WILL FIND THE NEWEST AND MOST FASHION—FORWARD
CLOTHING AND ACCESSORIES TO MAKE YOUR HOLIDAY
SHOPPING BRIGHT.

— JARROD & YOUNG —

MONTHLY PROMOTIONAL PLANS

Dept. # & Description ....

Month: .... LY Sales .... Plan .... % Increase ....

LY Sales .... Plan .... % Increase ....

General Comments: ....

....

....

....

....

MAJOR NEW TRENDS

1. ....

2. ....

3. ....

KEY ITEMS

Style #	Description	Vendor	Retail	Plan Unit Sales
....	....	....	....	....
....	....	....	....	....
....	....	....	....	....
....	....	....	....	....

PROMOTIONAL PLAN FOR MONTH

....

....

....

....

....

LOOKS TO BE PRESENTED IN THIS DEPARTMENT EACH WEEK

1. ....

2. ....

3. ....

FIGURE 7-5   JARROD & YOUNG'S ADDITION TO ADVERTISING SCHEDULE FORM

JARROD & YOUNG

ADDITION TO ADVERTISING SCHEDULE*

The following ad is to be added to schedule: (Date)

Date/Publication	Size of Ad	Dept.	Merchandise

*On additions to schedule, include the following information:

Gross Cost ....

Vendor Name ....   Amt. of Credit ....

Mdse. V.P. Signature

Sales Promotion V.P. Signature

Branch Store Ads: Mdse. Mgr. Signature

FIGURE 7-6 JARROD & YOUNG'S CHANGE IN ADVERTISING SCHEDULE FORM (ALSO USED FOR "KILLED ADS")

JARROD & YOUNG

CHANGE IN ADVERTISING SCHEDULE

The following ad is to be:

☐ rescheduled to: (Date) .... ☐ killed   ☐ held on wait order

Date/Publication	Size of Ad	Dept.	Merchandise

....
Mdse. V.P. Signature

....
Branch Store Ads: Mdse. Mgr. Signature

JARROD & YOUNG

ADVERTISING INFORMATION SHEET   Dept.# ....Ad#(for Adv. use) ....Page ....of ....

ART WORK / PHOTOGRAPHY	MEDIA INFORMATION			STORES COVERED BY AD			FOR VENDOR PAID ADS
Is Merchandise in Loan Room ☐ YES ☐ NO	Medium	Date	Size	Store	Full Asst.	Partial Asst.	Other requirements:
Do not request new art before checking if old art is available.				ALL			....
# of Illust. # of New # of Old							....
Date and medium in which old art last ran. Attach proof.							....
DATE MEDIUM							
Indicate specific item(s) to be illustrated, style #, model #, etc.:							....
....	If pickup, attach tear sheet.						If unusual vendor requirements, attach contract or pec. sheet.

COPY INFORMATION: **GIVE ALL FACTS CUSTOMER NEEDS TO PURCHASE.**

If partial assorted indicate below which items at which stores. If not available at store, mark NA.s

TYPE OF AD
(check one)   Z ☐ Sale   VI ☐ Regular Price Volume Response   DI ☐ Regular Price Institutional

☐ Mail Orders Filled   ☐ Phone Orders Filled   ☐ Use Coupon in Ad   ☐ Use Manuf. Name

Merchandise Description. Be specific, list each item. Asterisk items to be featured.	Style # (* if to be used in ad)	Colors, sizes, finishes, fiber content, dimensions, other pertinent information.	Quote phrase (if any)	Quote Price	Current Price	Advertised Price

What copy approach should be used?
....
....

What emphasis in illustrations?
....
....

Customer benefits of item(s). Why should customer buy items at R&S? Be concise. Bullet info when possible.
....
....
....
....
....

Delivery or handling charge?
....

The above merchandise and pricing information conforms to R&S advertising policy and Federal and local regulations.

Buyer ....Adm. or VP ....   Adv. (If Req.) .... Comparative Claims Rep. ....

FIGURE 7-8 JARROD & YOUNG'S VENDOR CHARGEBACK FORM

JARROD & YOUNG

CHARGE FOR ADVERTISING ALLOWANCE

ADDRESS	D-U-N-S (Dun's - #)	NO.
		47361

DATE	VENDOR D-U-N-S NO.	TRANS.	DEPT. NO.
		670	

Firm

Street

City   State   Zip Code

Item.. Direct Mail
                                     Magazine
                                     Paper

Firm Pays........................Of Ad   Date of Ad...................................
                                                          month   day

Vendor Authorized By

Send Checks To: Accounts Payable Dept., P.O. Box..
Overdue Payment Will Be Deducted From Our Payment.

To be filled in by
advertising statistics No. of Lines ....Charge per Line.....................Total Charge...........................Amount Due ....

Dept. Mgr. Signature .... Release Entry No.   Entry No. ....WOB ....

1. Dept. Mgr.: Send white, yellow & pink copies to Advertising with the Advertising Information Sheet.

2. Advertising Statistics: Fill in necessary date on form, send white & yellow copies to Accounts Payable Dept. with tear sheet attached to white copy. Retain pink copy for file.

FOLD ▼ HERE

FIGURE 7-9 JARROD & YOUNG'S NEWSPAPER FACT SHEET

JARROD & YOUNG
NEWSPAPER FACT SHEET

Art ☐   Photo ☐   Black & White ☐   Color ☐

Ad Date...........................City/Paper..Ad size.................................

Ad Date...........................City/Paper..Ad size.................................

Ad Date...........................City/Paper..Ad size.................................

Ad Date...........................City/Paper..Ad size.................................

Merchandise Available at these Stores:

☐ Des Moines   ☐ Ames   ☐ Iowa City   ☐ Davenport   ☐ Cedar Rapids   ☐ Council Bluffs   ☐ Sioux City   ☐ All

Style #...........................Item Description ....

....

....

Colors: ....Fabric: ....

Sizes: ....Price: ....
(More items? Use another fact sheet.)

Describe customer for whom merchandise was purchased (age, lifestyle, etc.): ....

....

....

What's most important to tell customer? ....

Unique qualities or benefits of merchandise: ....

....

Photo or Art Requests (what accessories to use, type or age of model, close-up on detail, etc.) ....

....

....

Return merchandise to store #: ....Dept. ....

COOPERATIVE ADVERTISING INFORMATION:

Must use this manufacturer's name ....in (Check one)

☐ Headline   ☐ Body Copy   ☐ Logo (logos only used if **absolutely** necessary!)

What else is required for payment? (fiber, fabric or other requirements): ....

....

....

(Attached co-op from 127; obtain from Supply Dept.)

Buyer's signature ....

Dept. name and number: ....Date:.................................

white to copy dept., yellow with merchandise, pink to buyer   F-126 FWP 10M 1-80

FIGURE 7-10   JARROD & YOUNG'S SIGN REQUISITION FORM

JARROD & YOUNG

SIGN REQUISITION

ALLOW 15 WORKING DAYS FOR COMPLETION OF SIGN

DEPT.	COLOR	AD DATE

1 SIDE	31/2 x 5	91/4 x 11	41/2 x 20	22 x 28	41/2 x 22
2 SIDES	51/2 x 7	11 x 14	14 x 22	41/2 x 6	21/2 x 11

DATE ORDERED	QUANTITY	Vertical Horizontal

INDICATE QUANTITY FOR EACH STORE

____ Des Moines   ____ Cedar Rapids ____ Iowa City
____ Council Bluffs ____ Sioux City ____ Ames ____ Davenport

LEAD IN LINE Start story with a reason to buy or customer benefit

KEY COPY What are you selling? Identify the item

SELLING POINTS List 3 sales features not obvious to customer

Our Low Price

Reg. Price

← Eye catching feature

← Identifies article
← Selling features

← Price

DUPLICATE OF THIS INFORMATION SHEET MUST GO TO SIGN SHOP

FIGURE 7-11 JARROD & YOUNG'S PROMOTIONAL EVENT RECAP FORM

JARROD & YOUNG

DEPT. NO.	EVENT			1st Day	2nd Day	3rd Day	4th Day	5th Day	6th Day	7th Day	8th Day	9th Day	10th Day	PLAN $ SALES ON SALE ITEMS T.Y.	ACT. $ SALES ON ITEMS L.Y.	PLAN $ TOTAL SALES	ACT. $ SALES T.Y.
	DATES THIS YEAR	DATES LAST YEAR	Last Year														
			This Year														

USE UNITS OR DOLLARS BY STORE AS PER DMM INSTRUCTIONS.
00 - On Order STK - In Stock (to be reduced)
SLD - Sold ACT - Actual On Hand (day of event)

	CLASS	COST	REGULAR RETAIL	SALE	$ SAVE																MARKDOWNS T.Y.	MARKDOWNS L.Y.	TOTALS Units	TOTALS Dollars	MEDIA
1						00																			
	Description:					STK																			
						ACT																			
						SLD																			
2						00																			
	Description:					STK																			
						ACT																			
						SLD																			
3						00																			
	Description:					STK																			
						ACT																			
						SLD																			
4						00																			
	Description:					STK																			
						ACT																			
						SLD																			
5						00																			
	Description:					STK																			
						ACT																			
						SLD																			
6						00																			
	Description:					STK																			
						ACT																			
						SLD																			
	TOTAL																								

FIGURE 7-12 JARROD & YOUNG'S NEWSPAPER FACT SHEET

JARROD & YOUNG
NEWSPAPER FACT SHEET

Art ☐   Photo ☐   Black & White ☐   Color ☐

Ad Date.............................City/Paper...Ad size.................................

Ad Date.............................City/Paper...Ad size.................................

Ad Date.............................City/Paper...Ad size.................................

Ad Date.............................City/Paper...Ad size.................................

Merchandise Available at these Stores:

☐ Des Moines   ☐ Ames   ☐ Iowa City   ☐ Davenport   ☐ Cedar Rapids   ☐ Council Bluffs   ☐ Sioux City   ☐ All

Style #..............................Item Description ....

....

....

Colors: ....Fabric: ....

Sizes: ....Price: ....
(More items? Use another fact sheet.)

Describe customer for whom merchandise was purchased (age, lifestyle, etc.): ....

....

....

What's most important to tell customer? ....

Unique qualities or benefits of merchandise: ....

....

Photo or Art Requests (what accessories to use, type or age of model, close-up on detail, etc.) ....

....

....

Return merchandise to store #: ....Dept. ....

COOPERATIVE ADVERTISING INFORMATION:

Must use this manufacturer's name ....in (Check one)

☐ Headline   ☐ Body Copy   ☐ Logo (logos only used if **absolutely** necessary!)

What else is required for payment? (fiber, fabric or other requirements): ....

....

....

(Attached co-op from 127; obtain from Supply Dept.)

Buyer's signature ....

Dept. name and number: ....Date:...................................

white to copy dept., yellow with merchandise, pink to buyer   F-126 FWP 10M 1-80

FIGURE 7-13   JARROD & YOUNG'S NEWSPAPER FACT SHEET

JARROD & YOUNG
NEWSPAPER FACT SHEET

Art ☐   Photo ☐   Black & White ☐   Color ☐

Ad Date............................City/Paper..Ad size..

Ad Date............................City/Paper..Ad size..

Ad Date............................City/Paper..Ad size..

Ad Date............................City/Paper..Ad size..

Merchandise Available at these Stores:

☐ Des Moines   ☐ Ames   ☐ Iowa City   ☐ Davenport   ☐ Cedar Rapids   ☐ Council Bluffs   ☐ Sioux City   ☐ All

Style #...............................Item Description ....

....

....

Colors: ....Fabric: ....

Sizes: ....Price: ....
(More items? Use another fact sheet.)

Describe customer for whom merchandise was purchased (age, lifestyle, etc.): ....

....

....

What's most important to tell customer? ....

Unique qualities or benefits of merchandise: ....

....

Photo or Art Requests (what accessories to use, type or age of model, close-up on detail, etc.) ....

....

....

Return merchandise to store #: ....Dept. ....

COOPERATIVE ADVERTISING INFORMATION:

Must use this manufacturer's name ....in (Check one)

☐ Headline   ☐ Body Copy   ☐ Logo (logos only used if **absolutely** necessary!)

What else is required for payment? (fiber, fabric or other requirements): ....

....

....

(Attached co-op from 127; obtain from Supply Dept.)

Buyer's signature ....

Dept. name and number: ....Date:................................

white to copy dept., yellow with merchandise, pink to buyer   F-126 FWP 10M 1-80

FIGURE 7-14   JARROD & YOUNG'S NEWSPAPER FACT SHEET

JARROD & YOUNG
NEWSPAPER FACT SHEET

Art ☐   Photo ☐   Black & White ☐   Color ☐

Ad Date.............................City/Paper...Ad size..................................

Ad Date.............................City/Paper...Ad size..................................

Ad Date.............................City/Paper...Ad size..................................

Ad Date.............................City/Paper...Ad size..................................

Merchandise Available at these Stores:

☐ Des Moines   ☐ Ames   ☐ Iowa City   ☐ Davenport   ☐ Cedar Rapids   ☐ Council Bluffs   ☐ Sioux City   ☐ All

Style #...............................Item Description ....

....

....

Colors: ....Fabric: ....

Sizes: ....Price: ....
(More items? Use another fact sheet.)

Describe customer for whom merchandise was purchased (age, lifestyle, etc.): ....

....

....

What's most important to tell customer? ....

Unique qualities or benefits of merchandise: ....

....

Photo or Art Requests (what accessories to use, type or age of model, close-up on detail, etc.) ....

....

....

Return merchandise to store #: ....Dept. ....

COOPERATIVE ADVERTISING INFORMATION:

Must use this manufacturer's name ....in (Check one)

☐ Headline   ☐ Body Copy   ☐ Logo (logos only used if **absolutely** necessary!)

What else is required for payment? (fiber, fabric or other requirements): ....

....

....

(Attached co-op from 127; obtain from Supply Dept.)

Buyer's signature ....

Dept. name and number: ....Date:......................................

white to copy dept., yellow with merchandise, pink to buyer   F-126 FWP 10M 1-80

FIGURE 7-15 JARROD & YOUNG'S SIGN REQUISITION FORM

JARROD & YOUNG

SIGN REQUISITION

ALLOW 15 WORKING DAYS FOR COMPLETION OF SIGN

DEPT.	COLOR	AD DATE

1 SIDE 3 1/2 x 5 ☐ 9 1/4 x 11 ☐ 4 1/2 x 20 ☐ 22 x 28 ☐ 4 1/2 x 22 ☐

2 SIDES 5 1/2 x 7 ☐ 11 x 14 ☐ 14 x 22 ☐ 4 1/2 x 6 ☐ 2 1/2 x 11 ☐

DATE ORDERED	QUANTITY	Vertical Horizontal

INDICATE QUANTITY FOR EACH STORE

____ Des Moines ____ Cedar Rapids ____ Iowa City
____ Council Bluffs ____ Sioux City ____ Ames ____ Davenport

LEAD IN LINE Start story with a reason to buy or customer benefit

KEY COPY What are you selling? Identify the item

SELLING POINTS List 3 sales features not obvious to customer

Our Low Price

Reg. Price

← Eye catching feature

← Identifies article
← Selling features

← Price

DUPLICATE OF THIS INFORMATION SHEET MUST GO TO SIGN SHOP

FIGURE 7-16 JARROD & YOUNG'S SIGN REQUISITION FORM 163

JARROD & YOUNG

SIGN REQUISITION

ALLOW 15 WORKING DAYS FOR COMPLETION OF SIGN

DEPT.	COLOR	AD DATE	1 SIDE	31/2 x 5	91/4 x 11	41/2 x 20	22 x 28	41/2 x 22
			☐	☐	☐	☐	☐	☐
			2 SIDES	51/2 x 7	11 x 14	14 x 22	41/2 x 6	21/2 x 11
			☐	☐	☐	☐	☐	☐

DATE ORDERED	QUANTITY	Vertical Horizontal	INDICATE QUANTITY FOR EACH STORE
		☐ ☐	___ Des Moines ___ Cedar Rapids ___ Iowa City
			___ Council Bluffs ___ Sioux City ___ Ames ___ Davenport

LEAD IN LINE Start story with a reason to buy or customer benefit

KEY COPY What are you selling? Identify the item

SELLING POINTS List 3 sales features not obvious to customer

Our Low Price

Reg. Price

← Eye catching feature

← Identifies article
← Selling features

← Price

DUPLICATE OF THIS INFORMATION SHEET MUST GO TO SIGN SHOP

FIGURE 7-17 JARROD & YOUNG'S SIGN REQUISITION FORM

JARROD & YOUNG

SIGN REQUISITION

ALLOW 15 WORKING DAYS FOR COMPLETION OF SIGN

DEPT.	COLOR	AD DATE	1 SIDE	31/2 x 5	91/4 x 11	41/2 x 20	22 x 28	41/2 x 22
			2 SIDES	51/2 x 7	11 x 14	14 x 22	41/2 x 6	21/2 x 11

DATE ORDERED	QUANTITY	Vertical Horizontal	INDICATE QUANTITY FOR EACH STORE
			___ Des Moines ___ Cedar Rapids ___ Iowa City
			___ Council Bluffs ___ Sioux City ___ Ames ___ Davenport

LEAD IN LINE Start story with a reason to buy or customer benefit

KEY COPY What are you selling? Identify the item

SELLING POINTS List 3 sales features not obvious to customer

Our Low Price

Reg. Price

← Eye catching feature

← Identifies article
← Selling features

← Price

DUPLICATE OF THIS INFORMATION SHEET MUST GO TO SIGN SHOP

CHAPTER EIGHT

Merchandising Reports and the Purchase Journal

OBJECTIVES

- *Read and interpret the merchandising reports used by a department store buyer.*
- *Detail how selling report information can be used for department projections and planning.*
- *Understand the functions of the purchase journal.*
- *Interpret the interrelationships of merchandising activities on departmental book inventory.*

ASSIGNMENT

"The Gallery" officially opened on August 1 as planned. The first market specific ad, used to introduce the department, generated enormous customer response for the initial two weeks of business. In between managing the floor and staff, you spent a good deal of time monitoring your business by reading the merchandising reports and the purchase journal.

You are now preparing for the September market week to purchase merchandise for next early Spring delivery (January and February selling). As part of your preparation, you have analyzed the merchandising reports to anticipate your customer's needs. Based on the current sales figures of "The Gallery," you and your merchandise manager agree to increase your plan for early Spring by 10%[13].

To arrive at an OTB for early Spring, use the six-month plan that you prepared in Chapter Two. Review the January and February planned figures, (i.e., sales, stock, markdowns, and retail purchases), and increase your planned sales by 10%. Your stock, markdowns, and retail purchase figures must be revised to meet your new sales goals.

You also review your department's book inventory by examining the purchase journal on a weekly basis. Conforming with store policy, you visit the accounts payable division to make certain that your department's records are correct and to verify all charges by signing the purchase journal sheets.

---

[13] An unlikely occurrence — the difference between planned figures and actual figures should vary within reasonable limits, otherwise there will stock dislocation (i.e., overstocked or understocked).

A department store buyer has access to a variety of tools that aid in the planning, buying, selling, and control of their business — the merchandising reports. It is necessary to decide the form, frequency, and type of information in the reports. Merchandising reports vary depending upon the type of merchandise, volume of a department, the number of branches, the volume of the organization, and the location of the units. Within one organization, different departments may use different types of merchandising reports or controls. A department that sells fashion merchandise would have information needs unlike a department that sells furniture or electronic equipment. However, all departments need to know certain basic information: the history of every piece of merchandise, the date it is received and removed from stock, (e.g., sold to a customer, returned to a manufacturer, or transferred to another location).

The purchase journal serves as an auditing tool for all merchandise charges. By verifying all department merchandise charges, the buyer (and/or assistant buyer) can prevent shortages and overages caused by bookkeeping errors.

Merchandising Reports — Tools for Planning, Buying and Selling

The three basic types of merchandise handled in a department store are:

- Fashion.
- Staple.
- Big ticket.

Each merchandise type requires specific information. Because the concern in this text is fashion, the review will be confined to fashion department requirements.

Fashion merchandise departments require the most current information, which is why a fashion buyer receives constant, up-to-date reports of merchandising activities. The premise behind this constant flow of information is that no store or department can function without controls. Information is the tool that the buyer can use to exercise merchandising decisions based on selling results — which is the reality of merchandising — and consumer acceptance, as compared with prior merchandise preparation and planning. Information from these reports is used to decide:

- What to buy.
- From whom to buy.
- When to buy.
- How much to buy.
- What and when to reorder.
- What and when to markdown.
- What, when, and where to transfer merchandise.

Merchandise reports help a buyer to analyze merchandise and merchandising activities so that decisions can be the most accurate. A carefully prepared system of segmenting merchandise (sub-classes) into units of consumer demand can give a buyer insight for:

- Trend spotting.
- Fast recognition of slow-selling segments of stock.
- Development of a constantly current direction for purchasing.
- Performance of narrowed stock elements, (i.e., sub-classifications).
- Accuracy of stock/sales ratio by sub-classification and the opportunity to increase or reduce ratio based on performance.
- Specific style performance.
- Accurate timing of promotions.

The fashion control systems used by most large stores with multi-branches are reports with detailed information, such as color, size, vendor, price, subclasses, style, and rate of sales. Departments that use more generalized reports take a physical count before placing a reorder, or for any merchandising activity that requires specific merchandise information that is not available from the printouts.

Control systems are dependent upon merchandising activities, (e.g., sales, markdowns, goods received, customer returns, etc.) to create merchandising reports. However, because the most important merchandising activity is sales, more selling reports are generated than any other type. The majority of department stores use register captured information from mechanical or barcode tickets. Register captured information is sales data that is fed into the register at the point of sale (POS).

Kimball tickets are an example of mechanical merchandise tickets. Kimball tickets are three-part, perforated tickets with information about the vendor, style, color, department, size, price, etc., which is attached to each garment in stock. Figure 8-1, page 170, is a sample KIMBALL TICKET from Dept. 349. When a garment is sold, one stub is removed and the information is input into the register, which, in turn, feeds into the store computer. The computer subsequently produces the sales records.

The BARCODE TICKET is a two-part ticket with merchandise information that is also attached to the garment (see Figure 8-2, page 170)[14]. When the garment is sold, the barcode is scanned by a wand or stylus, or is passed through an electronic eye. This information is fed directly into the store's information systems. Barcode ticketing provides faster and more accurate reporting, and can be linked to outside computer systems. When a retailer, textile company, and apparel manufacturer have a quick response agreement, barcode ticketing, and POS reporting are the links that provide immediate sales information to all three companies.

Selling information is fed into a store's system is reconfigured into different merchandising reports. In this text, several sample types of forms will be reviewed, some of which are currently being used by Jarrod & Young in other departments or are prototypes that are under consideration.

Figure 8-3, page 171, is a sample of a STYLE/SALES & ON-HAND REPORT FOR DEPARTMENT 349, "THE SPORTSWOMAN." It shows sales and on hand for merchandise sold. This report is distributed to buyers and department managers every Friday. Markdowns can be interspersed with regular styles by price line, shown separately, or not at all. Figure 8-3, page 171, is annotated (1) through (8) and reads:

(1) Dept. 349; All stores report.
(2) Class, A1.
(3) Vendor, 215.
(4) Style 4503.
(5) Current retail, 10.00.
(6) WTD sales — week to date sold 4, all stores.
(7) On hand — current 31, all stores.
(8) The breakdown for all stores L through U, example:
Store L — sold 1, on hand minus 1 (this is a reporting problem); Store M — sold 3, on hand 21; Store N — sold 0, on hand 0; etc.

---

[14] Figures 8-1 and 8-2 are also annotated for ease of comprehension.

FIGURE 8-1 KIMBALL TICKET

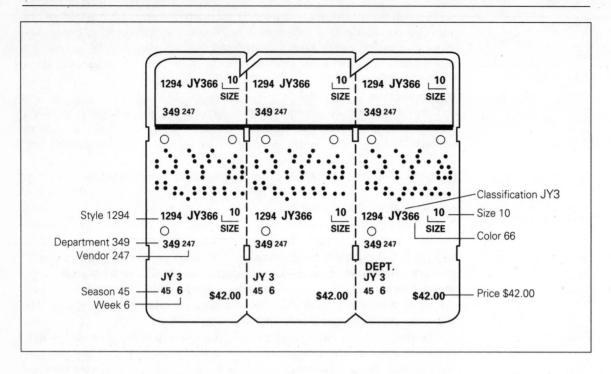

FIGURE 8-2 BARCODE TICKET

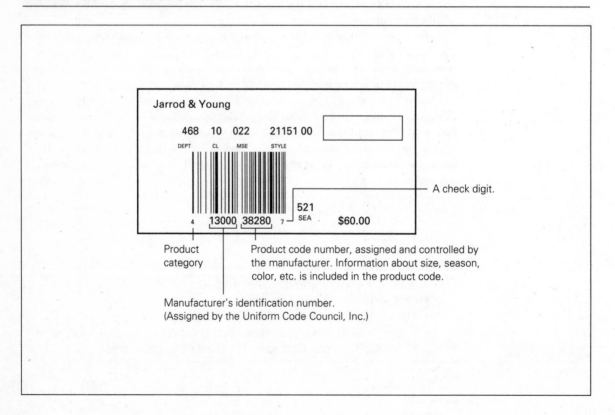

JARROD & YOUNG

STYLE/SALES & ON HAND REPORT — THE SPORTSWOMAN

Y (1.) DEPT 349   REG.   15-1   00-00   PAGE 1

CLASS CODES (2.)	VEND (3.)	STYLE (4.)	CURR. RETAIL (5.)	ALL STORES WTD SALES (6.)	ALL STORES ON HAND (7.)	(8.)L WTD	(8.)L OH	(8.)M WTD	(8.)M OH	(8.)N WTD	(8.)N OH	(8.)O WTD	(8.)O OH	(8.)P WTD	(8.)P OH	(8.)Q WTD	(8.)Q OH	(8.)R WTD	(8.)R OH	(8.)S WTD	(8.)S OH	(8.)T WTD	(8.)T OH	(8.)U WTD	(8.)U OH
A100	215	4503	10.00	4	31	1	-1-	3	21				3				13							1	8
	253	5191	12.00	1	3	1	2		1				30			3										
	262	621	11.00	6	220	1	41	1	39		27		45		1				1	2	5	2	37		26
	273	8823	17.00	1	169		33	-1	10		12	10	11		12		13		12		12		10		23
	378	600	5.99								14		10						7					8	9
		601		26	59	3	24		1	6	20		7			4	29					1	17
		1000		9	62	4	15			4						1	2					3	37
		2000		3	43		-3									1	9					2	19
	390	4000	9.00	45	233	10	4	6	37	2	84												
	399	934	12.00	7	214	1	2	3	48		42		23	4	12	4	7	2		2	40		42
		2009	13.00	3	22		-3		6		12		2	1		1	29				28		1
		2061	14.00	17	175		2		14	4	32	3	6	2	19	1	2	2	9	3	17		42
				2	40		7		7		8		8				9						10
		2040	15.00	3	93		20		37		34		22	2	19	-1	1	1		2	6	1	14
		2044		3	66	3	25	1	-7	1	25		13							2	35		10
		2049		7	136		-13	1	17	4	8		-5	2	17	1	31	1	11	2	18
		2057		10	57			1	6	1			7	2	18	1	9			2	10	1	12
		2060	17.00	5	33		46		14		9		16		4	3	-4				18		28
		2063	13.00	13	180	3	20	3	32		22		22		9	5	29			2	14	4	22
	431	3305		1	137		22		11				22		12		11		12	2	11	1	9
		3318		1	127				9								10				10		
		6227	16.00	-1	42	1	15		-2	-1	10		3		2						7		7
		7030		37	23		6		46		-1				6			3	8	3	57	2	6
		7051			413	4	100	5		1	49		25	1	43	1	26			1	18	1	70
	524	2722	11.00	2	40						14										-5		7
		100	8.00	15	365	1	71	1	36	3	35		36		35	2	34	2	8	3	31		90
		101		26	154	4	32	1	30	7	34	6	30				48	5	36	1	5	5	35
		102	8.99	4	236					2	46						48			5	76	5	72
		103		4	236					2	46									18	5	1	72
		104		16	239	6	22	12	24	3	47	2	28	2	28	1	31	1		1	34	4	72
	525	305	8.00	16	239				19	1	17	9	78	1	33				13
	560	850	7.99	1	56	3				13	5	2	8	1	16	16				8
		16	5.59	117	605	22	168		40	2	60		2	9	78	11	16				80
		1712	14.00	6	116		31		8	2	24		2	1	9		45			1	5	1	53
	3011	3011	9.00	1	16				17	2	13	1	14	5	45	10					66
		3013	16.00	24	380	6	49	1	24	5	5	2	36	2	33	1	1		9		16	1	15
		3081		2	25					1	4		-1							3		51
	4505	4505	12.00	5	154	3	2		5	2	5	1	14							4	10
	570	178	11.00	4	16		6		17		3		16	1	9				16	1	66
		186	11.00	3	48		5	2	43	2	1	1	8	1	10					4
	902	254	12.00	10	54		7	4	6	5	3		18			2	12			3	5
		292	10.00	26	148	2	20	1	-6	3		2	12	3	4	1		2		2	14	2	18
		341	11.00	13	64	1	11		-4	3	9	2	12	4	12	5		1		1	18	2	28
		1308	13.00	3	28		6	7		9	8	2	8	1	-1	4	7	10		8	2		3
		8206	11.00	5	34		1	-1		1	2		14	1	19	1	29			2	
	8278	8278		24	150	5	9	2	16	62	625	29	538	28	344	42	589	21	145	37	505	62	1137
SUB-CLASS		8278		491	6231	72	806	46	647							3		1		2	14	2	19
A400	110	3000	9.00	4	310	2	-5	1	55	3	52		59		11	1	-1	2	10	-1	49
	170	295	13.00	1	28		9			3	10			5	-5			2	-2
	186	2120	14.00	7	50					3	21			4	29			2	-1
		2154	10.00	15	18			-1		1	4		11					1	-2
	265	2337	8.00	12	227	1	95	2	34	5	45	2	48		36	4	-5	1	47	8	-8	2	94
		6462	11.00	26	538	1	14	2	4	9	58	1	58		7	1	47	3	33	2	2	8	7
		6489		22	60			4	7	4	7		6				3			2	9
	243	175	15.00	1	39			5	7	1	12								

0389 1-1 PG 272 D372 P P 1 RUN OF 04/20 PASS-1 M10-1

A buyer can get specific information about selling history by style, size, class, and color, from several different reports.

Figure 8-4, page 173, is a sample of COLOR/SIZE REPORT that shows sales by style, color, and size for each store as well as for all stores. It is specifically used for improved control over distribution of merchandise. Markdowns are not shown. This report is distributed on Monday and Thursday to buyers and department managers. Thursday's report will show sales the same as for week-to-date and current sales, (i.e., Monday, Tuesday, Wednesday). Monday's report will have total week sales in week-to-date columns and Thursday, Friday, Saturday in current columns. Figure 8-4, page 173, is annotated (1) through (7) and reads:

(1) Dept. 349 for week ending December 6, 1994.
(2) Class, G1.
(3) Vendor, 99.
(4) Style, 9.
(5) Current retail, $100.00.
(6) Sizes are listed within color: Color, 01; Size 12.
(7) Sold 1 in P at the beginning of the week (because it appears in WTD column only).

Figure 8-5, page 174, is a prototype of a STYLE REPORT DETAIL — RECEIVED/SOLD printout. Because this report is a selling history of one style, the buyer has a complete style summary of this style from this one report. Figure 8-5, page 174, is annotated (1) through (13) and reads:

(1) Style number, SW40A.
(2) Style description, Cotton V-neck (in blue).
(3) Vendor number and name, MA101, Majestic Sportswear.
(4) Season, Fall.
(5) Department, 04.
(6) Class, 1.
(7) Store location.
(8) On hand.
(9) Receive/Sold to date.
(10) Selling for this week and last week.
(11) Breakdown of received/sold by size.
(12) Style totals (received/sold all stores and received/sold by size all stores).
(13) Current on order quantities.

COLOR PROFILE ANALYSIS (see Figure 8-6, page 175), is a prototype printout used to highlight color performance on a season, department, class, region and store basis to help the buyer make transfers and future purchasing decisions. This report allows the buyer to respond to overall color preferences, instead of a specific color of a specific style or vendor. Sales are separated by price, (i.e., regular, markdown, and promotional), location, (i.e., region and store), and percent to the business, (i.e., by color, class, and department).

Figure 8-7, page 176, is a SIZE PROFILE INQUIRY prototype, which highlights size statistics by season, department, class, region, and store to assist in buying and transfer decisions. It features comparisons between sold and on-hand, can include or exclude markdowns and can thereby show the buyer those sizes that generated the most sales vs. those sizes that generated the most markdowns. This report can be particularly useful because it shows regional and store size preferences.

FIGURE 8-4 COLOR/SIZE REPORT, DEPT. 349, "THE SPORTSWOMAN"

JARROD & YOUNG

Y   DEPT 349   REG.   (1.) REPORT THRU 12/06/94   00-00   18-1   PAGE 1

DEPT/ CLASS (2.)	VEND (3.)	STYLE (4.)	SZ CLR	(5.) RETAIL	CURR	ALL STORES WTD SALES	SLS CURR	L WTD SALES	SLS CURR	M WTD SALES	SLS CURR	N WTD SALES	SLS CURR	O WTD SALES	SLS CURR	P WTD SALES	SLS CURR	Q WTD SALES	SLS CURR	R WTD SALES	SLS CURR	S WTD SALES	SLS CURR	T WTD SALES	SLS CURR	U WTD SALES	SLS CURR
G1 00	4	47	80	86.00		1	1	1	1																		
G1 00	99	9	01	100.00		1	0																				
			120														1										
	20	24	140			2	2	1	1	1				1	1					1	1					1	1
	24		140			1	1	1	1							1	1			1	1					1	1
			120			3	3	1	1																	2	2
			140			1	1																				
	69		180			2	2	1	1							1	1					1	1			
			100			1	0																				
			120			1	0																				3
			140			1	0																				
			TOTAL 97	TOTAL 86.00		13	9	5	4	1	1	-1		1	1	3	1	2	1							5	3
G1 00	99	24	60			-1	0																				
			80			2	0	1								1	1									2	1
			100			1	1									1	1	1	1							1	1
			160			1	1	1				-1				2	1	1										
			TOTAL 98	TOTAL 59.99		5	2																				
G1 00	99	23	120			1	1			-1	-1			1	1	1	1							2	1
			140			1	1	2	2					1	1	1	1			-1				1	1
			TOTAL 102	TOTAL 89.99		2	2	2	2	-1	-1													5	5
G1 00	99	23	80			1	1	1	1	-1	-1	-1		1	1									2	1
	24		100			2	1	2	2			1		2	1	1	1							1	1
			160			2	1	-1						2	1	1	1			-1	-1	1	1	1	1
			TOTAL	TOTAL		7	5	2	2					5						1	1			5	3
H4 00	124	1206	160	44.99P		-1	-1	-1		-1	-1	-1	-1	2	2	1	1			1					
	00		160			1	1	2				1		1	1					1					
	01		140																						
	10		80			3	2							2	2									1	1
			100			0	1							1	1									1	1
			120			0	0			1	1														
			140			2	2							1	1										
			160			3	3			1	1			5	4	1	1				3	3			
	24		180			6	5	-1						1	1					-1					
			100			1	1							1	1					1				1	1
			120			0	1	2		1	1	1		1	1					1				
			140			4	1							1	1									
			160			5	2	-1		1	1			2	2	1	1							
			100			0	0					-1												
			160			3	2							2							1	1		
	28		80			1	1	1	1	1	1			1	1							1	1
			100			1	1							1	1							-1	-1
			140			0	0																
			160			1	1							1	1	1						-1	-1
	41		80			1	0			1	1											-1	-1
			100			1	0			1	1			1	1							-1	-1
			120			4	0									1						-1	2

FIGURE 8-5 STYLE REPORT DETAIL — RECEIVED/SOLD

**STYLE REPORT DETAIL – REC'D/SOLD
WEEK ENDING OCT 08, 94**

(1.) STYLE SW40A COL 030

(2.) COTTON V – Neck Sweater Blue SEASON M FALL (4.)

(3.) VENDOR: MA010 Majesty Sportwear Inc. VENDOR STYLE SW40 — A

DATE OCT 09, 94 TIME 9:43 AM

PAGE: 1

(5.) DEPT 04 Sweaters (6.) CLASS 1 Cotton

SZ TY (7.) STORE	(8.) ON HAND	(9.) RECV/SOLD —TO DATE—	(10.) SOLD T.W.	L.W.	(11.) RECVD/SOLD BY SIZE XS	S	M	L	XL
001	29	44 / 15	3	8	8 / 2	10 / 4	10 / 6	10 / 2	6 / 1
002	26	46 / 20	11	5	8 / 3	10 / 4	10 / 6	10 / 5	8 / 2
003	33	54 / 21	8	10	10 / 3	12 / 7	12 / 8	10 / 2	10 / 1
004	24	52 / 28	9	11	10 / 7	12 / 6	12 / 7	10 / 6	8 / 2
005	22	46 / 24	12	7	8 / 2	10 / 3	10 / 6	10 / 8	8 / 5
COLOR TOTAL	134	242 / 108	43	41	44 / 17	54 / 24	54 / 33	50 / 23	40 / 11
ON ORDER	50				8	13	13	11	5
(12.) STYLE TOTAL	210	400 / 185	80	70	68 / 26	90 / 40	90 / 42	82 / 38	70 / 39
(13.) ON ORDER	88				14	22	22	20	10

© 1993 Richter Merchandising Services, Inc.

FIGURE 8-6   COLOR PROFILE ANALYSIS

SEASON : M FALL

COLOR PROFILE ANALYSIS - UNITS SOLD
WEEK ENDING OCT 08, 94

DATE OCT 09, 94   PAGE: 1
TIME 9:45 AM

DEPT CLASS	DESCRIPTION	COL GROUP	DESCRIPTION	STORE REGION		ON HAND	% ON ORDER	SALES T.W.	SALES L.W.	REGULAR	%	MRKDWN	PROMO	TOTAL	% OF TOTAL DEPT/CL
06	Ladies Dresses														
1	Cocktail	030	Blue	001	001	10	16.7	4	3	61	17.3	4	7	72	
					002	12	20.0	6	4	50	14.2	4	4	58	
					003	5	8.3	7	4	57	16.2	3	5	65	
	TOTAL REGION			001		27	45.0	17	11	168	47.7	11	16	195	
				002	004	13	21.7	3	7	90	25.6	7	7	104	
					005	20	33.3	1	2	94	26.7	5	7	106	
	TOTAL REGION			002		33	55.0	4	9	184	52.3	12	14	210	
	TOTAL COL. GROUP 030 (Blue)					60	100.0	21	20	352	100.0	23	30	405	53.2
	TOTAL CLASS	1	(Cocktail)			212		38	41	653		46	63	762	100.0
	TOTAL DEPARTMENT	06	(Ladies Dresses)			435		104	125	1907		70	82	2059	

© 1993 Richter Merchandising Services, Inc.

FIGURE 8-7 SIZE PROFILE INQUIRY

```
DATE:   OCT 9, 94

                              SIZE PROFILE INQUIRY
================================= AS AT OCT 08, 94 =================================

SEASON    M        FALL                                  REGULAR OR TOTAL  (R/T)  R
DEPT 04            Sweaters                  CLASS 1      Cotton
                   <<<<<<<<<<<<<<<<<< UNITS BY SIZE >>>>>>>>>>>>>>>>>>>>>>>>>>

SZ   REGION              XS     S     M     L     XL
TY      STORE                                                            TOTAL
-----------------------------------------------------------------------------
     001   001   SOLD    40    75    85    30    10                       240
                 ON HAND 70    90   100    85    60                       405

           002   SOLD    20    40    88    64    50                       262
                 ON HAND 90   125    90    40    40                       385

     002   003   SOLD    53    64    87    60    52                       316
                 ON HAND 40    58    46    22    26                       192

CR=NEXT,    CTLI=NEXT SIZE RANGE,    CTLII=NEXT CLASS,    CTLIII=NEXT DEPT,    CTLIV=EXIT
```

© 1993 Richter Management Services, Inc.

FIGURE 8-8   SALES SUMMARY REPORT

SALES SUMMARY REPORT
WEEK ENDING   OCT 08, 94

DATE   OCT 09, 94   PAGE: 1
TIME   9:45 AM

DEPT/ CLASS	DESCRIPTION	STORE NO.	ON HAND	% O.H.	% SOLD	THIS WEEK	LAST WEEK	2 WEEKS AGO	3 WEEKS AGO	LAST YEAR THIS WEEK	ON ORDER	REG	M/DOWN	PROMO
						--- UNIT SALES BY WEEK ---						*--- SALES TO DATE ---*		
02	Pants													
1	Dress	001	30	21.6	20.3	10	12	15	14	11	10	190	5	
		002	33	23.7	16.9	3	9	10	9	7	7	158	2	
		003	20	14.4	23.9	14	16	15	12	10	8	224	4	
		004	41	29.5	13.3	2	5	4	7	7	4	125	4	
		005	15	10.8	25.6	17	17	15	7	9	15	240	7	
	TOTAL CLASS 1		139	100.0	100.0	46	59	59	49	44	44	937	22	
2	Corduroy	001	45	21.2	20.7	8	7	5	12	11	7	135	10	15
		002	48	22.6	16.1	7	7	4	5	5	7	105	8	10
		003	25	11.8	17.1	11	8	8	4	8	9	112	8	12
		004	37	17.5	22.8	8	12	10	8	12	7	149	12	14
		005	57	26.9	23.3	4	7	9	11	7	5	152	8	12
	TOTAL CLASS 2		212	100.0	100.0	38	41	36	40	43	35	653	46	63
TOTAL DEPARTMENT	02 (Pants)		435			104	125	118	112	108	90	1907	70	82

© 1993 Richter Merchandising Services, Inc.

Figure 8-8, page 177, represents a SALES SUMMARY REPORT prototype, which is used to analyze sales trends by class for the last four weeks (or longer if desired). The sales summary report is a selling profile of an entire class of merchandise from assorted vendors in a single department. The sales history is reported by store, by week, by price type — regular, markdown, and promotional.

At the beginning of a new season there may be no stock on hand of a particular new sub-class. However, to ensure a stock/estimated sales balance, reorders must be calculated based on planned sales, the on-hand, and the on-order. Consequently, the buyer is in a position to evaluate planned commitments because these planned inventory figures by sub-class in dollars, units, price levels, and in colors and sizes are known (see Figure 7-5, p. 148). Additionally, because of this knowledge, the buyer can have the greatest possibility of avoiding the pitfalls of stock duplication, overstocking, or other merchandise dislocations.

Figure 8-9, page 181, CLASSIFICATION SUMMARY REPORT, is issued weekly to buyers and department managers. This report:

- Shows total units and dollars sold for each store for each classification.
- Projects sales (in units and dollars) for four weeks and three months.
- Shows actual sales for last year.
- Indicates what percentage of sales dollars or stock sold in that classification.
- Provides blank columns for all notes.

Figure 8-9, page 181, is annotated (1) through (8), and reads:

(1) Dept. 349, level 2, all stores.
(2) Report headings: units & dollars and percentage distribution.
(3) Units & dollars sold and on-hand for third week of November 1994.
(4) Class B3, cardigans.
(5) Units & Dollars, example: L sold 176 cardigans this year vs. 311 last year; this week sold 92 cardigans vs. 195 last year; 1080 cardigans in this classification on hand.
(6) Future weeks' sales, example: 4th week, November, 133; 1st week, December, 102; 2nd week, December, 202; 3rd week, December, 565; 3 future months sales: November, 444; December, 1170; January, 27.
(7) Under percentage distribution sales, example: cardigans accounted for 6% of the sales at L store this year and last year; 9% of this week's sales; 12% of stock (on hand) as before, the projected percentages are actual last year.
(8) Distribution given in dollars.

Figure 8-10, page 182, CLASSIFICATION STOCK STATUS (STORE B), is another example of how a store presents classification information. The buyer of this store, however, must have other records of planned sales in dollars and at price levels. Because classification information is of critical importance to a buyer's planning, two examples of store printouts from two different stores have been included. Figures 8-9 and 8-10 reflect these differences.

The CLASS/PRICE REPORT, Figure 8-11, page 183, is another type of classification report. This report is based on individual price lines within each classification. It is distributed twice monthly to buyers and department managers. It shows sales this year and last for all stores and projects four weeks and three month information (shows actual last year figures). Figure 8-11, page 183, is annotated (1) through (5), and reads:

(1) Dept. 349, 2nd week of April 1994 media date ending April 17, 1994, level A4.

(2) Sales trend, example: L sold 115 units at $7.00 this week this year vs. 38 units last year. L sold 67 units previous week last year; 48 this week; 280 units, on hand.

(3) Future weeks sales, example: last year's sales for the next 4 weeks were 17, 17, 15, 9.

(4) 3 future months sales, example: 36 units sold in May last year; 150 sold in June last year.

(5) Stock/sales ratio, example: 6, (i.e., 6 on hand to sell).

In Figure 8-12, page 184, a buyer is able to immediately identify the best sellers. The BEST SELLERS REPORT ranks the top five styles (total unit sales) in each classification and is distributed weekly to the merchandise vice president, divisional merchandise manager, buyer, and department manager. The pound (#) symbol in the report represents quick sellers. These styles sold 10% or better of the total subclassification and were received in the last three days. The asterisk (*) represents fast sellers. These styles sold 30% or better of the total sub-classification and were received in the last twelve days.

The FASHION FLASH REPORT for "The Sportswoman" (see Figure 8-13, page 185), is distributed on Tuesday and Friday to buyers and department managers. This report indicates net unit sales by style and store for the previous day only, (i.e., Monday and Thursday.) The buyer selects exception criteria (quantity) which determines minimum activity required for a style to appear on this report. Styles will appear on this report if they meet either of the following two conditions:

- Four or more pieces sold in all stores.
- Half the criterion was sold in any one store, (i.e, two in the sample given).

Figure 8-13, page 185, is annotated (1) through (7) and reads:

(1) Dept. 349, net sales of Monday 4/28/94.
(2) Class, example: A3.
(3) Vendor, example: 575.
(4) Style, example: 0682.
(5) Retail, example: $32.00.
(6) Styles sold 6 in all stores, example: L sold 3; P sold 1; R sold 1; S sold 1.

Figure 8-14, page 186, the LIFE HISTORY STYLE/STATUS REPORT, is the most comprehensive report generated from this fashion control system. It is distributed weekly to buyers and department managers. This report provides such information as:

- Cost, retail, markup percentage.
- Markdown information in units and dollars for all stores.
- Last action, (e.g., receipts, transfer, and order.)
- Total sales and receipts for life of the item.
- Current sales and stock levels for all stores.

Figure 8-14, page 186, is annotated (1) through (21) and reads:

(1) Dept. 349; week ending 11/15/94.
(2) Class B1.
(3) Vendor, 443.
(4) Style number, 3035.
(5) Style description, example: "Bus Dream".
(6) Cost, example: $6.00.
(7) Retail, example: $12.00.

(8) Markup, example: 50%.

(9) Last action, example: transfer on 10/25 (no indication of stores involved).

(10) Receipt, example: 173 pieces received 7 weeks ago.

(11) Last receipt, example: 6 weeks ago.

(12) Returns, example: 11 units have been returned.

(13) Sales, example: 85 units sold since classification arrived. The breakdown of these sales is contained in (14) through (17):

    (14) 4 weeks ago, example: 6 units sold.

    (15) 3 weeks ago, example: 9 units sold.

    (16) 2 weeks ago, example: 10 units sold.

    (17) Last week, example: 6 units sold.

(18) Current sales, example: all stores — 3; O — 1; T — 2.

(19) On hand, example: all stores — 88; L — 13; O — 14: P — 12; R — 15; T — 34.

(20) Last weeks: all stores — 6; L — 1; O — 2; P — 2; R — 1.

(21) Sold for life of classification, example: all stores — 85; L — 11; N — 11; O — 22; P — 12; R — 9; T — 13; U — 12.

The THREE-MONTH SALES SURVEY, Figure 8-15, page 187, is issued four times a year and presents sales by price line within classifications weekly and monthly for the three-month period. Markdowns either can be interspersed with other merchandise, shown separately from other merchandise, or not shown at all. Figure 8-15, page 187, is annotated (1) through (9) and reads:

(1) Dept. 349, L store, February, March, April.

(2) Month sales actual for February, example: L sold 10 blouses at $7.99 in February.

(3) Sales by week for February, example: 1st week, 6; 2nd week, 1; 3rd week, 1; 4th week, 2.

(4) Month sales actual for March, example: L sold 22 blouses.

(5) Sales by week for March, example: 1st week, 5; 2nd week, 8; 3rd week, 2; 4th week, 2; 5th week, 1.

(6) Month sales actual for April, example: L sold 109 blouses in April.

(7) Sales by week for April, example: 1st week, 1; 2nd week, 54; 3rd week, 32; 4th week, 22.

(8) 3 months total, example: 141 blouses sold in February, March, April.

(9) 6 months total, example: 747 blouses sold from February to July.

The HOT ITEM CONTROL SHEET, Figure 8-16, page 188, is not issued by a computer. The sales information is obtained usually from the kimball selling reports by the department clerical or assistant buyer who fills in the information by hand. The buyer is then able to keep abreast of the selling record and act accordingly.

Figure 8-17, page 189, is a WEEKLY MERCHANDISE AND OPEN-TO-BUY REPORT for a three-month period. Each month these figures give the buyer information concerning ending month inventory, on order for that month, balance of planned sales for that same month, planned ending inventory, and finally, the open-to-buy.

All of the amounts contained in Figure 8-17 are categorized by major classification. Using this information, the buyer can see at a glance those classifications that are performing best, and those that are not performing as planned. This is demonstrated by listing OTB figures followed by a — (minus sign). For example: designer separates show 126 —. These numbers represent a negative OTB and must be adjusted by the buyer. Also shown on this figure are markdowns by classification, inventory calculations by classification, transfers, merchandise in transit this week, markdowns, and all sales adjustments.

FIGURE 8-9 CLASSIFICATION SUMMARY REPORT, DEPT. 349, THE SPORTSWOMAN

JARROD & YOUNG

(1.) DEPT 349

LEVEL 2 - ALL STORES

NOV WK 3 1994

(2.) UNITS AND DOLLARS

(2.) PERCENTAGE DISTRIBUTION

DESCRIPTION		NOV TY	NOV LY	SALES TREND %CHG	PD %CHG	NOV TY	NOV LY	WK3 LY	%CHG	OH	CURRENT LIABILITY OO	OO	OTR	NOV WK4	DEC WK1	DEC WK2	DEC WK3	NOV	DEC	DEC	JAN	NOV TY	PD LY	THIS TY	WEEK LY	CURRENT LIABILITY OH	OO	NEXT 4 WKS	3 FUTURE MOS. NOV	DEC	JAN
(3.) MKDN DOLL		1.8	1.4	.3		.3	.9		3.1					.2	.4	1.8	1.6	1.6	1.8	14.8	7.5										
REG DOLL		38.1	25.3	14.6		14.6	5.4		109.9					7.0	13.5	31.8	45.1	22.3	31.8	06.6	6.8										
(4.) B3		(5.)	UNITS			***** CARDIGANS *****																									
	L	176	311	92	195				1080					133	102	202	565	444	1170		27		6	6	9	9	9	12		5	6	9	2
	M	138	184	52	44				765					87	69	180	370	271	801		65		7	6	9	9	11	12		11	6	11	2
	N	204	168	105	41				1121					171	141	283	414	339	1115		69		8	5	11	7	13	13		12	7	12	2
	O	148	250	69	121				1218					163	145	284	378	422	1085		85		6	8	7	11	15	15		15	4	14	3
	P	70	175	27	103				699					97	71	177	268	272	653		24		4	7	4	14	13	13		10	10	10	2
	Q	44	75	21	27				202					34	46	112	208	109	500		44		5	4	4	8	9	9		11	8	10	4
	R	94	98	44	54				708					120	101	167	218	213	504		26		6	6	7	8	15	15		11	8	9	1
	S	26	25	21	4				248					13	31	54	60	35	147		35		5	4	10	5	18	18		12	5	12	7
	T	82	164	41	97				574					155	20	118	296	339	661		48		5	8	7	10	12	12		12	11	10	8
	U	254	948	132	191				1078					266	324	381	381	1149	614		61		10	11	14	14	13	13		19	13	17	3
MKDN UNITS		72	191	13	104				100					96	201	163	120	287	1353		366												
REG UNITS		1164	1636	591	878				7593					1143	955	1781	3058	2774	6603		179												
B3			DOLLARS			***** CARDIGANS *****																									
	L	3.0	4.4	1.7	3.6				17.5					2.2	1.6	2.6	8.4	7.1	15.8		.7		6	7	10	11	18		10	7	10	1
	M	2.2	2.4	.9	1.5				12.2					1.5	1.1	2.4	5.0	4.3	33.1		.7		6	7	11	10	15		11	7	11	2
	N	3.3	2.7	1.7	1.5				18.6					2.7	1.9	3.6	5.6	5.4	14.6		.7		7	6	11	8	14		13	8	12	2
	O	2.5	3.4	1.2	1.9				20.0					2.6	3.1	3.7	5.4	6.5	14.5		.6		6	5	7	11	15		14	10	19	2
	P	1.2	2.4	.5	1.7				10.5					1.6	1.2	2.4	3.4	4.5	8.5		.3		4	10	4	17	15		12	9	11	1
	Q	.7	1.1	.3	.4				3.4					.5	.7	1.4	2.6	1.5	6.2		.5		7	8	7	10	11		11	9	9	6
	R	1.7	1.6	.8	.4				11.9					1.5	1.5	2.1	2.8	3.5	7.6		.3		7	5	10	9	17		14	9	13	1
	S	.4	.4	.4	.2				4.0					.2	.5	.8	.6	2.5	2.6		.4		6	5	11	6	20		13	5	13	6
	T	1.4	2.4	.7	1.6				9.3					2.5	3.1	1.5	4.5	8.6	8.6		.5		5	9	8	12	25		13	11	12	2
	U	4.1	5.6	2.2	3.2				17.8					4.4	5.4	6.2	5.8	10.0	18.5		.6		10	13	15	17	14		23	15	20	2
MKDN DOLL		.8	2.1	.2	1.1				1.2					1.0	1.9	1.6	1.2	3.1	13.7		3.5												
REG DOLL		19.7	26.8	18.2	14.9				125.0					19.1	16.3	24.6	42.8	45.8	43.4		1.4												
B4			UNITS			***** TEE SHIRTS *****																									
	L	90	50	19	12				404					113	68	37	161	163	369		45		3	1	1		4		3	2	3	1
	M	53	40	11	16				273					76	31	35	56	118	167		39		3	1	1	1	4		3	3	3	
	N	81	14	21	1				555					35	38	44	104	47	328		96		3	2	2	1	6		3	1	3	3
	O	72	64	18	17				363					80	23	8	14	149	56		48		3		1		4		1	1		1
	P	24	14	4					232					21	29	74	41	35	257		41		1		2		4		3	1	4	1
	Q	5	9		1				81					9	19	122	52	18	237		12			1	1		5		6	2	5	1
	R	38	23	6	2				160					42	32	15	34	65	129		28		2	1	1		5		2	1	1	1
	S	8	7	1	1				66					1			3	8	8		11		1	1			4			1	2	2
	T	60	18	5	7				164					21	11	46	108	39	275		92		4		1		5		9	1	4	5
	U	86	22	18	7				540					43	20	22	26	65	82		30		3	1	1	1	6		1	1		1
MKDN UNITS		69	52	17	19				1023					19	172	155	391	71	449		74												
REG UNITS		448	214	47	41				1875					422	100	302	278	636	908		360												
B4			DOLLARS			***** TEE SHIRTS *****																									
	L	.8	.7	.1	.2				2.9					1.7	.6	.3	1.4	2.3	3.2		.3		1				2		2	2	2	1
	M	.5	.5	.1	.2				2.1					1.1	.3	.3	.4	1.6	1.4		.2		1		1		2		2	1	1	1
	N	.7	.6	.2					3.1					.5	.4	.6	.7	.7	2.4		.6		1				1		1	3	2	3
	O	.8	.6	.1	.2				2.3					1.2	.2	.1	.1	2.0	.5		.6		1				1		2	1	2	3
	P	.2	.2						1.2					.3	.3	.4	.5	.5	1.6		.2				1		1		2		2	1
	Q								.7					.1	.4	.3	.3	.3	1.1		.1						1		2		3	
	R	.3	.3	.1					.7					.6	.1	.3	.3	.9	1.3		.1		1				1		2	2	3	
	S	.6	.2	.1	.1				.2					.3	.2	.3	.8	.1	1.8		.4		1	1			2		2	2	2	
	T	.7	.2	.1	.1				.7					.6	.2	.2	.2	.1	.8		.1						2		1	1	2	2
	U	.4	.4	.1	.1				3.1					.1	1.4	1.2	3.1	.5	7.9		.6				1		1		2	1	3	1
MKDN DOLL		4.2	3.1	.6					5.1					.6	1.3	1.7	1.8	.9	9.1		1.8												
REG DOLL									11.6					6.5				9.3															
B5			UNITS			***** VESTS *****																									
	L	17	104	3	47				72					32	33	97	89	136	271		36		1	2	2	2	2		3	2	2	1
	M	15	53	1	31				57					7	29	50	117	62	236		40		1	1	2	3	2		3	3	3	1
	N	43	80	17	27				86					25	49	108	75	103	278		31		2	2	1	5	1		3	3	3	1
	O	31	110	13	36				112					48	42	48	79	158	296		48		1	3	1		1		3	3	4	1

FIGURE 8-10   CLASSIFICATION STOCK STATUS REPORT (STORE B)

CLASSIFICATION STOCK STATUS

DEPARTMENT 118   WOMEN'S TOPS

Column groups (left to right): TWO MONTHS PRIOR — JULY | ONE MONTH PRIOR — AUGUST | CURRENT MONTH — SEPTEMBER | ONE MONTH FUTURE — OCTOBER | TWO MONTHS FUTURE — NOVEMBER | THREE MONTHS FUTURE — DECEMBER

Sub-columns per month: ON ORDER O.T.B. · OPENING STOCK · SALES · M/D · RECEIPT

Row structure for each classification: DATA BY WEEK (1, 2, 3, 4, 5) and MONTH (TY / PLAN / LY)

08 NOVELTY AND OUTERWEAR

Line		July Open	July Sales	July M/D	July Rec	Aug Open	Aug Sales	Aug M/D	Aug Rec	Sept Open	Sept Sales	Sept M/D	Sept Rec	OTB
TY		133	14	4	10	75	55	2	246	300	80	26	180	33 / 182
PLAN		150	60		100	100	20		220					
LY		228	35	3	666	805	88	2	381	1095	335		880	

Weekly (Sept) opening / sales: 265 / 12 · 348 / 11 · 337 / — · 311 / 26

Future months (Oct / Nov / Dec) — OTB, Opening, Sales, M/D, Receipt:
- October: OO 75, OTB 117; Opening TY 400, LY 1614; Sales TY 60, LY 532; M/D 51; Receipt 10 / -273
- November: OTB 17; Opening TY 350, LY 758; Sales TY 50, LY 306; M/D 5; Receipt -100 / 254
- December: OTB 17; Opening TY 200, LY 701; Sales TY 150, LY 736; M/D 22; Receipt 408

SWEATERS — TOTAL

Weekly (Sept) opening: 1026 · 1900 · 1844 · 1712; sales 43 / 56 / 147
- September: OO 1624; Opening TY 1800, LY 1095; Sales TY 480, LY 335; M/D 26; Receipt 930 / 880 ; OTB 80
- Aug: Opening 350/450/805; Sales 146/130/88; M/D 4/3/2; Receipt 824/1480/381
- July: Opening 140/150/228; Sales 42/60/35; M/D 4/3; Receipt 296/360/666
- October: OO 1382, OTB -1452; Opening 2250 / 1614; Sales 750 / 532; M/D 51; Receipt -150 / -273
- November: OTB -1352; Opening 1350 / 758; Sales 450 / 306; M/D 5; Receipt 100 / 254
- December: OTB -752; Opening 1000 / 701; Sales 1050 / 736; M/D 22; Receipt 600 / 408

09 SHELLS AND TANKS

Weekly (Sept) opening: 91 · 92 · 76 · 61; sales 22 / 15 / 13
- July: Opening 212/300/363; Sales 79/50/172; M/D 27/5; Receipt -13/140
- Aug: Opening 67/200/219; Sales 90/50/120; M/D 7/6; Receipt 121/372
- September: OTB 89; Opening 150/465; Sales 50/101; M/D 19; Receipt 30/29
- October: OO 108, OTB 11; Opening 130/374; Sales 30/58; M/D 6; Receipt 30/154
- November: OTB 11; Opening 130/464; Sales 30/71; M/D 9; Receipt 50/-81
- December: OTB 61; Opening 100/448; Sales 50/134; M/D 2; Receipt 50/-81

10 T-SHIRTS AND SCIVVIES

Weekly (Sept) opening: 298 · 222 · 215 · 194; sales 39 / 32 / 18
- July: Opening 313/400; Sales 150/90; M/D 21; Receipt -5/-10
- Aug: Opening 88/300; Sales 147/100; M/D 8; Receipt 364/50
- September: OTB 2; Opening 250; Sales 100; Receipt 50
- October: OO 22; Opening 200; Sales 70
- November: OTB 42; Opening 150; Sales 70; M/D; Receipt 20
- December: OTB 142; Opening 100; Sales 100; Receipt 100 / 3

TOTAL TOPS

- July: Opening 525/700/363; Sales 228/190/172; M/D 47/5; Receipt -17/-10/140
- Aug: Opening 155/200/219; Sales 238/150/120; M/D 15/6; Receipt 485/50/372
- September: OTB 92; Opening 400/465; Sales 150/101; M/D 19; Receipt 80/29
- October: OO 108, OTB 34; Opening 330/374; Sales 100/58; M/D 6; Receipt 50/154
- November: OTB 54; Opening 280/464; Sales 100/71; M/D 5; Receipt 20/64
- December: OTB 204; Opening 200/448; Sales 150/134; M/D 2; Receipt 150/-79

Weekly (Sept) opening: 388 · 314 · 290 · 255; sales 61 / 47 / 31

11 SOLID SHIRTS

- July: Opening 332/500/555; Sales 112/140/111; M/D 26/10; Receipt 38/140/40
- Aug: Opening 184/500/353; Sales 95/70/129; M/D 11/12; Receipt 379/-130/505
- September: OTB -439; Opening 300/718; Sales 100/284; M/D 15; Receipt 100/240
- October: OO -339, OTB -339; Opening 300/659; Sales 100/164; M/D 10; Receipt 100/95
- November: OTB -189; Opening 300/579; Sales 50/146; M/D 14; Receipt 150/214
- December: OTB -239; Opening 400/634; Sales 150/328; M/D 15; Receipt -50/179

Weekly (Sept): opening 457 / 447 / 499 / 688; sales 33 / 43 / 60

DOLLARS IN HUNDREDS

FIGURE 8-11 CLASS/PRICE REPORT, DEPT. 349, THE SPORTSWOMAN

JARROD & YOUNG

(1.) DEPT 349   LEVEL A4—ALL STORES   APR WEEK 2 1994

DESCRIPTION	APR TY	PTD LY	PREV WK TY	PREV WK LY	THIS WK TY	THIS WK LY	CURRENT OH	OO	APR	MAY	JUNE	APR WK1 PL	WK1 LY	APR WK4 PL	WK4 LY	MAY WK1 PL	WK1 LY	MAY WK2 PL	WK2 LY	APR	MAY	JUNE	STOCK SALES RATIO
6.99																							
L																						203	
M																						195	
N																						154	
O																						157	
P																						150	
Q																						80	
R																						68	
S																						25	
T																						104	
U																						104	
ALL ST																						1245	
7.00																							
L	115	38	67	18	48	20	280						17		17		15		9	72	36	150	6
M	121	39	52	21	69	18	266						17		14		11		13	75	36	134	4
N	158	21	50	4	68	12	173						14		15		12		6	50	36	136	3
O	239	44	147	27	42	22	167						20		11		8		6	80	24	148	2
P	126	11	44	6	77	5	114								3		2		1	14	4	45	3
Q	82		41		41	5	82					4			1		1			10	4	41	2
R	109	4	32	5	77	4	33										3			4	4	49	
S	48	5	23		25	5	144										2			5	3	48	6
T	66	4	32	3	34	1	189										3		2	4	6	104	6
U	184	45	82	16	102	24	221						38		31		18		12	114	48	147	8
ALL ST	1248	226	615	105	633	121	1674						110		47		75		44	433	201	1107	3
7.99																							
L																						51	
M																						56	
N																						54	
O																						59	
P																						34	
Q																						40	
R																						19	
S																						9	
T																						17	
U																						3	
ALL ST																						236	
8.00																							
L	87	102	51	40	-36	62	574						66		71		137		146	241	651	693	16
M	70	156	26	58	44	98	487						45		63		114		189	264	622	572	11
N	91	164	36	69	55	95	501						36		81		119		147	301	825	1385	7
O	225	209	91	77	415	124	680						102		75		173		215	383	845	1145	8
P	41	124	27	44	64	85	336						42		57		87		122	228	469	661	
Q	26	28	7	6	14	16	187						17		12		18		32	51	120	191	10
R	58	88	26	32	54	29	246						21		27		51		104	136	326	609	8
S	31	21	1	2	30	19	186						8		19		17		42	46	143	179	8
T	58	88	21	43	27	45	249						48		53		66		129	189	475	638	9
U	132	128	37	41	95	87	496						43		50		81		139	221	605	1393	5
ALL ST	859	1104	323	404	536	695	3942						450		506		853		1365	2062	4889	8902	7
9.00																							
L	18	24	10	11	8	13	82						4		12		17		16	45	58	104	3
M	24	40	11	30	13	10	67						8		11		21		30	54	124	24	5
N	21	32	7	14	14	25	62						10		20		57		35	83	145	85	3
O	65	75	27	36	38	34	144						23		12		35		40	110	157	115	4
P	30	16	14	4	16	12	153						5		3		17		20	24	65	27	10
Q	3	8		3	3	3	26						2		2		5		1	10	16	14	4
R	8	20	2	7	6	13	42						5		9		14		66	34	58	20	7
S	16	9	4	3	12		82								3		2		9	6	13	3	7
T	4	12	1	7	3	5	14						4		4		7		27	20	62	14	5
U	31	33	11	17	20	16	46						18		4		40		54	68	189	62	5
ALL ST	220	281	67	145	133	138	773						84		85		220		238	450	873	404	6
10.00																							
L	87	5	41	2	46	3	251								1					6	1	50	5
M	115	1	54		61	1	271						1		2						4	47	9
N	126	8	49	8	77	10	373						2		1				1	11	20	42	4
O	94	20	40	10	54	10	304						6		6		2		3	32	25	59	7
P	57	9	23	1	34	2	142						3				-1		1	2	6	41	5
Q	25		12		13		112								1					1		18	4
R	36	19	14	8	22	9	183						3		4		1		-1	20	5	38	8
S	18		9		4		123															4	14
T	38	4	12	3	21	1	170						1		1		1		1	6	4	35	8
U	81	7	12	2	54	7	322						3		2		1		5	12	24	56	5
ALL ST	677	61	281	34	396	27	2256						14		18		7		10	48	85	371	6

RUN DATE 04/18/94   RUN PAGE 725   LEVEL 4   MULTI STORES   MEDIA DATE W/E 04/17/94

(1.) DEPT 349   PAGE 6   APR WEEK 2 1994   **CLASS/PRICE REPORT**

FIGURE 8-12 BEST SELLERS REPORT, DEPT. 349, THE SPORTSWOMAN

JARROD & YOUNG

DEPT 349 THE SPORTSWOMAN

CLASS	VEND	STYLE	RETAIL	Description	ALL STORES SLS (CURR/PRWK/2AGO)	ALL STORES OH (CURR/2AGO)	L SLS	L OH	M SLS	M OH	N SLS	N OH	O SLS	O OH	P SLS	P OH	Q SLS	Q OH	R SLS	R OH	S SLS	S OH	T SLS	T OH	U SLS	U OH
F1				**PULLOVERS**																						
	713	04801	11.00	SOLID 1x1 RIB COWL	116 / 97 / 104	1016 / 365 / 397	13 / 14 / 27	133	14 / 11 / 7	141	12 / 9 / 129	188	12 / 5 / 12	1	22 / 4 / 6	173	6 / 0 / 7	102	14 / 34 / 9	123	10 / 11 / 2	54	5 / 0 / 8	20	12 / 9 / 10	71
*	713	04806	13.00	STRIPE 4 FIELD COWL	250 / 115 / 15	463 / 622 / 53	21 / 8 / 5	48	21 / 15	−35	44 / 33	63	43 / 6 / 8	77	29 / 23 / 1	73	20 / 5 / 3	41	21 / 22 / 1	59	2	2	13 / 3	72	31 / 11	58
	713	04814	15.00	ETHNIC YOKE	179 / 89 / 122	735 / 242 / 331	19 / 7 / 2	59	17 / 14 / 13	83	26 / 14 / 11	69	18 / 2 / 18	98	35 / 17 / 26	106	5		11 / 12	72 / 7	4 / 3	31 / 3	14 / 6	45 / 12	29 / 32	100
	713	04816	15.00	ZIG ZAG SCALLOP SKIVVY	101 / 42 / 63	650 / 260 / 316	5 / 4 / 3	56	2 / 5 / 2	72	10 / 7 / 11	88	6 / 3	65	13 / 6 / 12	105	29		43 / 13 / 12	55	4	31	7 / 6 / 6	62	11 / 6 / 16	87
#	713	04840	7.99		139	750	5	67	4	69	26 / 21	94	21	51	17 / 4	102	4	69	45	75	3	45	3	69	11	109
G1				**JACKETS**																						

FIGURE 8-13   FASHION FLASH REPORT, DEPT. 349, THE SPORTSWOMAN

JARROD & YOUNG

FASHION FLASH

(1.) DEPT 349   PAGE 1   NET SALES OF MONDAY   04-28-94   EXCEPTION CRITERIA 04

(2.) CLASS	(3.) VENDOR	(4.) STYLE	(5.) RETAIL	TOTAL (6.)	L	M	N	O	P	Q	R	S	T	U
A3	575	0682	32.00	6	3									
B1	617	9512	50.00	11	7	1	2		1		1	1		1
B1	617	9619	52.00	3	2	1								
B2	017	3209	64.00	4	1		1			1		1		
B2	027	2096	40.00	4			1		2					
B2	522	3672	38.00	5	5									
C1	017	2773	54.00	3	2	1	1							
C1	017	3339	66.00	8	2			3					2	1
C1	017	3354	66.00	4	2									-1
C1	027	2174	39.99	4	2							1		1
C1	410	1472	80.00	6	4	1		1			1			
C1	522	3725	33.00	3	3									
C1	802	2603	38.00	1	-1		3			-1				
C1	802	2407	38.00	2			2							
C1	802	3116	38.00	6	1	-1	3	1					1	1
C1	802	7146	17.00	2			-1							
C1	902	0855	49.00	7	7				1				1	
C1	902	0856	49.00	13	5	1	3	2					2	
C1	902	0884	49.00	4			2	1	1					
C8	003	0599	5.99	4	4									
C8	061	4462	29.99	8	5		1		1				1	
C8	061	4463	.00	14	6		1		2		3		1	
C8	061	4745	24.99	7	2		2							1
C8	061	4948	29.99	7	3	1		1			1		1	
C8	061	4949	29.99	2	2					1				2
C8	617	4109	29.99	5	2		2							
I9	617	9500	29.99	6	4							1		
I9	617	9503	29.99	3	3				1					

MONDAY   04-28-94   DEPT 349   PAGE 1   FASHION FLASH   PASS 01   PAGE 85

JARROD & YOUNG

Y (1.) DEPT 349 REG DISS SEQUENCE REPORT THRU 11-15-94

Life History Style/Status Report — Dept. 349, The Sportswoman. Columns include VEND, STYLE (STYLE NAME, CONDITION & DATE), CLASS CODES, DESTINATION DATE, COST (MU%, EST. RETAIL), CURR. RETAIL, 1ST INQUIRY (SALES, RECPT., RETURNS), RECENT SALES & STOCK HISTORY (4 WEEKS AGO, 3 WEEKS AGO, 2 WEEKS AGO, 1 WEEK AGO, LAST RECEIPT WKS AGO, FIRST RECEIPT WKS AGO), ALL STORES COMBINED (CURR SLS, ON HAND, PRV WKS, LIFE), and STORE DATA (CURRENT SALES & CURRENT ON HAND SALES HISTORY) with store columns L, M, N, P, Q, R, S, T, U.

VEND STYLE	STYLE NAME	MU% / EST.RET	CURR RET	1ST INQ SALES / RECPT / RET	ALL STORES CURR SLS / ON HAND / PRV WKS / LIFE	L	M	N	P	Q	R	S	T	U
443 3000		.00 / .0%	12.00	209 / 7297 / 7	162 / 7082 / 47 / 204	22 / 1167 / 31	22 / 743 / 37	27 / 1084 / 31	8 / 1008 / INV	16 / 520 / 17	7 / 412 / 7	15 / 525 / 16	117 / 3	25 / 509 / 30	14 / 997 / 23
443 3035 BUS DREAM		6.00 / 50.0%	12.00	85 / 173 / 11	3 / 88 / 6 / 85	13 / 11	INV	11	14 / 2 / 22	12 / 2 / 12		15 / 1 / 9		34 / 13	2
554 3036 SPACE THEATRE POPCORN		6.00 / 50.0%	12.00	66 / 114 / 4	53	24 / 8	8 / 1 / 16	9						
443 3037 ORIENTAL LADIES		6.00 / 50.0%	12.00	57 / 105 / 1	5 / 46 / 18 / 57	-2 / 2 / 2 / 2	2 / 25 / 5 / 19	16 / 2 / 10	15 / 2 / 10	1 / 11 / 11	5	1 / 7 / 7 / 4			12 / 11
443 3050 UMBRELLAS IN SNOW STORM		6.00 / 50.0%	12.00	149 / 208 / 6	9 / 59 / 4 / 144	2 / 12	1 / -1	3 / 7 / 28	4 / 20	3 / 10 / 26		10 / 1	17	INV	4 / 1
443 3041 ORIENTAL		6.00 / 50.0%	12.00	93 / 197 / 1	5 / 104	18 / 37	10	28	1 / 10		22 / 12	1 / INV	4 / 1 / 7 / 5	2	28 / 2 / 18
453 3042 DARK COLOR HILLSIDE		6.00 / 50.0%	12.00	95 / 226 / 4	11 / 127	13 / 41	INV / 11	14 / 27	14 / 5	2 / 27	1 / 10	1 / INV	7	INV	4 / 14
443 3044 LA CARPALE		6.00 / 50.0%	12.00	76 / 139 / 5	10 / 99	19 / 26	13	7 / 18	18	16 / 2		INV	5	3	10
443 3045 TV SHOW		6.00 / 50.0%	12.00	26 / 119	1 / 63	3 / 22	INV / 14	22	20 / 1	1					20
553 2950 VERMONT WINTER		7.75 / 49.9%	15.00		6 / 76	39 / 2 / 7	2 / 1 / 10	1	22 / 1						8
443 3057 RICEFIELD		7.75 / 49.0%	15.00	24 / 121	21 / 97	2 / 10	3 / 5	4 / 8	3 / 9	4 / 8	2 / 9	12	3 / 8 / 2	3 / 12	14 / 1 / 5
443 3055 RIVER AND TREE		7.75 / 49.0%	15.00	13 / 216	3 / 15 / 24 / 203	2 / 2	3 / 2	3 / 1	4 / 1	4 / 23	2 / 23	1 / 4	12	5 / 22	12
543 3021 WATERFALLS		7.75 / 49.0%	15.00		13	22 / 2	22 / 2	2	2	10 / 2	10 / 1	12 / 2		22 / 2	24
443 3052 AIRPLANE		7.75 / 49.0%	15.00	4 / 215	107 / 4 / 211	24 / 24	24 / 23	24 / 1	24	12 / 21	1 / 2	24 / 2	2	

FIGURE 8-15 THREE-MONTH SALES SURVEY, DEPT. 349, THE SPORTSWOMAN

JARROD & YOUNG

(1.) DEPT 349, L STORE

DATA ENDING WITH EOM.   JULY 1994

****** SHIRTS AND BLOUSES ******

CL / PR		BOP STOCK PLANS ACTUAL	(1.) FEBRUARY	(1.) MARCH	(1.) APRIL	3 MONTHS THIS PAGE	6 MONTHS TOTAL
A1	1.99 x						1
A1	2.99 x						11
A1	3.99 x			445		445	610
A1	4.99 x						21
A1	5.99 x			16	16	16	139
A1	6.99 x						1
A1	7.99 x	(2.) 10	(3.) 6	(4.) 22	(5.) 5 (6.) 109	(7.) 1 (8.) 141	(9.) 747
A1	8.99 x						2
A1	9.99 x	2	2	1	32	35	175
A1	10.99 x	9	1	13	4	22	24
A1	12.99 x	8	5	7	1	18	40
A1	19.99 x				1	1	2
A1	.00	54	31	6	1	61	41
A1	3.99	1			1	2	7
A1	5.99	15	1	1384	73	1472	1473
A1	6.99				24	24	4
A1	7.99	12		1274	36	1322	1331
A1	8.00				1	1	4
A1	8.99	11		14	1	26	29
A1	9.00	2		30	12	44	75
A1	9.99						-1
A1	10.00	33	8	32	11	76	76
A1	10.50			1		1	1

DEPT 349   PAGE 5

RUN DATE 08/23/94   RUN PAGE 511

FIGURE 8-16 HOT ITEM CONTROL SHEET

JARROD & YOUNG

	Feb/Aug	March/Sept	April	May	June/Dec	
STORE L						
OO*			120	125		
REC*			120			
S*			10 / 15 / 20			
OH*			45 / 75			
PS			50	100		

Dept	Description	Cost	Retail	Class	House	House No.	Style
350	Man-Tailored Shirt	12.25	25.00	55	Jones Sportswear	411	711

* OO – On order, REC – Received, S – Sold, OH – On hand, PS – Planned Sales

WEEKLY MERCHANDISE AND OPEN-TO-BUY REPORT
OPEN-TO-BUY CALCULATIONS AND 2 FOLLOWING MONTHS

	DEPARTMENT TOTAL	13 BSC SEPRTS Amt	%	21 MOD SEPRTS Amt	%	39 DES SEPRTS Amt	%	47 CASUAL TOPS Amt	%	54 JEANS Amt	%	62 SKIRTS Amt	%	70 BSC PANTS Amt	%	88 JACKETS Amt	%	96 DRESS TOPS Amt	%	05 PROMO PANTS Amt	%
AUG END INV	10494	1305	12	966	9	440	4	1478	14	972	9	398	4	2752	26	1278	12	499	5	405	4
ON ORDER	1875	187	10			401	21	730	39	87	9	15	2	311	32	87	9	18	2	558	30
BAL PL SLS	982	158	16	118	12	65	7	123	13	1100	9	545	4	2100	17	1650	13	800	7	400	3
PL END INV	12275	1880	15	1350	11	650	5	1800	15	215		162		341-		459		319		563-	
OTB	888	546		502		126-		285-													
SEP ON ORDER	3837	384	10	1008	26	120	5	906	24	456	18	90	2	887	23	329	9	234	6	90	4
PLAN SLS	2605	150	6	376	14			276	11			40	2	841	32	198	8	58	2		
PL END INV	14679	2272	16	1863	13	827	6	2312	16	1086	7	588	4	2192	15	1794	12	938	6	807	6
OTB	1172	159		119-		297		118-		442		7-		46		14		38-		497	
OCT ON ORDER	5377	738	14	1110	21	622	12	980	18	307	9	90	2	770	14	293	5	418	8	356	7
PLAN SLS	3561	405	11	514	14	130	4	445	13			60	2	1069	30	327	9	116	3	188	5
PL END INV	15866	2709	17	2271	14	946	6	2460	16	1076	7	598	4	2161	14	1863	12	965	6	817	5
OTB	629-	104		188-		373-		387-		297		20-		268		104		275-		158-	
3 MONTH OTB	1431	808		195		202-		790-		954		136		27-		576		6		224-	
ON ODR BEYOND TOTAL COMM	1383							250						624		59		81			
TOTAL COMM	22966	2614	11	3454	15	1463	6	4344	19	972-	4	577	3	5033	22	1958	9	1232	5	1319	6

Markdowns

	Amt	%	13 BSC SEPRTS Amt	%	21 MOD SEPRTS Amt	%	39 DES SEPRTS Amt	%	47 CASUAL TOPS Amt	%	54 JEANS Amt	%	62 SKIRTS Amt	%	70 BSC PANTS Amt	%	88 JACKETS Amt	%	96 DRESS TOPS Amt	%	05 PROMO PANTS Amt	%
MONTH TY		14.7	99	3.0	312	10.0	144	16.9	207	10.2	20	.9	26	8.9	261	4.5	230	13.3	192	16.1	2	.8
TO DATE PLAN																						
SEASON TY	1493	7.2																				
TO DATE PLAN		10.0																				

INVENTORY CALCULATIONS BY CLASS

INV. CALC BY CLASS	DEPARTMENT TOTAL	13 BSC SEPRTS	21 MOD SEPRTS	39 DES SEPRTS	47 CASUAL TOPS	54 JEANS	62 SKIRTS	70 BSC PANTS	88 JACKETS	96 DRESS TOPS	05 PROMO PANTS
BEG INVENTORY	10771	1352	991	456	1509	1005	400	2825	1306	515	412
PURCHASES	162	1	44	118	1	2	0	2	0	0	0
TRANSFERS IN	10		2				3				
INTRANSIT T/W	601	292	110		32	29	0	0	3	0	133
MARKUPS	2-	0	0		0		0		1-		0
TRANSFERS OUT	10				1	2	0		0		0
INTRANSIT L/W	763	292	154	118	32	29	3	2	3	0	133
MARKDOWNS	272	46	25	16	31	31	2	71	27	16	7
SALES											
ADJUSTMENTS	4-	0	1	0	0	1-	0	2-	1-	0	0
END INVENTORY	10494	1305	966	440	1478	972	398	2752	1278	499	405

WEEK ENDING 01-09/94   DIVISION 32   DEPARTMENT 485

Figure 8-18, page 192, is a sample of a six-month MERCHANDISE STATISTICS REPORT of a complete classification reported by a major sportswear department. Each month is categorized by week, (i.e., February 4 weeks, March 5 weeks, April and May 4 weeks each, June 5 weeks, and July 4 weeks) and weekly results are given in addition to a monthly total. This report is a dollar report only, and does not show units. Also shown are this year's results (TY), Plan, and last year's results (LY).

Using April results as an example (outlined in heavy lines) read across Figure 8-18:

10th WEEK OF SEASON (1st Week of April Business) [15]

Average Store:

TY = $610 (.61)
Plan = 570 (.57)
LY = $800 (.80)

Weekly:

TY = $311,300 (311.3)
Plan = $291,000 (291.0)
LY = $369,600 (369.6)

Cumulative:

TY = $2,639,000 (2639)
Plan = $3,742,000 (3742)
LY = $4,088,000 (4088)

Percent Change:

Plan vs. LY = − 29%
Actual vs. LY = − 24%

Cumulative MU%:

TY = 55.6%
LY = 56.2%

Markdowns (dollars):

TY = $108,000 (108)
Plan for the Month = $30,000 (30)

Markdowns (Percent):

TY = 34.6%
LY = 8.2%

Merchandise Receipts:

TY = − $224,000 (− 224)

(This is a negative figure because a style was moved from Spring stock to "pack and hold" for another season.)

LY = $47,000 (47)

Inventory (Total Dollars):

TY = $4,983,000 (4983)
Plan = $4,043,000 (4043) planned

EOM stock:

LY = $6,543,000 (6543)

Inventory (Average Store):

TY = $9,800 (9.8)
LY = $14,200 (14.2)

On Order:

TY = $505,000 (506) on order for Spring
TY MU% = 57.7% of 506 on order

April OTB:
= $46,000 (46)

---

[15] All figures on the merchandise statistics report are in 000's.

There are some secondary forms that are generated as a result of selling information. Figure 8-19, page 193, Vendor Performance Analysis prototype is an example of a secondary selling report. The buyer is able to judge the performance, and therefore profitability, of each vendor.

MERCHANDISING APPLICATION

Figure 8-20, pages 194-197, Style/Sales History for Dept. 345, "The Gallery", is a report by classification, by manufacturer, by price, and by units for the period August 1 to August 31.[16]

It will be necessary for you to supply:

- House Numbers (column 1).
- Style Numbers (column 2).
- Retail Prices (column 3).

By conforming this report (Figure 8-20) to your selected figures, the report can be used to fit your merchandising efforts such as your purchases (selected styles), your designated house numbers, and your established retail prices. You will be able to identify the styles of your selection, to rationalize the selling rate of each style, and to prove the need of particular information as a necessary tool of merchandising.

Based on the sales records and anticipated events for the period, your assignment is to:

- Establish a dollar OTB for November/December.
- Allocate a dollar OTB for each classification.[17]
- Support the allocation of OTB in dollars for each classification with appropriate data.[18]
- Indicate whether new sub-classifications are needed or if current ones are obsolete.

For the blouse classification only, break the allotted OTB figure into subclassifications and then into units for each price point. (Shirts are considered a sub-classification of blouses.)

The Purchase Journal — Auditing Your Book Inventory

The purchase journal is generated by the control department. A copy of each department's purchase journal is also kept in the accounts payable office. It lists all invoices and charge-backs that were processed through accounts payable during the previous week. The files are available on Thursday and are to be checked before the end of the week. They must be signed every week by the buyer.

Also on file are all copies of invoices and charge-backs listed in the purchase journal. Attached to each invoice is a Key-Rec (see Figure 8-21, page 199) on which the receiving department, the invoice office, and accounts payable have made entries.

---

[16] This is a report from one of nation's leading retail organizations, altered to fit the circumstances of "The Gallery." The reality of current merchandising events and retail forms is such that these factors far outweigh the disadvantages of having the buyer (student) supply information that is always part of such a report.

[17] Using proper forms.

[18] See Figure 8-20, pp. 194.

FIGURE 8-18 MERCHANDISE STATISTICS REPORT

MERCHANDISE STATISTICS REPORT — TOTAL SWEATERS — SPRING 1994

WEEK # 10

Column groups: **DOLLAR SALES (000'S omitted)** — Average Store (T.Y./PLAN/L.Y.), Weekly (T.Y./PLAN/L.Y.), Cumulative (T.Y./PLAN/L.Y.); **PERCENT** (Plan vs L.Y., Change Act vs L.Y.); **CUM MU%** (T.Y./L.Y.); **MARKDOWNS** — Dollars (T.Y./PLAN/L.Y.), Percent (T.Y./L.Y.); **MERCHANDISE RECEIPTS** (T.Y./L.Y./PLAN); **INVENTORY** — Dollars (T.Y./PLAN/L.Y.), Average Store (T.Y./PLAN/L.Y.); **ON ORDER** (T.Y., T.Y. MU%)

M/W/O/N/E/T/H #	AvgSt T.Y.	AvgSt PLAN	AvgSt L.Y.	Wkly T.Y.	Wkly PLAN	Wkly L.Y.	Cum T.Y.	Cum PLAN	Cum L.Y.	%Plan vs L.Y.	%Chg Act vs L.Y.	CumMU% T.Y.	CumMU% L.Y.	Mkdn$ T.Y.	Mkdn$ PLAN	Mkdn$ L.Y.	Mkdn% T.Y.	Mkdn% L.Y.	Rcpt T.Y.	Rcpt L.Y.	Rcpt PLAN	Inv$ T.Y.	Inv$ PLAN	Inv$ L.Y.	InvAS T.Y.	InvAS PLAN	InvAS L.Y.	OnOrd T.Y.	OnOrd MU%
F 1	0.25	0.22	0.29	126.0	109.5	134.2	665	906	1125	-25.0	-13.7	56.9	56.0	15	MONTH	4	11.9	3.1	1464	498		4133		6026	8.2		13.0	2418	57.1
E 2	0.30	0.31	0.41	149.4	154.6	189.5	814	1060	1315	-25.2	-22.0	57.0	56.0	135	205	224	49.0	69.3	721	779		4585		6395	9.1		13.8	2270	57.2
B 3	0.36	0.41	0.55	184.2	205.2	252.1	998	1265	1567	-25.4	-26.9	57.1	56.0	157	30.0	444	34.2	77.1	-240	840		4139		6764	8.2		14.6	2454	57.7
4	0.37	0.42	0.57	189.0	214.7	263.7	1187	1480	1831	-25.5	-29.3	56.7	56.2	170	S.T.D. 310	484	26.2	57.7	862	1268		4798	4386	7728	9.5	8.7	16.7	2872	57.0
FEB total	1.28	1.35	1.82	649	684	840				-26.1	-40.1			214	20.9	702	18.0	38.4	2806	3386	3494 OTB =		19	(431)			FEB 0.		0.0
M 5	0.36	0.71	0.77	181.4	358.6	356.0	1369	1839	2187	-7.6	-53.3	56.5	56.2	88	MONTH	83	48.7	23.3	531	221		5060		7510	10.0		16.2	2693	56.5
A 6	0.37	0.78	0.88	188.4	393.4	407.3	1557	2232	2594	-9.7	-55.6	56.3	56.1	131	410	529	35.5	69.4	844	62		5672		6718	11.2		14.5	2034	56.5
R 7	0.49	0.79	0.82	251.6	403.6	382.6	1809	2636	2976	-7.8	-50.5	55.8	56.0	452	20.8	785	72.7	68.5	476	584		5576		6664	10.9		14.4	1363	57.4
8	0.53	0.83	0.74	268.9	425.4	344.1	2078	3061	3321	-3.3	-45.6	55.6	56.1	602	S.T.D. 720	944	67.6	63.3	283	859		5441		7020	10.6		15.2	1029	57.2
9	0.49	0.76	0.86	249.6	390.0	397.6	2327	3451	3718	-5.1	-45.1	55.6	56.7	646	20.9	989	56.7	52.4	479	319		5626	4573	6896	11.0	8.9	15.0	545	57.9
MAR total	2.24	3.87	4.08	1140	1971	1888				-15.4	-42.7			860		1691	37.0	45.5	2614	2045	2568 OTB =		0	(1,053)			MAR 0.		0.0
A 10	0.61	0.57	0.80	311.3	291.0	369.6	2639	3742	4088	-29.0	-24.0	55.6	56.2	108	MONTH 750	30	34.6	8.2	-224	47		4983		6543	9.8		14.2	506	57.7
P 11	0.00	0.55	0.82		291.0	379.2	0	4033	4467	-31.2	-100.0	ERR	56.2		65.8	643	0.0	85.9	0	-9				5542	0.0		12.0		ERR
R 12	0.00	0.51	0.75		269.0	346.9	0	4302	4814	-31.7	-100.0	ERR	56.2		S.T.D. 1470	854	0.0	78.0	0	256				5240	0.0		11.4		ERR
13	0.00	0.54	0.68		289.0	313.8	0	4591	5128	-29.1	-100.0	ERR	56.0		32.0	926	0.0	65.7	0	76			4043	4931	0.0	7.6	10.7		ERR
APR total	0.61	2.17	3.06	311	1140	1410				-19.2	-41.0	ERR		968		2617	36.7	51.0	-224	370	1360 OTB =		46	0			APR 0.		506.2
M 14	0.00	0.68	0.83		360.5	383.3	0	4952	5511	-18.3	-100.0	ERR	56.1		MONTH 655	53	ERR	13.9	0	564				5058	0.0		10.9		ERR
A 15	0.00	0.60	0.73		319.1	338.4	0	5271	5849	-18.1	-100.0	ERR	56.1		51.2	385	ERR	53.4	0	47				4435	0.0		9.5		ERR
Y 16	0.00	0.60	0.73		319.1	338.3	0	5590	6188	-18.0	-100.0	ERR	56.1		S.T.D. 2125	583	ERR	55.0	0	48				3947	0.0		8.5		ERR
17	0.00	0.53	0.64		281.3	299.4	0	5871	6487	-18.1	-100.0	ERR	56.1		36.2	669	ERR	49.2	0	5			2775	3566	0.0	5.2	7.7		ERR
MAY total	0.00	2.40	2.93	0	1280	1359				-18.9	ERR	ERR		0		3286	0.0	50.7	0	664	667 OTB =		667	0			MAY 0.		0.0
J 18	0.00	0.53	0.58		283.0	269.0	0	6154	6757	-8.7	-100.0	ERR	56.1		MONTH 335	45	ERR	16.7	0	0				3251	0.0		7.0		ERR
U 19	0.00	0.51	0.56		273.6	260.9	0	6428	7018	-8.7	-100.0	ERR	56.1		27.3	299	ERR	56.3	0	0				2737	0.0		5.9		ERR
N 20	0.00	0.49	0.53		259.0	247.7	0	6687	7265	-8.8	-100.0	ERR	56.1		S.T.D. 2460	385	ERR	49.4	0	0				2403	0.0		5.2		ERR
E 21	0.00	0.43	0.46		231.6	215.1	0	6918	7468	-8.2	-100.0	ERR	56.1		34.6	472	ERR	47.5	0	0				2185	0.0		4.7		ERR
22	0.00	0.34	0.40		181.8	188.0	0	7100	7659	-9.4	-100.0	ERR	56.2			491	ERR	41.6	0	0			1211	1973	0.0	2.3	4.2		ERR
JUN total	0.00	2.30	2.54	0	1229	1173				-17.5	ERR	ERR		0		4036	0.0	52.7	0	0	0 OTB =		0	0			JUN 0.		0.0
J 23	0.00	0.26	0.42		140.9	195.5	0	7241	7866	-37.2	-100.0	ERR	56.2		MONTH 255	45	ERR	10.0	0	0				1758	0.0		3.8		ERR
U 24	0.00	0.25	0.44		134.2	202.9	0	7375	8063	-39.9	-100.0	ERR	56.2		54.1	138	ERR	34.7	0	-280				1436	0.0		3.1		ERR
L 25	0.00	0.20	0.40		106.1	186.4	0	7481	8218	-43.2	-100.0	ERR	56.4		S.T.D. 2715	262	ERR	44.8	0	0				1086	0.0		2.3		ERR
Y 26	0.00	0.17	0.29		89.8	134.9	0	7571	8349	-43.0	-100.0		56.4		35.9	329	ERR	45.7	0	0			485	884	0.0	0.9	1.9		ERR
JUL total	0.00	0.88	1.55	0	471	690				-19.7	ERR			0		4036	0.0	48.3	0	-280	0 OTB =		0	0			JUL 0.		0.0

FIGURE 8-19 VENDOR PERFORMANCE ANALYSIS

VENDOR PERFORMANCE ANALYSIS - BY VENDOR
WEEK ENDING OCT 08, 94

SEASON : M FALL
DATE OCT 09,94 TIME 9:48 AM PAGE: 1

VENDOR : BR010 The Shoe Company

DEPT: 05 Ladies Shoes

CLASS DESCRIPTION	TOTAL $ SOLD		% SOLD REG DOL		UNITS SOLD		% SOLD REG UNIT		% INIT MARKON		% GROSS MARGIN		DOLLARS RECEIVED		% RECD/PURC		% RETURNS	
	TY	LY	TY	LY	TY	LY	TY	LY	TY	LY	TY	LY	TY	LY	TY	LY	TY	LY
CLASS: 1 High Heel	142,875	130,144	90.2	88.6	1,705	1,732	96.1	93.2	52.4	51.1	50.1	50.8	190,125	180,145	90.5	88.1	1.5	4.2
: 2 Flat Heel	111,125	104,457	95.7	91.0	1,949	2,009	88.6	83.4	50.8	50.5	50.2	48.7	150,172	140,123	95.7	97.2	2.1	2.4
: 3 Casual	57,193	48,615	91.1	84.5	1,505	1,393	90.7	89.6	51.7	50.2	51.4	49.7	75,145	80,125	98.9	98.1	1.8	1.7
TOTAL DEPARTMENT	311,193	283,216	92.3	88.8	5,159	5,134	91.7	88.4	51.6	50.6	50.6	49.7	415,442	400,393	95.0	94.5	1.8	3.1
TOTAL VENDOR	410,145	390,271	88.7	85.3	6,795	7,045	86.4	83.2	50.7	50.1	50.2	49.4	547,512	510,874	94.3	94.0	2.1	2.7
TOTAL SEASON	955,024	961,701	91.4	87.2	25,792	25,673	90.4	85.9	52.1	51.3	51.9	49.9	2074185	2023134	98.7	95.3	1.9	2.6

FIGURE 8-20 STYLE/SALES HISTORY FOR DEPT. 345, THE GALLERY

JARROD & YOUNG

DEPT 345   THE GALLERY   WEEK ENDING ....

HOUSE	STYLE	RETAIL	SALES						THIS WEEK'S STORE SALES					
			WKS FRM 1ST SALE	LIFE TOTAL	3 WEEKS AGO	2 WEEKS AGO	1 WEEK AGO	THIS WEEK	DM DES MOINES	A AMES	SC SIOUX CITY	D DAVENPORT	CR CEDAR RAPIDS	CB COUNCIL BLUFFS
SHORT SLEEVE SHIRTS														
				93	33	30	17	13	5	1	2	2	1	2
				47	14	13	9	11	2	1	2	2	2	2
				33	8	9	5	11	5	1	1	1	2	1
				39	9	16	5	9	3	2	1	1	1	1
				21	6	5	3	7	1	1	1	3		1
				67	22	18	20	7	3			1	1	2
				42	14	10	11	7	3	1	1		1	1
				36	13	8	9	6	2	1	1		1	2
					19	12	12	6	1	1		2		2
					9	9	5	5	1	1	1	1		1
DESIGNER BLOUSES														
				39			16	23	14	1	2	1	2	3
				13			3	10	5	1	1	1		2
				19			9	10	3		1	3	1	2
				14			5	9	3		1	3	1	1
				15	6	3	2	4	4					
				33	10	8	10	5	2		1		1	1
VESTS														
				144	44	46	32	22	11	1	4	1	1	4
				69	29	16	8	16	5	2	2	2	2	3
				82	27	29	16	10	5	1	1		1	2
				50	12	17	12	9	4	1	2		1	1
				29	5	6	11	7	3	2	1	1		
				90	35	25	20	10	3		3	1		3
				23	5	5	4	9	1	2	1	3		2
				39	8	7	17	7	2	1	1	1	1	2
				33	12	9	8	4	2				1	1
					5	6	16	7	7	1	2	2	1	3
BASIC PANTS														
				86	25	27	23	11	5	1	2		1	2
				63	22	19	12	10	3	1	2	1	1	2
				44	17	12	6	9	4		1	1	1	2
				31	7	11	5	8	3	1	1	1	1	1
				39	15	14	6	4	1	1	1			1
				41	18	12	7	4		1			1	2
				57	28	15	11	3	1				2	
TURTLENECK PULLOVERS														
				475	84	91	121	179	61	19	24	23	20	32
				393	47	98	109	139	59	11	19	19	10	21
				202	31	60	56	(55)	28	3	5	6	3	10
				133	35	21	28	49	25	5	5	3	4	7
				111	34	25	21	31	15	2	3	2	3	6
				132	29	44	37	22	15		1	1	1	4
				103	27	30	23	23	11	2	3	1	2	4
				32	7	9	2	14	7	6	1			
				119	28	34	38	19	10	1	2	1	2	3
				38	9	9	12	8	4			2		2

DEPT 345   THE GALLERY   WEEK ENDING ....

HOUSE	STYLE	RETAIL	WKS FRM 1ST SALE	LIFE TOTAL	3 WEEKS AGO	2 WEEKS AGO	1 WEEK AGO	THIS WEEK	DM DES MOINES	A AMES	SC SIOUX CITY	D DAVENPORT	CR CEDAR RAPIDS	CB COUNCIL BLUFFS
								SKIVVIES						
				222			83	(139)	69	12	13	10	12	23
				312		72	132	108	54	9	10	17	6	12
				579	158	167	150	104	53	8	7	9	16	11
				96		17	35	44	20	3	4	2	4	11
				664	600	586	333	145	72	12	15	11	12	23
				234	35	87	72	40	18	4	5	2	4	7
				291	82	89	81	39	16	4	3	3	6	7
				20	5		5	10	9					1
				19	3	4	4	8	2	1	1	1		3
				39	1	11	16	11	11					
								CARDIGANS						
				362	74	104	93	(91)	44	8	9	6	10	14
				146	41	44	32	(29)	9	2	3	5	4	6
				53	10	11	21	11	5	2	1	1	1	1
				70	21	22	18	9	5	2	1	1		
				12	3	2	2	5	1				1	3
				32	3	10	8	11	11					
								MAN-TAILORED SHIRTS						
				288	65	107	66	(50)	24	5	4	3	6	8
				53			23	(30)	12	3	3	2	3	7
				43		15	14	14	2	1	4	2	1	4
				27	3	9	7	8	5	1		1	1	
				25	14	2	4	5	3					2
				34	11	7	8	8	3	1	1	1	1	1
				31	11	12	2	6	1	2	1			2
				10			4	6	2	2	1		1	1
				6		1		5	1			2	2	1
				18	8	7	-1	4		2		1	1	
								SKIRTS						
				466	171	144	107	(44)	20	7	5	3	4	5
				104	38	35	14	(17)	13		1	1	1	1
				70	29	16	11	14	7	1	4		1	1
				14			2	12	3	3		6		1
				22	1	5	8	8	6			1		1
				32	10	11	5	6	3	1		1		1
				23	10	2	4	7			1	4		2
				28	11	5	6	6	2			3		1
				13	4	3	2	4	3			1		
				19	5	5	5	4	2	1		1		

HOUSE	STYLE	RETAIL	SALES						THIS WEEK'S STORE SALES					
			WKS FRM 1ST SALE	LIFE TOTAL	3 WEEKS AGO	2 WEEKS AGO	1 WEEK AGO	THIS WEEK	DM DES MOINES	A AMES	SC SIOUX CITY	D DAVENPORT	CR CEDAR RAPIDS	CB COUNCIL BLUFFS
				LONG SKIRTS										
				130	37	37	34	22	9	2	2	4	2	3
				151	44	55	36	16	8	2	3	1	2	
				56	18	1	12	13	5	4	2			2
				62	13	20	19	10	2	3	1	1	2	1
				55	19	15	14	7	5		1			1
				25	2	9	8	6	1		1	1	1	2
				17	6	4	3	4	2			1		1
				31	12	8	7	4	2		2			
				26	13	7	2	4	2	1				1
				SKIRTS-FASHION										
				79	10	24	21	24	13	3	2	4	1	1
				61	8	20	17	16	4	3	3	2	2	2
				21	4	9	4	4	3			1		
				21	6	10		5	5					
				44	12	16	9	7	2	1		1	1	2
				17	5	5	2	5	3		1	1		
				21	3	6	7	5				2	1	2
				12		1	6	5	2					3
				10	2	4		4	1			1	1	1
				11	3	3	2	3	1					2
				JACKETS										
				226	38	77	67	44	21	6	5	3	4	5
				189	54	51	56	28	14	3	2	4	2	3
				30	5	8	9	8	4		1	2		1
				97	19	23	19	(36)	17	2	3	3	4	7
				79	28	20	25	(6)			3			1
				290	123	73	66	(28)	11	2	1	5	3	6
				29			15	14	4	2	2	1	4	2
				7	1	2	1	3	1			1		1
				10	2	4	1	3	2		1			
				80	32	21	18	9	3		3		2	1
				SKIRTS-NOVELTY										
				173	45	40	52	36	14	5	2	4	5	6
				116	36	21	13	(46)	16	6	6	5	6	8
				103		5	55	43	11	6	6	4	7	9
				95	31	15	21	(28)	11	5	7	4		1
				27	4	6	7	10	2	2	1	1	2	2
				60		2	37	21	7	1	4	2	2	5
				12	3	2	2	5	2	1	1	1		
				12	1	3	2	6	4		1		1	
				88	23	22	35	8		1	3	1	1	2
				38		2	24	12	3	1	1	3	2	2

HOUSE	STYLE	RETAIL	WKS FRM 1ST SALE	LIFE TOTAL	SALES 3 WEEKS AGO	2 WEEKS AGO	1 WEEK AGO	THIS WEEK	DM DES MOINES	A AMES	SC SIOUX CITY	D DAVENPORT	CR CEDAR RAPIDS	CB COUNCIL BLUFFS
								BODY SUITS						
				224	69	68	47	40	18	3	2	8	3	6
				206	68	46	52	(40)	11	8	4	3	4	10
				166	53	43	41	(29)	14	3	2	4	2	4
				40			17	23	4	1	2	5	2	7
				76	8	14	33	21	7	2	1	6	3	2
				58	20	14	12	12	2	2	3	2	1	1
								PANTS-FASHION						
				138	30	34	37	37	13	9	4	3	2	6
				122	36	20	36	30	16	8		4	1	1
				166	32	56	46	32	10	2	4	9	5	2
				144	46	37	38	23	10	2	2	1	4	4
				284	111	87	63	23	11	1	2	3	1	5
				127	35	46	27	19	9		3	1	4	2
				105	28	31	26	20	4	1	1	4		10
				94	28	37	13	16	1	3		3	4	5
				42	11	13	10	8	1	1	2	1	2	1
				17	5	4	4	4	1		1	1	1	
								DRESSY BLOUSES						
				171	40	31	40	60	25	12	1	9	5	8
				178	32	32	55	59	24	6	6	15	4	4
				170	48	38	45	39	6	6	7	7	6	7
				376	109	113	96	58	22	8	5	4	4	15
				226	81	58	55	32	11	5	3	6	2	5
				81	26	24	8	23	5	10	3	1	1	3
				42			25	17	8		4			5
				25	45	48	16	16	3	2	2	3	2	4
				93		8	26	59	20	10	10	11	4	4
				58	19	19	9	11	4	5	2			

In ready-to-wear departments, the "lineup" (buyer's copies of orders) plus the copy of key-rec received from the distribution center are used as a reference to check the purchase journal for accuracy. At this point, the buyer's job is to determine that:

- The entry belongs to the department.
- The vendor name and number are correct.
- "Own freight" is reasonable.
- The cost and retail are correct.
- The markup percentage is reasonable and bears a correct relationship to the cost and retail — which is a good guide to accuracy.
- Discount and anticipation, if applicable, have been taken.
- Freight costs were deducted.
- Inappropriate charges such as special handling charges and shipping charges are deducted.
- When an invoice is canceled totally by a charge-back, the invoice and the charge-back are both processed without retail. When an invoice is canceled partially by a charge-back, both the invoice and the charge-back must be completely retailed. (Reference: See Chapter Two, Student Review, for Retail Method of Inventory.) If either of these cases exist, the buyer must be sure that the charge-back, listed in the proper block of the "key-rec," appears on the purchase journal.

When you have determined that all the entries are correct, you then sign off "on the apron" in the space provided, thereby certifying that it is correct. The buyer uses the Purchase Journal Correction Form (see Figure 8-22, page 201) to correct any discrepancies found in the purchase journal.

If there is any question about an entry, the accounts payable supervisor can advise the buyer of the proper procedure. Buyers and/or assistant buyers should keep records of all changes to be made, and check subsequent purchase journals to see that the corrections were "journalized", (i.e., are recorded in the journal).

Return to Vendor

Occasionally, merchandise must be returned to the vendor (RTV) for any of a variety of reasons. Whenever merchandise is RTV'ed, accounts payable generates an invoice that gives the exact details of this transaction to the buyer for the record, which will help to avoid shortage or overage. This is the buyer's record until it appears on the purchase journal. The circumstances and procedures for returning merchandise is covered in Chapter Eleven.

PURCHASE JOURNAL APPLICATION

A careful study of all charges to your department discloses an error. A shipment of skirts that was ordered and received by department 375 was charged to your department. The details are:

Resource:	Mad Maxx
Invoice Number:	#4273-S
Receiving Number:	5592-362-K
Cost:	$550.00
Retail:	$1200.00

Use Figure 8-22, page 201, Jarrod & Young's Purchase Journal Correction Form to correct the error.

FIGURE 8-21 JARROD & YOUNG'S KEY-REC

FIGURE 8-21 JARROD & YOUNG'S KEY-REC

FIGURE 8-22   JARROD & YOUNG'S PURCHASE JOURNAL CORRECTION FORM

───────────────────────── **JARROD & YOUNG** ─────────────────────────

To: Buyers

In reviewing your *Purchase Journal*, errors may be corrected by preparing this form and submitting it to the Buyer's Liason Executive in the Accounts Payable Office. Clip the invoice(s) or other documents to this form to facilitate processing the correction.

Department Number .... Date

Submitted by .... Ext.

CHECK TYPE OF CORRECTION

☐ Invoice retail extended incorrectly

    Vendor ....Receiving # ....

☐ Invoice/RTV/Document retailed incorrectly (see notation on invoice(s) attached)

    Vendor ....Receiving # or RTV # ....

☐ Wrong department charged/credited. Journalized as Department #

    Should be department # ....(Invoice/RTV/Document attached)

    Cost $ ....Retail $ ....Discount $ ....

☐ Incorrect cost

    Vendor ....Invoice/RTV/Document # ....

    Cost shown as $ ....Cost should be $ ....

☐ Incorrect discount

    Vendor ....Invoice/RTV/Document #................

    Discount shown as ....% Discount should be %.................

    Discount shown as % ....Discount should be % ....

☐ Other (provide details)

CHAPTER NINE

Branch Store Merchandising & Communications

OBJECTIVES

- *Discuss the differences and similarities between branch and flagship merchandise requirements.*
- *Explain the role of the branch store executive in the major merchandising activities.*
- *Suggest methods to improve communication and teamwork among branch and flagship executives.*

ASSIGNMENT

"The Gallery" opening is scheduled within the week, and because every buyer must visit each branch at least once every two weeks, you plan to make your first visits to the branch stores within the next three days: two branches per day plus one visit on the third day.

You intend to establish a firm base for comprehensive and continuous communication with all concerned personnel, particularly with all the department managers and sales associates that are assigned to "The Gallery."

STUDENT REVIEW

Branch stores are post-World War II phenomena that continue to grow in number and national importance. The pre-eminence of this type of department store is such that the independently owned single store department store virtually is extinct. Because different stores operate in diverse manners, the size of branch stores and methods of operation lack uniformity between different organizations. Organizational structures, for the most part, provide for appropriate management in charge of the personnel of all branch stores, which can include a complete division for the branch store with a vice president who may be based in the main store. The difficulties in branch store management are the same as those associated with any operation that becomes decentralized. The two major problems most often associated with branch store management are:

- The levels of consumer responses for some goods tend to vary. Demographically and psychologically, narrowed trading areas can have distinct characteristics that may not be satisfied with merchandise that is commonly purchased.
- Merchandising activities such as markdowns, merchandise transfers, reorders, selling points of merchandise, and information on advertised merchandise require a degree of skill in communication that is often lacking in large branch store operations.

Many department store retailers are taking a more centralized approach (adapted from chain stores) to improve communications between store locations.

The buyer is not only a merchandising executive, but is also a manager and an effective communicator. To be an effective manager, the buyer must be visible, available, approachable, in addition to being a source of information and encouragement. For a branch to function profitably, a buyer must establish and maintain an essential two-way communication process between the flagship and branch stores. The buyer must foster a branch store manager's sense of importance and help to develop team work among the staff. As an executive who is also a motivator, the buyer should show leadership by extending praise for a job well done, and when necessary, also offer special, constructive suggestions to help to improve the performance of an underachieving branch.

APPLICATION

Prior to your branch store visits, prepare an outline for an oral presentation to the personnel of each branch store visited. Keeping in mind the significant and unique problems of branch store merchandising, your presentation should cover:

- The merchandise that will be stocked and why is has been chosen.
- How and which merchandise should be emphasized.
- How advertised merchandise will be handled.
- How markdowns will be taken.
- Why and how goods will be transferred from store to store.
- The process of reordering.
- How messages should be transmitted from branches and how they will be responded to by the main store.
- How team work best can be accomplished.

Following each branch store visit, you are to complete a JARROD & YOUNG'S BUYER'S BRANCH STORE VISIT EVALUATION. Submit the original to the vice-president in charge of branches and a duplicate to your merchandise manager and keep one copy for your file (use Figure 9-1, page 205 for your evaluation).

FIGURE 9-1   JARROD & YOUNG'S BUYER'S BRANCH STORE VISIT EVALUATION

JARROD & YOUNG

Store   Date

Who was present during your visit:

(1.) General observations of divisional set-up:

(2.) General observations of your department:

(3.) Requested changes to be made or requested improvements:

(4.) Analysis of business:
(a.) Volume

        Last week .... Last Week ....
          (Actual)   (Plan)

        Season to Date .... Season to Date ....
          (Actual)   (Plan)

        Store % Inc/Dec Sales to Date ....

        Dept. % Inc/Dec Sales to Date................

(a.) Classification performance (include best sellers with sales last week and sales to date, on hand, on order):

      (i.) Highlights:

      (ii.) Deficiencies:

(5.) Condition of stock rooms (i.e., RTV'S, excess stock):

(6.) Competition: Store's name

Observations (i.e., new resources, promotional items, classification set-up):

CHAPTER TEN

Taking Markdowns

OBJECTIVES

- *List and explain the legitimate and expected reasons buyers plan and take markdowns.*
- *Identify potential reasons for excessive markdowns.*
- *Demonstrate the ability to select merchandise from the stock to markdown and to detail the reasons for the markdown.*
- *Complete the correct paperwork to carry out the markdowns.*

ASSIGNMENT

It is the third week in September and the department has been in operation for seven weeks. Business is performing as planned, you are confident, and your merchandise manager is pleased. You have been keeping abreast of your daily sales results and your current open-to-buy status.

At this time, an analysis of each classification and sub-classification is necessary because markdowns are required on certain styles to accelerate sales and maintain your planned turnover. Additionally, your on order is coming in as planned. Your assignment is to take the appropriate markdowns on an on-going basis.

STUDENT REVIEW

Markdowns are a necessary part of the process of maintaining a profit center. In fact, a six-month plan provides a percent of net sales for this specific purpose. If markdowns were a negative factor and held against a buyer, it would inhibit the necessary risk-taking in buying and, consequently, stocks would tend to be staid and too basic. Markdowns help the buyer keep the stock exciting for the customer.

Although markdowns are recognized as necessary, useful, and unavoidable, merchants are all too aware of the tremendous loss of profits as a result of markdowns. Consequently, there is pressure to reduce markdowns. At the same time, markdowns give buyers the ability to take risks with new untested merchandise and keep fashion departments fresh and current-looking for their customers. This dichotomy explains the importance that GMROI has assumed in store fashion operations today. Emphasis on speedy deliveries, smaller quantities of initial receivings, and faster responses to sales to replenish stores have assisted buyers in reducing markdowns.

The original pricing of merchandise is really a temporary decision that is subject to revision based on consumer response, competitive activity, and new market developments. Some of the causes for markdowns are:

- Merchandise that is purchased to make a fashion statement at the beginning of the season, knowing that it will sell only after a downward price adjustment.
- Merchandise that is broken in size and color.
- Promotional purchase remainders.
- Failure of consumers to respond to particular styles, colors, or fabrics due to localized resistance.
- Promotional merchandise that fits into special occasions, (i.e., store events such as Founders' Day, Assistant Buyers' Day, Columbus Day, etc.).
- Meeting the competition's markdowns.
- Repositioning of stock that is in line with new market cost, (i.e., knock-offs, manufacturers' lowered prices, etc.).
- Consolidation of price lines.
- The selling of shopworn goods.

Markdowns, however, can become a problem for the buyer when they are in excess of planned figures. The buyer's performance, in this case, is open to criticism. Some reasons that illustrate a buyer's poor performance, which can tend to create excessive markdown figures are:

- *Overbuying* — purchasing more merchandise of a specific type than the department can sell.
- *Underbuying* — buying an inadequate color and size assortment of the right item(s). This situation does not give the customer the opportunity to be satisfied and will result in broken assortments.
- *Poor merchandise timing* — receiving goods too early or too late in the season.
- *Accepting merchandise not as ordered* — size, color, and even style substitution.

Therefore, being aware of economic conditions, market developments, sales results, customer returns, and having continuous communication with sales personnel make it possible for a buyer to maintain the planned markdown percentage to net sales.

There are three price change forms that are used by Jarrod & Young. You will have an opportunity to use all three in Applications A and B.

APPLICATION A

Because you have analyzed the style/sales history for Dept. 345 (see Chapter Eight), you are now ready to prepare markdowns. Your six-month plan shows how many dollars you planned to take on markdowns. You have identified two categories for price changes: (1) markdowns for clearance, and (2) markdowns for the store-wide Autumn Festival, which will be a promotional markdown. The clearance markdowns are on an assortment of merchandise from late August deliveries that now have broken sizes, colors, and fabrics. This merchandise should be deeply marked down to encourage a complete sell out. The promotional markdowns, however, are temporary price changes on merchandise that will be marked up, (i.e., a markdown cancellation) after the Autumn Festival ends.

Refer to the orders you placed (see Chapter Six) for style number and delivery dates. Next, using the two copies of the Sale Notification Form, (see Figures 10-1 and 10-2, pages 211-213), compile two lists of merchandise that are currently in stock that are ready for markdown: one list for clearance and one list for promotion. Be prepared to explain why you selected the merchandise for a specific category of markdown. Your DMM/GMM should sign your completed sales notifications before you proceed.

Additionally, you also must complete a Notice of Price Change Form (Figure 10-3 and Figure 10-4, pages 215-217), to implement the markdowns in the store systems. Clearance and promotional styles must be recorded on the two separate price change forms. It is essential to fill in the information in the type of price change box in the middle of the sheet. The DMM and the buyer must sign the form to complete the process.

Finally, you need to complete the Point of Sale Notice Forms (see Figures 10-5 and 10-6, pages 219-221), that will be the markdown reference at each "Gallery" register. Although markdown information is in the system, the point of sale notice is a handy reference for part-time and/or new sales associates.

APPLICATION B (FOLLOW-UP)

One week has passed and because your markdown sales have been very strong, your clearance merchandise is almost sold out. The Autumn Festival will end in two days, and consequently, you must complete a Notice of Price Change Form (see Figure 10-7, page 223) to cancel the markdown on the promotional merchandise only and return it to the original price. Make sure the styles listed are not clearance styles. Your DMM's should sign-off on your sheets.

FIGURE 10-1   JARROD & YOUNG'S SALE NOTIFICATION FORM

JARROD & YOUNG

SALES NOTIFICATION

FROM				INVENTORY USE
Buyer Group	Buyer Signature	Phone	Date	S.N. Number
				Date Entered

Please Issue A Sales Notice Containing The Information Below. Refer To Item   On Sales Notice Summary.

1. SALES DATES	3. SALES NOTICE FORM (ONLY ONE PER PAGE):	4. PERCENTAGE OFF
From To	See M.N. 20-6000 for descriptions.	
	☐ A. Ticketed Merchandise	If Percent Off Sale Enter Percent Amount In Box.
2. STORES AFFECTED:	☐ B. Non-Refundable Merchandise	
☐ All	☐ C. Paster Tickets	Use A Separate Sale Notification Form For Each Percent Off.
☐ All Except Circled Stores	☐ D. Multiple Items	
DM CR AMES CB	☐ E. Corner Cut Sales	
IC SC	☐ F. Sales Check Merchandise Only	
	☐ G. Sales Check & Non-Sales Check	
	☐ H. Free Item	

Description of Merchandise (including Price Range When Applicable)	DEPT	LINE	VENDOR	STYLE	CURRENT RETAIL	NO. OF UNITS	SALE PRICE

Merchandise Manager Signature   Date

Dmm Signature   Date

If Sale is to Begin	Sun	Mon	Tue	Wed	Thu	Fri	Sat
Inventory Must Receive This Form By Previous	Mon	Mon	Tue	Wed	Fri	Fri	Mon

X212-20 REV 11-86 02200.

FIGURE 10-2 JARROD & YOUNG'S SALE NOTIFICATION FORM

JARROD & YOUNG

SALES NOTIFICATION

FROM				INVENTORY USE
Buyer Group	Buyer Signature	Phone	Date	S.N. Number
				Date Entered

Please Issue A Sales Notice Containing The Information Below. Refer To Item _____ On Sales Notice Summary.

1. SALES DATES	3. SALES NOTICE FORM (ONLY ONE PER PAGE):	4. PERCENTAGE OFF
From To	See M.N. 20-6000 for descriptions.	

3. SALES NOTICE FORM (ONLY ONE PER PAGE):

See M.N. 20-6000 for descriptions.
- ☐ A. Ticketed Merchandise
- ☐ B. Non-Refundable Merchandise
- ☐ C. Paster Tickets
- ☐ D. Multiple Items
- ☐ E. Corner Cut Sales
- ☐ F. Sales Check Merchandise Only
- ☐ G. Sales Check & Non-Sales Check
- ☐ H. Free Item

2. STORES AFFECTED:
- ☐ All
- ☐ All Except Circled Stores

DM   CR   AMES   CB
IC   SC

4. PERCENTAGE OFF

If Percent Off Sale Enter Percent Amount In Box.

Use A Separate Sale Notification Form For Each Percent Off.

Description of Merchandise (including Price Range When Applicable)	DEPT	LINE	VENDOR	STYLE	CURRENT RETAIL	NO. OF UNITS	SALE PRICE

Merchandise Manager Signature	Date
Dmm Signature	Date

	Sun	Mon	Tue	Wed	Thu	Fri	Sat
If Sale is to Begin	Sun	Mon	Tue	Wed	Thu	Fri	Sat
Inventory Must Receive This Form By Previous	Mon	Mon	Tue	Wed	Fri	Fri	Mon

X212-20 REV 11-86 02200.

FIGURE 10-3 JARROD & YOUNG'S NOTICE OF PRICE CHANGE FORM

JARROD & YOUNG

NOTICE OF PRICE CHANGE

FIGURE 10-4 JARROD & YOUNG'S NOTICE OF PRICE CHANGE FORM

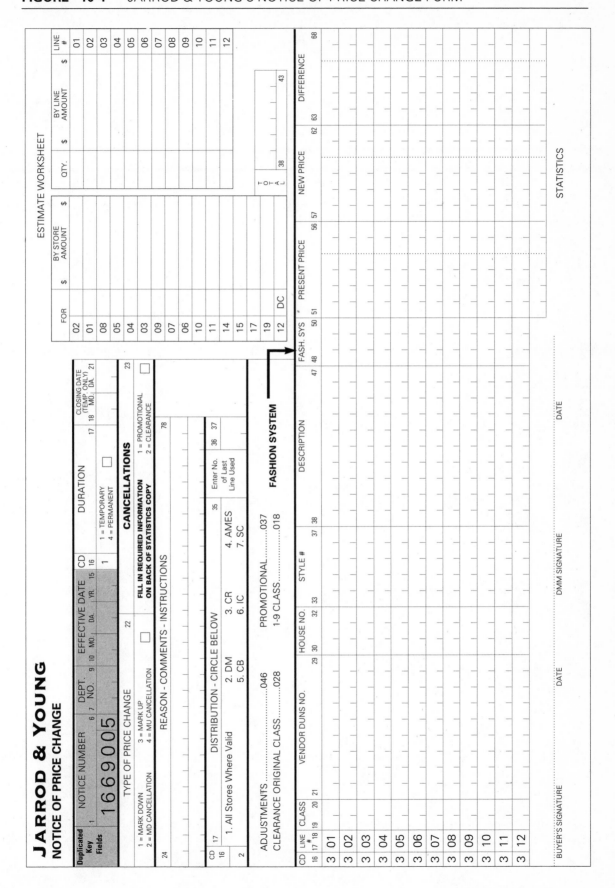

FIGURE 10-5 JARROD & YOUNG'S POINT OF SALE NOTICE FORM

JARROD & YOUNG

POINT OF SALE NOTICE

Division   Department

                                                           Lead Time 5 Working Days
Event

Effective Dates: .... Stores: ☐ All ☐ DM ☐ CR ☐ Ames ☐ CB ☐ IC ☐ SC
                 From   To

CLASS FR - TO	VDR	STYLE	DESCRIPTION	REG. PRICE	SALE PRICE	%OFF

PRICE REVISION TO BE TAKEN FROM

☐ Special Sale Markdown Report

ESTIMATED MARKDOWN DOLLARS

BUYER'S SIGNATURE   DATE   PHONE EXT.

DMM SIGNATURE   DATE

APPROVAL SIGNATURE   DATE

FIGURE 10-6   JARROD & YOUNG'S POINT OF SALE NOTICE FORM

JARROD & YOUNG

POINT OF SALE NOTICE

Division   Department

Lead Time 5 Working Days

Event

Effective Dates: .... Stores: ☐ All ☐ DM ☐ CR ☐ Ames ☐ CB ☐ IC ☐ SC
           From   To

CLASS FR - TO	VDR	STYLE	DESCRIPTION	REG. PRICE	SALE PRICE	%OFF

PRICE REVISION TO BE TAKEN FROM

☐ Special Sale Markdown Report

ESTIMATED MARKDOWN DOLLARS

BUYER'S SIGNATURE   DATE   PHONE EXT.

DMM SIGNATURE   DATE

APPROVAL SIGNATURE   DATE

FIGURE 10-7 JARROD & YOUNG'S NOTICE OF PRICE CHANGE FORM

JARROD & YOUNG
NOTICE OF PRICE CHANGE

ESTIMATE WORKSHEET

		BY STORE AMOUNT		QTY.	BY LINE AMOUNT	LINE #
FOR	$		$		$	$
02						01
01						02
08						03
05						04
04						05
03						06
09						07
07						08
06						09
10						10
11						11
14						12
15						
17						
19						
12 DC						

T O T A L 38 43

Duplicated Key Fields	NOTICE NUMBER 6 7	DEPT. NO. 9	EFFECTIVE DATE MO. 10 DA. YR. 15	CD 16	DURATION CLOSING DATE (TEMP. ONLY) MO. DA. 17 18 21
1	1669005			1	

TYPE OF PRICE CHANGE 22

1 = MARK DOWN 3 = MARK UP
2 = MD CANCELLATION 4 = MU CANCELLATION

1 = TEMPORARY
4 = PERMANENT

CANCELLATIONS 23

FILL IN REQUIRED INFORMATION ON BACK OF STATISTICS COPY

1 = PROMOTIONAL
2 = CLEARANCE

24 REASON - COMMENTS - INSTRUCTIONS 78

CD 16 17

DISTRIBUTION - CIRCLE BELOW

2 1. All Stores Where Valid

2. DM	3. CR
5. CB	6. IC
	4. AMES 037
	7. SC 018

Enter No. of Last Line Used 35 36 37

ADJUSTMENTS ....046 PROMOTIONAL 037
CLEARANCE ORIGINAL CLASS ....028 1-9 CLASS 018

FASHION SYSTEM

CD 16	LINE # 17 18	CLASS 19 20 21	VENDOR DUNS NO.	HOUSE NO. 29 30	STYLE # 32 33 37 38	DESCRIPTION	FASH. SYS 47 48	PRESENT PRICE 50 51	NEW PRICE 56 57	DIFFERENCE 62 63 68
3	01									
3	02									
3	03									
3	04									
3	05									
3	06									
3	07									
3	08									
3	09									
3	10									
3	11									
3	12									

STATISTICS

BUYER'S SIGNATURE _____ DATE _____

DMM SIGNATURE _____ DATE _____

CHAPTER ELEVEN

Other Merchandising Activities

OBJECTIVES

■ *Demonstrate through the completion of the appropriate forms the ability to:*
(1) Return goods to vendors.
(2) Transfer merchandise from store to store.
(3) Cancel orders.
(4) Revise delivery dates of previously written orders due to change in delivery or market conditions.
■ *Differentiate between domestic buying requirements and offshore buying requirements and the various methods that are used by buyers to buy foreign-made merchandise.*
■ *Select merchandise for promotion and then follow up with the necessary paperwork through the store's channels of distribution to the final conclusion.*

ASSIGNMENT

Although you have practiced and learned most of the major, recurring activities of a buyer's job, there are supplementary responsibilities that have not been covered. To maintain the high level of efficiency that leads to maximum sales results, well-balanced stock, and a better-than-average profit, you must be alert to and take action concerning:

■ Transferring goods to store units to consolidate a merchandise assortment.
■ Maintaining careful records of merchandise charged to but not physically in the department (see Chapter Nine).
■ Canceling orders within accepted industry practices (see Chapter Six).
■ Revising, rewriting, or changing purchase orders previously placed to alter the quality of merchandise, improve delivery, or to substitute new styles for those that will not be cut.
■ Obtaining the best market terms, which includes cooperative advertising money that remains within the guidelines of sound merchandising principles (see Chapter Seven).

- Arranging with vendors for the return of goods that were delivered not as ordered, and/or that are below store specifications.
- Acquiring knowledge to purchase merchandise from foreign markets (see Chapter Nine).

You are now required to perform some of these responsibilities to resolve your assignments, (i.e., Applications A and B).

STUDENT REVIEW

Transferring goods — Although commitments and careful planning take into consideration individual store characteristics such as size, location, past records, and any known particular consumer attitudes, generally, there is some variance in consumer response to merchandise. Additionally, from the middle to the end of a season, some styles in inventory are in broken sizes and colors, and cannot be filled in because of lateness in the season, or because manufacturers are no longer producing that merchandise. It is a sound merchandising step to transfer this merchandise to one location, either to the flagship or a branch store, where it can better balance an assortment. This consolidation of merchandise to one location will help to continue the selling momentum of fast-sellers and/or can be in preparation for a promotional event.

Each Monday, a buyer reviews the merchandising reports (i.e., style status report, color profile analysis, sales summary report) and lists the styles that should be consolidated. Branch department managers also review the merchandising reports and prepare lists of transfer requests — in and/or out of the department — to discuss with the buyer. The buyer then decides the styles and the branches that will participate in these transfers. For example, a branch that had excellent initial sales of a style may be picked to receive the stock from all other branches to continue the selling momentum. Or, a branch that outperforms all others with markdowns may receive a larger share of transfer stock for a sales event. The buyer's major consideration in transferring merchandise is ascertaining where the stock will sell best.

The Interstore Merchandise Transfer Form (see Figure 11-1, page 231), is completed and distributed after the buyer (or assistant buyer) talks with the department branch managers. Multiple styles can be transferred under one number on the form, as long as the "From" and "To" branch locations are the same. If there are transfers between two branch stores, it must be approved by the buyer either by phone or fax. Two copies of the form accompany the transfer shipment to the warehouse, (i.e., copies 2 and 3) and separate copies go to internal audit and the buyer.

The Outstanding Transfer List Print-out (see Figure 11-2, page 232), is printed after the transfers are completed, but before it is reported in the purchase journal. When a transfer is "journalized", (i.e., is reported in the purchase journal), it is deleted from the outstanding transfer list.

Additionally, accounting entries must be changed to reduce the retail inventory of the store making the transfer and to increase the inventory of the store receiving the merchandise.

Goods on loan — The retail method of inventory requires an accountability of every unit of a department's stock. In a retail operation, merchandise can be temporarily transferred to another department for use in:

- Window displays of departmental merchandise.
- Displays in other departments.
- Fashion shows.
- Inter-departmental promotions.
- Advertising.

Merchandise should never be released without the use and completion of the store-prepared forms. The merchandise is owned by the store and even though the transferring activities are normal and the merchandise will be returned eventually, the buyer is held responsible for having all the merchandise that is charged to the department in the department physically, or, in the event of transfers for whatever reason, having a record of the pieces that are physically in the possession of another department.

Canceling orders — An order is a contract that should be honored. As an industry practice, a manufacturer can deliver goods three days after the written order completion date. Keeping this in mind, a buyer should write every order with a specific cancellation date. Additionally, desired starting dates for delivery also should be specified, and the vendor made to adhere to these specified dates.

The buyer routinely refers to the OPEN PURCHASE ORDER REPORT (see Figure 11-3, page 233) to stay alert for orders or partial quantities that are approaching the cancellation dates. When a buyer cancels an order, the order is removed from the receiving department's file of orders. This eliminates the possibility of unwanted, late-delivered merchandise being accepted. If the merchandise is presented to the receiving department and there is no order on file, they contact the buyer for instructions; if the buyer or assistant buyer is not available, the merchandise is refused. The carrier (transportation company employee) will take the goods back to the carrier's distribution center, and the manufacturer is contacted. The manufacturer may make an effort to have the buyer reinstate the canceled order or write a new one. Failing in this effort, the carrier will be instructed by the maker to return the goods to their shipping facility.

During periods when business is off and when the department is not in an open-to-receive position, it is a fairly common practice for a buyer to request permission of manufacturers to cancel or hold up orders. In some instances, when a buyer of an important store is "hurting," despite the manufacturer's unhappiness, this request is granted.

It must be stressed that stores require that a manufacturer and buyer come to an agreement prior to cancellation before the contracted (purchase order) cancellation date. Unethical business practices are not tolerated by stores or manufacturers. They are aware of the long-term value of good resource relationships. To the manufacturer, the economic value of a retailer is that of a channel of distribution: the manufacturer makes available what the stores can buy and sell to obtain volume and profit, and it is to both their benefits that a store should safeguard their reputation as fair, reputable trading associates. Figure 11-4, page 234, is a sample ORDER CANCELLATION FORM used by Jarrod & Young to terminate purchase orders.

Changing delivery dates — When the pace of a department's business changes, the rate of inventory delivery must change to accommodate the business. By revising delivery dates, a buyer can accelerate or delay the delivery of on-order merchandise to match more closely the department's performance. An AUTHORIZATION TO CHANGE DELIVERY PERIOD ON PURCHASE ORDER FORM (see Figure 11-5, page 235), is used to revise a purchase order delivery date or delivery period. This form is completed after the buyer and manufacturer discuss and agree on a revised delivery date or delivery period.

Returning merchandise to vendors — Once a store accepts merchandise it owns the goods. This means that the title to the goods passes to the store. If, for any reason, the store (represented by the buyer) wishes to change the ownership of goods, there must be a contractual provision by mutual agreement to return goods to the vendor (RTV). Therefore, it is necessary for the buyer to advise a manufacturer of the reason(s) for the request to return goods by the store and why the return should be accepted. Valid reasons for requesting return of goods are that:

- The merchandise has been received but it is not as ordered (i.e., style, color, size, quality, specifications, and serviceability).
- The delivery of goods in such assortments, which do not allow for proper stock composition, (e.g., broken sizes and colors).
- Delivery of merchandise that is too late, (e.g., when a shipment that is overdue is accepted by receiving in error).
- The merchandise was received damaged.

Invalid reasons for requesting return of goods are:

- Merchandise that was sold in good faith that does not sell as well as the buyer's estimation (although some manufacturers will accede to the request, or voluntarily suggest a merchandise exchange to maintain a position in the store).
- Merchandise that is damaged after it is in stock.

Figure 11-6, page 236, is the RTV REASON CODES used by Jarrod & Young's buyers when filling out a RTV form. If permission to return goods is granted, the vendor will forward a sticker or give a return authorization number. Subsequently, the merchandise is collected, packed carefully, and returned with the manufacturer's sticker (or authorization number) and a completed RTV FORM (see Figure 11-7, page 237). A charge-back form is completed by the receiving manager, which takes the merchandise out of the department's retail figures, and subsequently, a claim is made against the manufacturer (see CLAIMS TRANSFER, Figure 11- 8, page 238). Finally, a print-out of the RTV claim is sent to the buyer, receiving department, accounts payable department, and the vendor as verification of the return transaction (see RETURN TO VENDOR NEGOTIABLE SHIPPED DOCUMENT, Figure 11-9, page 239).

When the manufacturer and buyer cannot agree about disputed merchandise, the buyer may complete a HOLD PAYMENT FORM (see Figure 11-10, page 240), to prevent accounts payable from issuing payment. It may be necessary to bring in the DMM to negotiate a resolution.

Foreign buying — Stores began to import foreign-made fashion apparel in unprecedented quantities after 1960. Over the years, every type of retail operation has participated in stocking and selling imported merchandise. Markets of greatest importance have shifted from country to country, and the total yearly retail import penetration has reached huge proportions. Practically all classifications of fashion apparel are produced abroad, and are sold by domestic retailers. Because foreign buying is an important part of the current merchandising environment, a buyer must be conversant with:

- The type of merchandise that is most suitable for overseas production and each store's specific needs.
- The required delivery lead time, (i.e., production and transportation time required) and the planning process, which includes the timing of merchandise for stock inclusion.
- The details of first cost and the addition of other costs involved in arriving at total cost and the level at which merchandise must be priced for retail acceptance. Figure 11-11, JARROD & YOUNG'S QUOTATION FOR OFF-SHORE OR OVERSEAS PURCHASE form, page 241, shows the elements of pricing for foreign merchandise.

Foreign-made merchandise can be purchased by either visiting foreign markets, by giving a commitment to the resident buying office representative who pools client store orders and travels abroad, or by placing a commitment with a foreign manufacturer's agent who is located in the domestic market. This text is concerned with the first two methods. It is the buyer's assignment and responsibility to select and arrange for the purchase of specific merchandise, in such quantities that are appropriate to future demand, and ensuring that this selection is within the limits of a dollar plan. Of course, this should be consistent with the planned classifications. Specification buying demands much more extensive product and fashion knowledge because the buyer in many aspects takes on the functions of a manufacturer's stylist.

Revising on-order money — Manufacturers do not produce all styles. The most heavily booked styles will be produced while marginally ordered styles will not be cut. It follows that some styles that buyers have ordered may never be produced, and part of the OTB can be tied up with no profit results. Most manufacturers will contact buyers and request the use of these dollars for styles that will be cut. If the buyer elects to switch the money to the manufacturer's suggested styles this could be called an automatic revision because this transaction involves no additional order writing or revision of on-order dollars.

Another revision circumstance is when a trend for which a buyer has made a commitment does not develop but the goods are still undelivered. In this case, the buyer may request that the manufacturer switch the unwanted styles for others, thereby canceling the unwanted ones.

Cooperative advertising money — Sales promotion activity is a method to accelerate selling. Some manufacturers offer stores advertising support. In some instances, this strategy is to encourage a buyer's support in introducing a new fashion development, or assure stock and advertising prominence. The degree of dollar support is a reduction of the cost of doing business for the retailer and is advantageous for both the buyer and the store because accelerated sales and a lessening of departmental expense can mean improved earning.

When an arrangement is made for cooperative advertising support, the buyer must alert the proper personnel in the store to make charge-backs so that the cost of the arranged advertising is not borne by the department (see Chapter Seven). Advertising is a necessary but controllable expense, and as such, is the buyer's responsibility to control.

APPLICATION A

Your merchandising reports indicate that "The Gallery" had an average 75% sell-through for all merchandise ordered from Anne Lauren. The flagship store in Des Moines, had the best stock turnover for the department. The Cedar Rapids branch store had the second best stock turnover. You decide to consolidate the remaining Anne Lauren merchandise in the flagship and Cedar Rapid locations with the flagship store receiving 70% of the remaining branch stock, and Cedar Rapids receiving 30%.

Your goal is to have a balanced assortment in the Des Moines and Cedar Rapid stores. Remember that you may have to transfer all of a style into only one location if the remaining total quantity is small.

Refer to the MULTI-STORE PURCHASE ORDER FORM that you completed in Chapter Six for the Anne Lauren style numbers, price, and original quantities that were ordered for each branch. The current quantities are 25% of the original units placed. Calculate the current quantities, by style, for each branch. When you have completed your calculations, add all the branch quantities (by style) together to get a total style quantity. Decide how you plan to divide the units between Des Moines and Cedar Rapids. Keep in mind that Des Moines and Cedar Rapids already have 25% of their own original quantity left.

Next, complete the Interstore Merchandise Transfer Forms (see Figures 11-12 and 11-13, pages 243-245), which will move all of the Anne Lauren merchandise into the flagship and/or Cedar Rapids store from the branches.

APPLICATION B   Your selling reports indicate that business with Elan has slowed. You negotiate a cancellation for the smallest remaining quantities on order for September. Complete the Order Cancellation Form (see Figure 11-14, page 247), and have your DMM sign it.

FIGURE 11-1 JARROD & YOUNG'S INTERSTORE MERCHANDISE TRANSFER FORM

JARROD & YOUNG

INTERSTORE MERCHANDISE TRANSFER

Department Number: ....

DATE OF TRANS.	STYLE NUMBER	FROM BRANCH	TO BRANCH	UNIT AMOUNT	$ AMOUNT	TRANSFER NUMBER	DATE RECEIVED	JOURNAL SHEET DATE

....

Authorized by (Signature)

....

Approved by Buyer/Date

Copy 1 – Internal Auditing
Copy 2 – Branch Dept. Manager
Copy 3 – Warehouse
Copy 4 – Des Moines Buyer

FIGURE 11-2 JARROD & YOUNG'S OUTSTANDING TRANSFER LIST PRINT-OUT

OUTSTANDING TRANSFER LIST AS OF OCT 08, 94

DATE OCT 09, 94 PAGE: 1
TIME 5:31 PM

1) BY FROM STORE - WITH DETAILS

FROM STORE	TO STORE	TRANSFER NUMBER	TYPE	TRANSFER DATE	SKU NO.	STYLE NO.	COL	SIZE	QUANTITY	PRICE	RETAIL AMOUNT	COST AMOUNT	TRANSFER REASON
001	002	000002	1	OCT 08, 94	0015149	SW10	030	XS	4	22.55	90.20	40.00	001 Slow Moving
					0015156	SW10	030	S	4	22.55	90.20	40.00	
					0015164	SW10	030	M	5	22.55	112.75	50.00	
					0015172	SW10	030	L	3	22.55	67.65	30.00	
					0015180	SW10	030	XL	2	22.55	45.10	20.00	
003	001	000001	1	OCT 07, 94	0014555	200XT	020	R - 40	3	440.00	1,320.00	825.00	003 Fast Moving
					0014563	200XT	020	R - 42	3	440.00	1,320.00	825.00	
					0014571	200XT	020	R - 44	3	440.00	1,320.00	825.00	
					0014589	200XT	020	R - 46	3	440.00	1,320.00	825.00	
					0014662	200BK	020	T - 38	1	440.00	440.00	275.00	
					0014670	200BK	020	T - 40	1	440.00	440.00	275.00	
					0014688	200BK	020	T - 42	1	440.00	440.00	275.00	
					0014696	200BK	020	T - 44	1	440.00	440.00	275.00	
					0014704	200BK	020	T - 46	1	440.00	440.00	275.00	

FIGURE 11-3 JARROD & YOUNG'S OPEN PURCHASE ORDER REPORT

OPEN PURCHASE ORDER REPORT

DATE AUG 15, 94
TIME 9:49 AM
PAGE: 1

DEPARTMENT	05	Ladies Shoes
CLASS	1	Dress Shoes - High Heel
VENDOR	BR010	The Shoe Company
		John Byron
		(618) 256-8965

P.O. NUMBER	001000	
ORDER DATE	MAY 12, 94 NET 45 DAYS	
DELIV. DATE	AUG10, 94	
CANCEL. DATE	AUG 30, 94 VIA U.P.S.	
SPECIAL NOTE		
BUYER	001	
SUPPLIER STYLE NO.	ANGELA	
OUR STYLE	1001 FALL	
DESCRIPTION	ANGELA #2 SEASON: M TYPE: 2	
FOB COST	45.00	
LANDED COST	60.00	
RETAIL PRICE	125.00	
DIST FORM	005 SHIP TO: 000 FOR: 000 Warehouse	

QUANTITY BY SIZE

SZ COL TP STR		4.0	4.5	5.0	5.5	6.0	6.5	7.0	7.5	8.0	8.5	9.0	9.5	TOTAL
020 2A 001 Black	ORD	12	12	12	24	24	24	24	24	24	24	24	24	252
	REC	6	6	6	18	18	18	18	18	18	18	18	18	180
	BAL	6	6	6	6	6	6	6	6	6	6	6	6	72
2A 002	ORD	12	12	12	24	24	24	24	24	24	24	24	24	252
	REC	12	12		12	12	24	24						96
	BAL			12	12	12			24	24	24	24	24	156
TOTAL SZ TP	ORD	24	24	24	48	48	48	48	48	48	48	48	48	504
	REC	18	18	6	30	30	42	42	18	18	18	18	18	276
	BAL	6	6	18	18	18	6	6	30	30	30	30	30	228

TOTAL COL		4.0	4.5	5.0	5.5	6.0	6.5	7.0	7.5	8.0	8.5	9.0	9.5	TOTAL
	ORD	60	60	60	96	96	96	96	96	96	96	96	96	1044
	REC	24	24	24	48	48	48	48	36	36	36	36	36	444
	BAL	36	36	36	48	48	48	48	60	60	60	60	60	600

TOTAL STYLE		4.0	4.5	5.0	5.5	6.0	6.5	7.0	7.5	8.0	8.5	9.0	9.5	TOTAL
	ORD	96	96	96	132	132	132	132	132	132	132	132	128	1472
	REC	36	36	36	72	72	72	72	72	72	48	48	48	684
	BAL	60	60	60	60	60	60	60	60	60	84	84	80	788

CRD QTY 1472   REC QTY 684   BAL QTY 788   REC$ 30,780.00   BAL COST 135,460.00   BAL RET 98,500.00   MU% 52.00

FIGURE 11-4   JARROD & YOUNG'S ORDER CANCELLATION FORM

JARROD & YOUNG

666917

....
Vendor Name (Print)

....
Street

....
City   State   Zip Code

RE: ORDER CANCELLATION

PLEASE CANCEL THE   ☐ Balance   ☐ Line Items   OF THE ORDER LISTED BELOW AT THE STORES INDICATED

Store Codes

☐1	Des Moines	☐7	Davenport	☐1		☐7
☐2	Cedar Rapids			☐2		
☐3	Ames			☐3		
☐4	Council Bluffs			☐4		
☐5	Iowa City	☐0	All	☐5		☐0
☐6	Sioux City			☐6		

Merchandise received against these orders after this date will be returned at your expense. Thank you for your cooperation.

....
Reason

....
Approved By   Buyer

....
Order Number

....
Dept. No.   Date   Vendor No.

LINE NO.	UNIT RETAIL	UNIT COST	STYLE	QUANTITY

B921-63 REV. 4/86L

FIGURE 11-5   JARROD & YOUNG'S AUTHORIZATION TO CHANGE DELIVERY FORM

JARROD & YOUNG

AUTHORIZATION TO CHANGE DELIVERY PERIOD ON PURCHASE ORDER

PURCHASE ORDER NO.	DEPARTMENT	CONTROL NUMBER
1 6	7 9	

REVISED DELIVERY DATE	REVISED DELIVERY PERIOD	VENDOR NAME
16 21		

STORE (Circle)

		WHS	4
&		Y	80
28		43	

INSTRUCTIONS:

1. Buyer forwards approved form in duplicate to Control Desk, B.O.

2. Check Here _____ if delivery period is being changed on an order being shipped via Ideal Hanging Corp.

3. Control Desk validates and distributes: Original to Reproduction Section, Duplicate to Buyer.

4. Reproduction Section prepares and distributes to circled stores. Note: If No. 2 has been checked, send a copy to Ideal Hanging Corp.

5. Receiving Office Supervisor is to change period on purchase order and attach copy of form to purchase order.

REQUESTED BY (Buyer):	TEL. EXT:
APPROVED BY (Merchandise Manager):	DATE:

XG921-68 REV 6-83 567000

FIGURE 11-6 JARROD & YOUNG'S RETURN TO VENDOR (RTV) REASON CODES

JARROD & YOUNG

RTV REASON CODES

REASON: Three letter code identifying the reason the merchandise is being returned to the vendor **AND who pays the freight charges outbound**.

Reason	Description	Frt. Out/HC Responsibility	Frt.-in* Respons.
DAM	Damaged Merchandise	VENDOR	VENDOR
WRG	Wrong Merchandise	VENDOR	VENDOR
NOR	Not Ordered	VENDOR	VENDOR
CAN	Order Cancelled	VENDOR	VENDOR
LAT	Received Late	VENDOR	VENDOR
AGV	Agreement—vendor pay	VENDOR	N/A
AGS	Agreement—store pay	STORE	N/A
SMV	Sample—vendor pay	VENDOR	N/A
SMS	Sample—store pay	STORE	N/A
JBV	Job Out—vendor pay	VENDOR	N/A
JBS	Job Out—store pay	STORE	N/A

*Freight In will be charged back to the vendor ONLY if the store payed the original inbound freight.

FIGURE 11-7 JARROD & YOUNG'S RETURN TO VENDOR (RTV) FORM

JARROD & YOUNG

JARROD & YOUNG'S RETURN TO VENDOR (RTV)

Received At (Store Name) .... ☐ Ship To .... ☐ Ship Direct From Store ....

For Consolidation RTV No. ....

Buyer .... Date .... EXT. .... DIV. .... DEPT. .... Page .... Of ....

SHIP TO

VENDOR NAME

STREET ADDRESS (NOT SHOWROOM OR P.O. BOX)

CITY   STATE   ZIP CODE

VENDOR REPRESENTATIVE'S PHONE NO.

CHARGE TO

AUTHORIZED BY (VENDOR)

VENDOR NAME

AUTHORIZATION NO.

STREET ADDRESS

LABEL REQUIRED   ☐ NO   ☐ YES

CITY   STATE   ZIP CODE

TERMS

%	DAYS	EOM

D & B NUMBER

DEBIT BALANCE CONTROL

APPROVAL NUMBER

APPROVED BY

WHO PAYS THE FREIGHT?   ☐ Vendor   ☐ Store

DMM approval   Date

GMM approval   Date

Traffic Dept. approval

☐ ESTIMATE   ☐ MAXIMUM   ☐ DAMAGES ONLY   ☐ CARTONS   ☐ HANGERS   ☐ HANGER PACKS

$ _____ $ _____

*Attach "HOLD" if more than $5,000

STORE

ENTER ACTUAL QTY. SHIPPED

1	2	3	4	5	6	7	0

MARK BOXES BELOW FOR EACH STORE AFFECTED—ENTER MAXIMUM OR ESTIMATE FOR EACH STYLE

UNIT COST	UNIT RETAIL	EST. QTY.	LP/RTV QTY.

$ _____ $ _____

MERCHANDISE DESCRIPTION

SKU NUMBER

CLASS	VENDOR	STYLE	UNIT

DATE REC'D

TOTAL CTNS

LIB PARK LOCATION

TOTAL RECEIVED /RTV

/RTV SHIPMENT

TOTAL CARTONS

TOTAL WEIGHT

COST

MARK (X) REASON FOR RETURN

☐ DAM   ☐ WRG   ☐ NOR   ☐ CAN   ☐ LAT   ☐ AGV   ☐ AGS   ☐ SMV   ☐ SMS   ☐ JBV   ☐ JBS   ☐ Other

RTV Number (Store Direct) ....

Transfer Number (Consolidation) ....

Total Pieces ....

Total CTNS. ....

For another supply, request F137 (10/85) from the supply department

FIGURE 11-8   JARROD AND YOUNG'S CLAIMS TRANSFER FORM

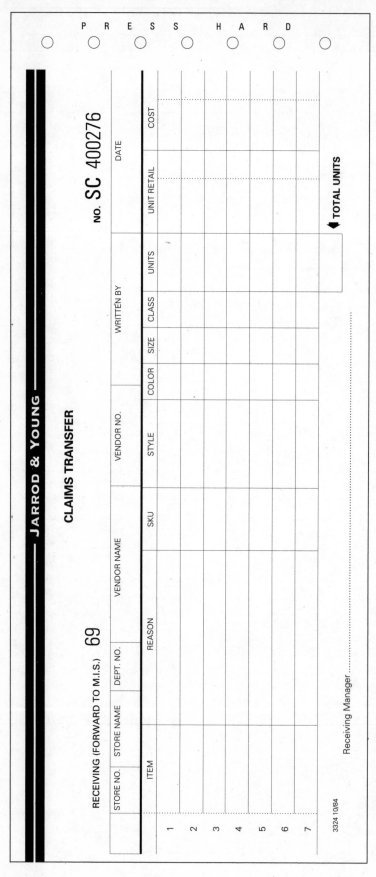

JARROD & YOUNG

VENDOR COPY

RETURN TO VENDOR NEGOTIABLE SHIPPED DOCUMENT

SHIPPED FROM: Des Moines,Iowa CONSOL LOC - 0005

DUNS NO.: 096133434 90
RTV NO.: 0000065
DEPT.: 0505

RTV CREATED ON: 07/14/1993
RTV SHIPPED ON: 07/21/1993

REASON FOR RTV: DAMAGED (V)
VENDOR TERMS: R 30 0.00

VENDOR AUTH.: E. MOORE
AUTH. CODE: TEST1234
AUTH. ON: 07/12/1993

RTV NO.: 0000065

CHARGE YVES DE LA MONACO
TO: B N Y FINANCIAL CORP
P.O. BOX 13728
NEWARK, NJ 07188

DUNS NO.: 096133434 90

SEND YVES DE LA MONACO/INACTIVE
TO: YLM
121 VENDOR RETURN ST.
RETURN ROOM NY 20000

DUNS NO.: 096133434 70

LIN	CLS	MKSTY	CLR	SZ	VNDR-STYLE	DESCRIPTION	RTV QTY	UNIT COST	TOTAL COST
1	005	06800	000	00000	6800	100% BABY ALPACA, VICUNA	1	$969.00	$969.00
2	013	06965	000	00000	6965	DB WOOL BLACK	1	$393.00	$393.00
3	014	06032	000	00000	6032	UNLINED CHAR/TPE MELANGE	1	$626.00	$626.00
4	014	06996	000	00000	6996	GRY/BLK/GRN MELANGE EXCL	0	$404.00	$0.00

MERCHANDISE COST:	$1988.00
HANDLING CHARGE:	$15.00
FREIGHT CHARGE IN:	$12.00
FREIGHT CHARGE OUT:	$30.00
TTL MERCHANDISE PLUS CHGS:	$2045.00

TOTAL NUMBER OF CARTONS: 2
TOTAL WEIGHT: 10 01

CARRIER NAME: UPS
SHIP VIA: UPS
FOB: X
BILL OF LADING: TEST

COMMENTS: ANY MERCHANDISE RETURNED TO FROM THIS INVOICE MUST BE REBILLED TO US INDICATING DEPARTMENT AND INVOICE NUMBER, AND RETURNED TO THE LOCATION INDICATED.

CLAIMS FILED FOR SHORTAGES, DAMAGES, AND NO DELIVERIES MUST BE MADE WITHIN 15 DAYS OF RECEIPT OF INVOICE OR STATEMENT OR RECEIPT OF SHIPMENT.

*** END OF SHIPPED DOCUMENT - 08/20/93 ***

FIGURE 11-10   JARROD & YOUNG'S HOLD PAYMENT FORM

JARROD & YOUNG

HOLD PAYMENTS

Mdse. Div. Code	Vendor Name
Mdse. Mgr. Signature	Vendor Number

Held by (Buyer's Name)	Date
Amount $	Period of Hold
Reason for Hold	

RELEASED	
By	Date
Reason for Release	

HOLD	**RELEASE**
Received By	Received By
Date	Date

L232-64 REV. 11/74 L.   **BUYER COPY**

JARROD & YOUNG

Vendor

Street

Country

Commodity

Mfrs. Item

Total Quantity Ordered

Ex-Factory Cost, per _____

Foreign Inland Freight

F.O.B. Dock Origin

Agent's Commission

Master Pack

Duty % (   )

Ocean Freight

Insurance Rate

Broker's Fees Conference

Wharfage and Handling

Non-Conference

Cartage

U.S. Port Landed Cost

Inland Freight

Total Charges Per _____

GENERAL INFORMATION

Is label or other identification of merchandise required:
City & State

Pre-Ticketed: ☐ YES   ☐ NO

PACKING:

1. Unit Pack

2. Units per Inner Pack

3. No. of Cartons

4. Weight per Master Pack

5. Dimensions

6. Cube

7. Ocean Freight Rate

(a) Contract
(b) Conference
    Non-Contract

(c) Rate

8. Latest Shipping Date

9. Cancellation Date

10. Approx. U.S. Arrival Date at

11. Quantity

12. RN Number

MARKS:

Dept. No.

Order No.

Code No.

U.S. Port

Numbers 1/up

FIGURE 11-12 JARROD & YOUNG'S INTERSTORE MERCHANDISE TRANSFER FORM

JARROD & YOUNG

INTERSTORE MERCHANDISE TRANSFER

Department Number: ....

DATE OF TRANS.	STYLE NUMBER	FROM BRANCH	TO BRANCH	UNIT AMOUNT	$ AMOUNT	TRANSFER NUMBER	DATE RECEIVED	JOURNAL SHEET DATE

....
Authorized by (Signature)

....
Approved by Buyer/Date

Copy 1 – Internal Auditing
Copy 2 – Branch Dept. Manager
Copy 3 – Warehouse
Copy 4 – Des Moines Buyer

FIGURE 11-13 JARROD & YOUNG'S INTERSTORE MERCHANDISE TRANSFER FORM

JARROD & YOUNG

INTERSTORE MERCHANDISE TRANSFER

Department Number: ....

DATE OF TRANS.	STYLE NUMBER	FROM BRANCH	TO BRANCH	UNIT AMOUNT	$ AMOUNT	TRANSFER NUMBER	DATE RECEIVED	JOURNAL SHEET DATE

....

Authorized by (Signature)

....

Approved by Buyer/Date

Copy 1 – Internal Auditing
Copy 2 – Branch Dept. Manager
Copy 3 – Warehouse
Copy 4 – Des Moines Buyer

FIGURE 11-14 JARROD & YOUNG'S ORDER CANCELLATION FORM

═══════════ **JARROD & YOUNG** ═══════════

666917

Vendor Name (Print)

Street

City   State   Zip Code

RE: ORDER CANCELLATION

PLEASE CANCEL THE ☐ Balance   ☐ Line Items   OF THE ORDER LISTED BELOW AT THE STORES INDICATED

Store Codes

1	Des Moines	7	Davenport		1		7
2	Cedar Rapids				2		
3	Ames				3		
4	Council Bluffs				4		
5	Iowa City	0	All		5		0
6	Sioux City				6		

Merchandise received against these orders after this date will be returned at your expense. Thank you for your cooperation.

Reason

Approved By   Buyer

Order Number

Dept. No.   Date   Vendor No.

LINE NO.	UNIT RETAIL	UNIT COST	STYLE	QUANTITY

B921-63 REV. 4/86L

CHAPTER TWELVE

Completion of the First Year of Operation

OBJECTIVES

- *Identify methods for improving vendor performance.*
- *Read and interpret the elements of a financial statement as a guide to department performance.*
- *Discuss the effect of each financial element listed on the department's net income.*
- *Develop strategies to increase department profits and decrease expenses.*

ASSIGNMENT

Congratulations! You and "The Gallery" have reached a milestone by successfully completing your first year. George Johnson is impressed with your performance as a buyer. The merchandising vice president, Carolyn Millar, has personally expressed her confidence in the future growth of "The Gallery" under your leadership. However, like all great merchants, Ms. Millar and Mr. Johnson want even better results next year.

The VP and DMM have scheduled an appointment with you to review the department's operating results. They are interested in forming strategies to increase profits in "The Gallery", and decrease its expenses. You are asked to make recommendations that will improve the department's net profit during the next six months.

STUDENT REVIEW

At the end of each season, management (and buyers) evaluate a department's profitability — what is commonly referred to as the "bottom line." Additionally, a department's profitability is one of the methods used by management to evaluate a buyer's performance. The profitability of a department is more than having money in excess of expenses — it is using all resources as efficiently as possible to run the business. Generally, the standards used to measure a department's efficiency are:

- Gross margin.
- Vendor performance.
- Turnover.
- Shortage.
- Number of transactions.
- Sales per square foot.
- Merchandise returns.
- Trade discount percents.
- Markdowns.
- Total of direct and indirect expenses (that are necessary to run the department) as a percent to sales — salaries, selling commissions, advertising, maintenance & repairs, etc.
- And, of course, **Sales**.

A STATEMENT OF INCOME (see Figure 12-1, page 251) and the OPERATING STATEMENT (see Figure 12-2, page 252), give the most comprehensive reports of a department's — or an entire store's — performance. Additional reports covered in previous chapters that also are used to analyze a business are vendor analysis, GMROI, and classification summaries.

APPLICATION

As preparation for the meeting with Ms. Millar and Mr. Johnson, familiarize yourself with the elements of the prototype STATEMENT OF INCOME (see Figure 12-1, page 251) and the sample OPERATING STATEMENT (see Figure 12-2, page 252). Prepare two preliminary lists: (1) inexpensive and effective ideas for increasing sales, and, (2) transactions that contribute to expenses in the department, which can be controlled or reduced. Review the appropriate *Buyer's Workbook* chapters to recall the different functions and purposes of the categories on Figures 12-1 and 12-2.

A form has been provided (FUTURE BUSINESS RECOMMENDATIONS AND STRATEGIES, Figure 12-3, page 253) for all store buyers to complete before the meeting. You must provide four specific recommendations to improve sales and four specific strategies to decrease expenses[19] in "The Gallery" during the next six months. Include a brief explanation or reason for all recommendations and strategies.

---

[19] Fortunately, some of the expenses incurred by "The Gallery" during the first year were due to its start-up, and will not be repeated next year.

FIGURE 12-1 STATEMENT OF INCOME

STATEMENT OF INCOME
AS OF SEPT 30, 94

STORE: Broadway

PAGE   1

PRINTED: OCT 02, 94

	MONTH BUDGET	(%)	MONTH ACTUAL	(%)	Y-T-D BUDGET	(%)	Y-T-D ACTUAL	(%)
Sales	134,000	103.1	152,073	103.2	825,000	103.1	972,372	103.3
Less: Returns	4,000	3.1	4,755	3.2	25,000	3.1	30,647	3.3
Net Sales	130,000	100.0	147,318	100.0	800,000	100.0	941,725	100.0
Cost of Goods Sold:								
Opening Inventory	212,700		187,840		250,000		257,372	
Purchases	105,000		107,315		410,000		416,174	
Freight In	2,100		2,174		8,200		8,892	
Less: Closing Inventory	252,200		223,818		252,200		223,818	
Cost of Goods Sold	67,600	52.0	73,511	49.9	416,000	52.0	458,620	48.7
Gross Profit	62,400	48.0	73,807	50.1	384,000	48.0	483,105	51.3
Store Expenses								
Advertising	800	0.6	1,314	0.9	5,600	0.7	10,358	1.1
Selling Salaries	15,600	12.0	18,215	12.3	96,000	12.0	116,773	12.4
Sales Commissions	2,600	2.0	3,120	2.1	16,000	2.0	19,776	2.1
Rent	7,800	6.0	7,800	5.3	48,000	6.0	48,000	5.1
Depreciation	1,100	0.8	1,100	0.7	7,600	1.0	11,975	1.3
Electricity	600	0.5	812	0.6	4,000	0.5	5,226	0.6
Delivery Charges	1,000	0.8	1,450	1.0	7,500	0.9	9,284	1.0
Maintenance & Repairs	400	0.3	874	0.6	3,200	0.4	7,612	0.8
Store Supplies	400	0.3	512	0.3	2,800	0.4	5,897	0.6
Over and Short	300	0.2	588	0.4	1,600	0.2	2,825	0.3
Window Displays	1,000	0.8	1,708	1.2	7,500	0.9	12,648	1.3
Stationery / Wrapping Supplies	500	0.4	694	0.5	3,400	0.4	6,650	0.7
Taxes and Licenses	700	0.5	830	0.6	4,800	0.6	5,712	0.6
Total Operating Expenses	32,800	25.2	39,017	26.5	208,000	26.0	262,736	27.9
Operating Income	29,600	22.8	34,790	23.6	176,000	22.0	220,369	23.4
Head Office Overhead Allocation	10,400	8.0	12,227	8.3	64,000	8.0	79,104	8.4
Net Income	19,200	14.8	22,563	15.3	112,000	14.0	141,265	15.0

FIGURE 12-2 FIGURE 12-2. JARROD & YOUNG'S OPERATING STATEMENT

JARROD & YOUNG

OPERATING STATEMENT   Dept...Period.................19..........

	Period				Year to Date			
	This Year		Last Year		This Year		Last Year	
	Amount	%	Amount	%	Amount	%	Amount	%
1. No. Transaction & % Chg.								
2. % Mdse. Returns								
3. Avg. Sale & T.O. Rate								
4. Begin. Stock- (Retail) & MU%								
5. Purchases- (Retail) & MU%								
5a. Transportation Costs								
6. End. Stock- (Retail) & MU%								
7. Markdowns & %								
8. Shortage Allowance								
9. Employee Discounts								
10. Total Reductions & %								
11. Net Sales & % Chg.								
12. Cost of Sales								
13. Workroom Cost								
14. Gross Margin & %								
15. Discounts & % to Cost Purchases								
16. Gr.M., Disc. & Gr.In.T.Load-%								
17. Gross Inc. & Payroll Tax								
18. Tax & Ins. on Mdse.								
19. Rent-Store & %								
20. Rent-Warehouse								
21.								
22. Production Costs								
23. Fashion & Mdse. Shows								
24. Newspaper Cost & %								
25. Cuts & Electros								
26. Other Advertising								
27. Direct Mail								
28. Window & Special Display								
29. Signs								
30.								
31. Buying Salaries								
32. Clericals								
33. Stock Records								
34. Interest on Stock								
35. Travel								
36. Other Buying								
37.								
38.								
39. Salespeople Sal. & %								
40. Stock & Clerical Salaries								
41. Wrapping & Packing								
42. Other Selling								
43. Delivery								
44.								
45. Total Direct Expense & %								
46.								
47. Indirect Expense								
48. Total Expense & %								
49. Net Profit & %								

Note: Details are missing, but you can fill them out after researching retail standards.

JARROD & YOUNG

Buyer Name   Date

Department Name   Department Number

Four Recommendations for Improving Future Business

(1.)

(2.)

(3.)

(4.)

Four Strategies for Decreasing Future Expenses

(1.)

(2.)

(3.)

(4.)

SOFTWARE TO ACCOMPANY
The Buyer's Workbook

The diskette included with *The Buyer's Workbook* contains seven spreadsheet templates for use with the text. To use the software, you must have an IBM-compatible personal computer with MS-DOS installed, which runs either Lotus 1-2-3® and WordPerfect®, or WordPerfect® Works, which is an integrated software package that incorporates word processing and spreadsheets. The spreadsheet templates are formatted for use with either Lotus 1-2-3® (used in conjunction with WordPerfect® for the "README" files) or WordPerfect® Works software programs. One of these programs will have to be installed on your computer to use the spreadsheet templates.

To work with the spreadsheet templates, you will need to have a basic understanding of how to operate a MS-DOS personal computer system. For example, you should know how to open, save, modify, and print documents. Additionally, you should be familiar with certain spreadsheet terminology including: columns, rows, cells, and formulas. If you are not familiar with these terms, you should read the software manual or ask your instructor or academic computing center for additional information.

The spreadsheet templates included on this diskette are the following:

(1) A six-month plan file named SIXMO.
(2) A season markdown percent by month file named MARKDO.
(3) A buyer's inventory reconciliation sheet file named BUYIN.
(4) Four merchandise report files named GALL1, GALL2, GALL3, GALL4.
(5) A first year operating statement file named OPSTAT.

The spreadsheet templates are formatted already with the column and row headings. It is recommended that you make a backup copy of the spreadsheet templates before you begin to work. All of the information contained in the spreadsheets can be modified and adjusted for your individual projects. Just input your data into the appropriate cells and print out your report.

The computer assignments relate to the merchandising principles discussed in the following chapters of *The Buyer's Workbook*:

SIXMO, BUYIN, MARKDO ► Chapter Two
GALL1, GALL2, GALL3, GALL4 ► Chapter Eight
OPSTAT ► Chapter Twelve

You should understand the principles discussed in each chapter before using the computer spreadsheet templates to execute your workbook assignments. Working with the spreadsheet templates will help you develop your computer skills by creating professional-looking spreadsheet projects.

If *The Buyer's Workbook* software was not included with your book and you wish to place an order, or if you want to order additional copies, please write to:

Fairchild Books and Visuals
Dept. SW, 7 West 34th Street
New York, NY 10001

Or call our Toll-Free order number:

▶ (800) 247-6622 (outside New York)
▶ (212) 630-3880 (in New York, Mon. - Fri., 9:00 - 5:00 EST)
▶ (212) 630-3880 (outside the contiguous U.S.)

Or Fax:

▶ (212) 630-3868

You must have an IBM-compatible personal computer with MS-DOS.
You must have Lotus 1-2-3® and WordPerfect® or WordPerfect® Works.
Be sure to specify disk size below:

(56367-027-5) for 3.5 inch diskette
(56367-028-3) for 5.25 inch diskette